The Living Death of Modernity
Balzac, Baudelaire, Zola

LEGENDA

LEGENDA is the Modern Humanities Research Association's book imprint for new research in the Humanities. Founded in 1995 by Malcolm Bowie and others within the University of Oxford, Legenda has always been a collaborative publishing enterprise, directly governed by scholars. The Modern Humanities Research Association (MHRA) joined this collaboration in 1998, became half-owner in 2004, in partnership with Maney Publishing and then Routledge, and has since 2016 been sole owner. Titles range from medieval texts to contemporary cinema and form a widely comparative view of the modern humanities, including works on Arabic, Catalan, English, French, German, Greek, Italian, Portuguese, Russian, Spanish, and Yiddish literature. Editorial boards and committees of more than 60 leading academic specialists work in collaboration with bodies such as the Society for French Studies, the British Comparative Literature Association and the Association of Hispanists of Great Britain & Ireland.

The MHRA encourages and promotes advanced study and research in the field of the modern humanities, especially modern European languages and literature, including English, and also cinema. It aims to break down the barriers between scholars working in different disciplines and to maintain the unity of humanistic scholarship. The Association fulfils this purpose through the publication of journals, bibliographies, monographs, critical editions, and the MHRA Style Guide, and by making grants in support of research. Membership is open to all who work in the Humanities, whether independent or in a University post, and the participation of younger colleagues entering the field is especially welcomed.

ALSO PUBLISHED BY THE ASSOCIATION

Critical Texts
Tudor and Stuart Translations • New Translations • European Translations
MHRA Library of Medieval Welsh Literature

MHRA Bibliographies
Publications of the Modern Humanities Research Association

The Annual Bibliography of English Language & Literature
Austrian Studies
Modern Language Review
Portuguese Studies
The Slavonic and East European Review
Working Papers in the Humanities
The Yearbook of English Studies

www.mhra.org.uk
www.legendabooks.com

RESEARCH MONOGRAPHS IN FRENCH STUDIES

The *Research Monographs in French Studies* (RMFS) are selected, edited and supported by the Society for French Studies. The series seeks to publish the best new work in all areas of the literature, language, thought, history, politics, culture and film of the French-speaking world and to cover the full chronological range from the medieval period to the present day. Proposals are accepted for monographs of up to 85,000 words, while proposals for 'short' monographs (50,000–60,000 words), a traditional strength of the series, are still welcomed.

Editorial Committee
Diana Knight, University of Nottingham (General Editor)
Robert Blackwood, University of Liverpool
Jane Gilbert, University College London
Katherine Ibbett, Trinity College, Oxford
Shirley Jordan, Newcastle University
Max Silverman, University of Leeds

Advisory Committee
Wendy Ayres-Bennett, Murray Edwards College, Cambridge
Celia Britton, University College London
Ann Jefferson, New College, Oxford
Sarah Kay, New York University
Michael Moriarty, University of Cambridge
Keith Reader, University of Glasgow

PUBLISHED IN THIS SERIES

20. *Selfless Cinema? Ethics and French Documentary* by Sarah Cooper
21. *Poisoned Words: Slander and Satire in Early Modern France* by Emily Butterworth
22. *France/China: Intercultural Imaginings* by Alex Hughes
23. *Biography in Early Modern France 1540–1630* by Katherine MacDonald
24. *Balzac and the Model of Painting* by Diana Knight
25. *Exotic Subversions in Nineteenth-Century French Literature* by Jennifer Yee
26. *The Syllables of Time: Proust and the History of Reading* by Teresa Whitington
27. *Personal Effects: Reading the 'Journal' of Marie Bashkirtseff* by Sonia Wilson
28. *The Choreography of Modernism in France* by Julie Townsend
29. *Voices and Veils* by Anna Kemp
30. *Syntactic Borrowing in Contemporary French*, by Mairi McLaughlin
31. *Dreams of Lovers and Lies of Poets: Poetry, Knowledge, and Desire in the 'Roman de la Rose'* by Sylvia Huot
32. *Maryse Condé and the Space of Literature* by Eva Sansavior
33. *The Livres-Souvenirs of Colette: Genre and the Telling of Time* by Anne Freadman
34. *Furetière's* Roman bourgeois *and the Problem of Exchange* by Craig Moyes
35. *The Subversive Poetics of Alfred Jarry*, by Marieke Dubbelboer
36. *Echo's Voice: The Theatres of Sarraute, Duras, Cixous and Renaude*, by Mary Noonan
37. *Stendhal's Less-Loved Heroines: Fiction, Freedom, and the Female*, by Maria C. Scott
38. *Marie NDiaye: Inhospitable Fictions*, by Shirley Jordan
39. *Dada as Text, Thought and Theory*, by Stephen Forcer
40. *Variation and Change in French Morphosyntax*, by Anna Tristram
41. *Postcolonial Criticism and Representations of African Dictatorship*, by Cécile Bishop
42. *Regarding Manneken Pis: Culture, Celebration and Conflict in Brussels*, by Catherine Emerson
43. *The French Art Novel 1900-1930*, by Katherine Shingler
44. *Accent, Rhythm and Meaning in French Verse*, by Roger Pensom
45. *Baudelaire and Photography: Finding the Painter of Modern Life*, by Timothy Raser
46. *Broken Glass, Broken World: Glass in French Culture in the Aftermath of 1870*, by Hannah Scott
47. *Southern Regional French*, by Damien Mooney
48. *Pascal Quignard: Towards the Vanishing Point*, by Léa Vuong
49. *France, Algeria and the Moving Image*, by Maria Flood
50. *Genet's Genres of Politics*, by Mairéad Hanrahan
51. *Jean-François Vilar: Theatres Of Crime*, by Margaret Atack
52. *Balzac's Love Letters: Correspondence and the Literary Imagination*, by Ewa Szypula
53. *Saints and Monsters in Medieval French and Occitan Literature*, by Huw Grange
54. *Laforgue, Philosophy, and Ideas of Otherness*, by Sam Bootle
55. *Theorizing Medieval Race: Saracen Representations in Old French Literature*, by Victoria Turner

www.rmfs.mhra.org.uk

The Living Death of Modernity

Balzac, Baudelaire, Zola

Dorothy Kelly

LEGENDA

Research Monographs in French Studies 63
Modern Humanities Research Association
2021

Published by Legenda
an imprint of the Modern Humanities Research Association
Salisbury House, Station Road, Cambridge CB1 2LA

ISBN 978-1-78188-650-2 (HB)
ISBN 978-1-78188-654-0 (PB)

First published 2021

All rights reserved. No part of this publication may be reproduced or disseminated or transmitted in any form or by any means, electronic, mechanical, photocopying, recording or otherwise, or stored in any retrieval system, or otherwise used in any manner whatsoever without written permission of the copyright owner, except in accordance with the provisions of the Copyright, Designs and Patents Act 1988, or under the terms of a licence permitting restricted copying issued in the UK by the Copyright Licensing Agency Ltd, Saffron House, 6–10 Kirby Street, London EC1N 8TS, *England, or in the USA by the Copyright Clearance Center, 222 Rosewood Drive, Danvers MA 01923. Application for the written permission of the copyright owner to reproduce any part of this publication must be made by email to legenda@mhra.org.uk.*

Disclaimer: Statements of fact and opinion contained in this book are those of the author and not of the editors or the Modern Humanities Research Association. The publisher makes no representation, express or implied, in respect of the accuracy of the material in this book and cannot accept any legal responsibility or liability for any errors or omissions that may be made.

Trademark notice: Product or corporate names may be trademarks or registered trademarks, and are used only for identification and explanation without intent to infringe.

© *Modern Humanities Research Association 2021*

Copy-Editor: Charlotte Brown

CONTENTS

	Acknowledgements	ix
	List of Abbreviations	x
	Introduction	1
1	Balzac and the Living Death of Modernity	9
	The Ghostly Present: Balzac's *Adieu*	9
	Le Colonel Chabert: Buried in the Present	15
	La Peau de chagrin: Shopping, Phantasmagorias, and Veils	19
	Illusions perdues and *Splendeurs et misères des courtisanes*	27
	The Living Death of the Provinces	28
	Living Death in Paris: Selling Books, Selling Bodies	29
	Power, Change, and Living Death	35
2	Baudelaire: Woman, the City, and Living Death	52
	Memory, Love, and Poetry as Living Death: 'Le Flacon'	53
	'Une charogne': Poetry and the Living Dead Woman	57
	Fetish and Androgyny: The Poet's Relation with Woman	62
	Woman, Death, and the City: 'À une passante' and 'Le Cygne'	71
	Endless Living Death	80
	Allegory and the Living Dead	82
3	Zola: Heredity and Social Living Death	95
	The Inheritance of Death in *La Fortune des Rougon* and *La Bête humaine*	95
	The Living Death of Reification: Shopping, Money, and Illusion	110
	Thérèse Raquin: Commerce and Living Death in Modern Paris	110
	La Curée: Dispossession and Living Death	114
	Au Bonheur des Dames: The Living Death of Shopping	128
	Conclusion: Bare Life and the Living Death of Modernity	147
	Bibliography	155
	Index	167

ACKNOWLEDGEMENTS

Parts of Chapter 1 appeared in the article 'The Living Death of the Past: Body Parts, Money, and the Fetish in *La Peau de chagrin*', *Lingua Romana: A Journal of French, Italian and Romanian Culture*, 8.1 (Fall 2009) (no pagination) <https://linguaromana.byu.edu/2016/06/20/the-living-death-of-the-past-body-parts-money-and-the-fetish-in-la-peau-de-chagrin/> [accessed 10 October 2020].

Parts of Chapters 1 and 2 appeared in the book chapter 'Balzac, Gender, and Sexuality: *La Cousine Bette*', in *The Cambridge Companion to Balzac*, ed. by Owen Heathcote and Andrew Watts (Cambridge: Cambridge University Press, 2017), pp. 111–26 <https://doi.org/10.1017/9781107588929.011> [accessed 10 October 2020].

Parts of Chapter 2 appeared in the article 'Toxic Doxa in Baudelaire: "À celle qui est trop gaie" and "Une charogne"', *Symposium: A Quarterly Journal in Modern Literature*, 66.4 (2012), 194–205 <https://www.tandfonline.com/doi/full/10.1080/00397709.2012.733629> [accessed 10 October 2020].

The author gratefully acknowledges the generous support of the late James Winn, Susan Mizruchi, and the Boston University Center for the Humanities for the fellowships that enabled the completion of this book. My gratitude also goes out to Diana Knight, for her thorough and valuable observations and suggestions for the manuscript, and to Graham Nelson for his careful guidance.

D.K., Boston, January 2021

LIST OF ABBREVIATIONS

CH   Honoré de Balzac, *La Comédie humaine*, ed. by Pierre-Georges Castex, Pierre Citron, Bibliothèque de la Pléiade, 12 vols (Paris: Gallimard, 1976–81)
OC   Charles Baudelaire, *Œuvres complètes*, ed. by Claude Pichois, Bibliothèque de la Pléiade, 2 vols (Paris: Gallimard, 1975–76)
RM   Émile Zola, *Les Rougon-Macquart*, ed. by Henri Mitterand, Bibliothèque de la Pléiade, 5 vols (Paris: Gallimard, 1960–67)

Translations from the literary texts are the author's own. Translations have been kept as close as possible to the word order in French, to allow for simpler access to English speakers.

INTRODUCTION

'Parfois encore, dans cette morte, dans cette vieille femme blême qui paraissait n'avoir plus une goutte de sang, des crises nerveuses passaient' [Again at times, through this dead woman, through this pallid old woman, who seemed not to have a single drop of blood left, ran nervous attacks].[1] Here Dide, the primal mother of Zola's *Rougon-Macquart* series, is a living woman who is dead: 'cette morte'. She is neither a ghost nor a zombie; she is simply an old woman. What does it mean that this living woman is dead? That is the question posed in this book. It does not explore paranormal phenomena, nor ghosts and vampires, but rather the recurring theme or trope of living death used for believable, realistic characters and situations in nineteenth-century works.

Although Balzac's early realist writing and Zola's naturalist fiction purport to represent reality, certain characters, such as Dide, and certain physical places and things in their realist works are described in surprising ways as both alive and dead, as a living presence of death. Baudelaire's poetry, which represents the new and jarring changes in Paris and their effects, nevertheless represents memory of the past as something that returns, like Lazarus from the dead. His poems explore the symbolic, rather than literal richness of metaphorical skeletons and revenants. Thus, the central goal of this study is to understand, through close readings of important literary texts written in this period of industrialization and modernization, during this advent of 'the new', how and why literary texts repeatedly employ this image of a living dead person, or of a dead past that returns to haunt the present in physical ways. Living death takes on surprisingly many guises in these works and spans a number of different contexts, which establish themselves and combine in unique ways in each author. Thus, the term, 'living death', is flexible and inclusive of a wide range of contexts, but always anchored in the paradoxical union of life and death.

This period in French history has time and again been described rightly as a period of rapid and deep transformations of society: industrialization, growth of commerce, new forms of transportation and communication, and more. However, there is another side to this as well, which is richly analyzed by David Harvey, whose balanced view of the extent of this change can function as a historical and allegorical background to the complexities of these literary texts. He finds two different aspects of what is considered to be a radical break in French culture and society caused by the 1848 Revolution and the changes wrought in Paris by Haussmann. On the one hand, the extreme newness of Haussmann's architectural projects destroyed the familiar old Paris, both in physical spaces and in human activities in those spaces. Yet Harvey shows, on the other hand, that the ideas for city planning were not as new and revolutionary as thought: the new was, in fact, constructed from the old. As Harvey argues, Haussmann himself was in part responsible for this 'myth' of the new: 'He needed to build a myth of a radical break around himself and the Emperor — a myth that has survived to the present day — because he needed to show that what went before was irrelevant; that neither he nor Louis Napoleon was in any way beholden to the thinking or the practices of the immediate past'.[2]

Harvey goes on to say that many of the plans for city and architectural change had been drawn up before Haussmann took over, and Haussmann, rather than scrapping these plans altogether, actually used and modified them by increasing their scale, enlarging them. Haussmann greatly expanded on the existing ideas, such as the plans for Les Halles, whose replacement had been intensely discussed earlier during the July Monarchy, and then were taken up later by Haussmann (p. 12).[3] As Harvey affirms, 'we must search (as Saint-Simon and Marx insist) for the new in the lineaments of the old' (p. 10). However, he goes on to note, 'While Haussmann's myth of a total break deserves to be questioned, we must also recognize the radical shift in scale that he helped to engineer, inspired by new technologies and facilitated by new organizational forms' (p. 13). The revolutionary forms are new, yet contain within them the presence of past forms. Harvey goes on to say something similar about Balzac, who 'helps us identify the deep continuities that underlay the seemingly radical break after 1848' (p. 17). This structure of deep continuity lodged in a radically changed environment appears in the texts explored here in various incarnations of our concept of living death: the past is inescapable and present in the present moment.

This continuity also manifests itself in the cycles of political change in the France of the time. Balzac lived during the dizzying and repetitive substitutions of one regime for another in the first half of the nineteenth century, interspersed with uprisings and revolution. Baudelaire, writing in the middle part of the century, witnessed many of these changes, ending with the failure of the republic and the coming to power of another empire. Zola, in the latter part of the century, witnessed yet another cycle come to a close with the downfall of Napoleon III and the establishment of the Third Republic, during which the spectre of the monarchy continued to haunt the political scene. This recycling of history provides a backdrop for the literary texts, which do not necessarily depict its repetitions directly. However, the return of the past in images of the living dead captures what seemed to be the impossibility of moving beyond a past that refused to die and continued to return. The trope of living death provides the means of representing a history, personal or societal, that cannot be repressed or destroyed.

In modern literary criticism, Walter Benjamin's use of the phantasmagoria is perhaps the most well-known symbol of modernity that has an association with the return of the dead. On the one hand, it is clear that, as a result of Benjamin's work, which gives great importance to the material contexts of literary texts, many scholars have explored the ways in which the changes brought about by the modern social, political, and material world, the 'new,' were represented in texts written during that time. From new fashion, new Paris, new journalism, new literary themes, to the new affordability of books, this scholarship has enormously enriched our understanding of nineteenth-century literature and culture.

However, there is a countercurrent in Benjamin's work that matches the countercurrent of our literary texts and also Harvey's work, which is evident in Benjamin's use of that symbolic example of the phantasmagoria. Benjamin's term familiarized us with this modern, pre-cinematic, visual spectacle, which was a device that projected images onto or through a screen. Most important for us here, these images were often of skeletons, ghosts, or famous dead people. The following passage from the book *L'Optique* of 1867 describes Robertson's phantasmagorias, in which famous dead people appeared out of nowhere:

> Le fantôme s'avançait jusque sous les yeux du spectateur, et, au moment où celui-ci allait jeter un cri, disparaissait ave une promptitude inimaginable. D'autres fois, les spectres sortaient tout formés d'un souterrain, et se présentaient d'une manière inattendue. Les ombres des grands hommes se pressaient autour d'une barque et repassaient le Styx, puis, fuyant une second fois la lumière céleste, s'éloignaient insensiblement pour se perdre dans l'immensité de l'espace [...]. 'Robespierre', disait le *Courrier des spectacles* du 4 ventôse an VIII, 'sort de son tombeau, veut se relever [...]. Des ombres chéries viennent adoucir le tableau: Voltaire, Lavoisier, J.J. Rousseau, paraissent tour à tour'.[4]

> [The phantom moved forward until it was right in front of the spectator, and, just as the spectator was about to cry out, it disappeared with incredible speed. At other times, spectres came out completely formed from below ground, and appeared unexpectedly. The shades of great men gathered around a boat and traversed the Styx again, then, fleeing for a second time the light of heaven, gradually moved away to be lost in the immensity of space [...]. 'Robespierre', as written in the *Courrier des spectacles* of the 4 ventôse year VIII, 'emerges from his tomb, wants to rise up again [...]. Other loved shades arrive to lighten the scene: Voltaire, Lavoisier, J.J. Rousseau, appear in turn'.]

In this new form of spectacle, the dead return, thus combining what is a 'modern' spectacle with the reappearance of the dead past. As Benjamin notes in another context, the new seems to be a repetition: 'This semblance of the new is reflected, like one mirror in another, in the semblance of the ever recurrent. The product of this reflection is the phantasmagoria of "cultural history"'.[5] Louis Auguste Blanqui becomes for Benjamin the thinker who represents most clearly the frightening aspect of this return of the past:

> In the same period, the most dreaded adversary of this society, Blanqui, revealed to it, in his last piece of writing, the terrifying features of this phantasmagoria. Humanity figures there as damned. Everything new it could hope for turns out to be a reality that has always been present; and this newness will be as little capable of furnishing it with a liberating solution as a new fashion is capable of rejuvenating society.[6]

Thus, Benjamin's phantasmagoria is the new, this technology of the visual spectacle, which generates what seems to be the 'living dead'. In this way, living death is the complication of the idea of newness.

By projecting ghosts and dead luminaries, the phantasmagoria dragged the dead from the past into a present, modern illusion that seemed to bring the person back to life before one's eyes. Similarly, our authors express not only the state and effects of the new, but also the contrary presence of the dead, of death, or of the dead past in that new, present moment. This phantasmagorical aspect of modernity manifests itself in a variety of ways. Here again, Benjamin is important as he highlights the growing domination of commodities and shopping in the nineteenth century. Using Marx, he helps to elucidate the relation between the phantasmagorical phantom and this changing culture in his description of the nature of the commodity. In *The Arcades Project*, he provides a quotation from Otto Rühle, who quotes Marx, on the phantasmagoria and the commodity:

> Once escaped from the hand of the producer and divested of its real particularity, it ceases to be a product and to be ruled over by human beings. It has acquired a 'ghostly objectivity' and leads a life of its own [...]. Cut off from the will of man, it aligns itself in a mysterious hierarchy, develops or declines exchangeability, and, in accordance with its own peculiar laws, performs as an actor on a phantom stage [...]. Things have gained autonomy, and they take on human features [...]. Marx speaks of the fetish character of the commodity. 'This fetish character of the commodity world has its origin in the peculiar social character of the labor that produces commodities... It is only the particular social relation between people that here assumes, in the eyes of these people, the phantasmagorical form of a relation between things'.[7]

In their works, our authors represent this phantasmagorical social relation in their representations of buying and selling, where commercial things display that ghostly humanness. In one Balzac text, used clothing on sale has been imprinted with the image of its dead owner, and one can see that phantasmagorical person in the item. In one of his poems, Baudelaire describes a book for sale on one of the stalls of the quays, in which images of skeletons till the earth, working on after death. In Zola's *Au Bonheur des Dames*, mannequins seem to have more life than the sales-clerk who must serve as a mannequin for a customer. Furthermore, the living dead state of the human is embodied in the works of all three authors in the figure of the prostitute, a human for sale as a kind of commodity, as well as in the representation of authors as prostitutes, who must betray their ideals to earn money.[8] This prostitution also reaches into the world of high society, particularly in the case of women who are traded in the marriage market. In these texts, human and commodity can meld into a living-dead state.

In a different way, as a result of the increasing availability of commodities over the course of the nineteenth century, shopping begins to infiltrate everyday life. A Balzac character, having decided to drown himself as soon as night falls, needs to kill time and goes 'window shopping' in a store, where he enters an odd, hallucinatory state between life and death, when the objects on display come alive. In a poem about mourning the dead past, Baudelaire describes the baubles that could be seen in a shop window. Zola infuses living death into both old-fashioned, small speciality stores as well as into the new and modern large department stores.

The growing desire for the commodities sold in these stores results, in some of these texts, in a loss of free will and therefore of humanity, represented by characters who exist in a kind of living death. The increasing lure of the commodity spectacle gnaws away at human will in the need to possess it and the money that will allow its purchase. Even Balzac, early in the century, shows how, when society becomes dominated by money, it creates subjects who have lost their humanity, most notably in *Splendeurs et misères des courtisanes*. For Zola, women can become possessed by their desire to buy, mechanically pursuing their need, and thereby becoming a kind of machine emptied of human will. These examples illustrate some of the varied ways that the living death of the new commodity culture manifests itself in the texts of these authors. All three symbolize the growth of this culture and the reification of the human being through images of the living dead.

The use of the oxymoronic combination of life and death in these works also effaces the borders between various other contradictory terms, thus revealing problems of liminality. For instance, the powerful spectacles of modernity can create a world of illusions making it difficult to distinguish what is real from that illusion. Zola's Renée at the end of *La Curée* wakes up to her reality, after having lived in a kind of dream state. She perceives that she is 'dead', when she is actually still alive. Through this problematic of determining what is real, these texts highlight the increasing understanding of the artificiality of identity, which opposes the notion of a natural, corporeal and unified human individual. Balzac's Chabert most aptly represents this understanding of the constructed nature of identity when even the presence of his physical body cannot overturn the social decree that he is dead, and he must live on as someone who has died. Certain Baudelaire poems reveal the reality that lies beneath the artificial surface of social life, represented in one poem by a female skeleton dressed in elegant clothes at a party. She makes it clear that the living people at the party are the same, that they are also the living dead. This artificiality of identity is often linked with money, particularly in its new paper forms, and with the problem of distinguishing what is natural and real from what is artificial and constructed. Natural identity disappears into clothing and the artifice of appearance, identity dissolves, class distinctions disappear, creating a symbolic, living death of identity and of reality.

In these texts, physical human spaces, neighbourhoods, and buildings can preserve and entomb a past, which then creates a hallucinatory appearance of that past in the present moment. Threshold spaces, such as the edge of a forest, can embody the ambiguous space between the present and an undead past. Material possessions and things, such as a watch or a piece of clothing, can embody the dead person who owned them, making the ghost of that person seem to return in the present. Ruins of buildings can embody the living death of the person who lives amid those ruins. A razed section of Paris can in its emptiness conjure up the past and the beings that lived there, who become strangely present.

In these texts trauma manifests itself as a form of living death; a character remembers a traumatic experience or repeats the traumatic experience of the 'dead' past in bodily and psychological symptoms, thus living in a state that combines the dead past with present. A room in an apartment can make present the past as it brings back a traumatic experience that occurred there and continues to return. In several of these texts, the traumatic event is re-experienced because of a city area or another kind of space, and the character, through symptoms or words, returns to that dead past to live it again.

These traumas at times revolve around the death of a loved one or the end of love itself. It can take the form of a continuing repetition in the present of a past traumatic event related to that person, as when Stéphanie repeats the last word she called out to her loved ones and when Andromache mourns at an empty tomb. This can be a way of living in the dead past. In a different fashion, it can be a conscious memory of dead love that returns, phantom-like, yet physically in the present through the suggestions given by senses, such as smell, particularly in Baudelaire. It can be the apparent phantomic return of an ancestor in the physical body of another person who resembles that ancestor. In this case, it is the past that returns in a physical way in the present. If trauma in modernity has consistently been linked to the wound caused by the shock of the new, in the analyses here, the emphasis is not the shock of the new but the shock of the return of the dead past in the new, in the present, or the disappearance of this present into the stronger pull of the dead past.[9]

In another way, living death manifests itself in physical ways in the concept of heredity, which seems to materialize the presence of dead ancestors in the human body itself. For authors in the first part of the century, the understanding of this physical continuity with past family members stems in part from early theories of the evolution of humans over time, before any real understanding of heredity or evolution as we know it. Balzac used and expanded transformism (an early theory of evolution) into the idea of the physical legacy of ancestors. As the century progressed, more accurate understandings of evolution ratified the idea of the constructed nature of human identity as formed physically through heredity. The trope of living death in this case expresses this understanding that we are physically made of the past: we are our ancestors through bodily inheritance from them, and our identities are a combination of those dead ancestors and our lived, personal experience.

The determinism of heredity finally relates to the gradual discoveries at that time not only of natural selection and evolution, but also of the importance of 'nurture,' of the power of the social and political realms to control and actually create human identity and behaviour. This is the discovery of what Pierre Bourdieu calls the 'habitus', a 'present past', as Richard Terdiman calls it, that determines human action.[10] The promise of the new reveals itself to be a sham as authors show that the present is in fact 'la présence active des expériences passées' ['the active presence of past experiences'].[11]

The textual analysis begins with Balzac to explore in general how a number of characters in his works seem to be both living and dead. Although Balzac is not always included in the list of modern writers, his observations and criticisms of the replacement of religious faith by the worship of money make of him an early witness to the social and economic transformations that occurred in his century. In the literary analyses to follow, the first characters analyzed are those who have suffered from the trauma of war: Stéphanie in *Adieu* and Chabert in *Le Colonel Chabert*. The focus then turns to Paris and its relation to the living dead, in which two characters on the brink of suicide, Raphaël de Valentin and Lucien de Rubempré, are saved and return to life, until finally they both, in a certain way, succeed in killing themselves. Their interim lives are an intensified mode of existence, and their (at least partially) aristocratic lineages supply an allegorical, historical meaning for their 'return' from the dead. Balzac also represents both characters as being immersed in the changing culture of nineteenth-century Paris, in which shopping, money, and artifice are rapidly taking over the daily life of the city, surprisingly even in the early 1831 novel, *La Peau de chagrin*.

Chapter 2, on Baudelaire, consists of close readings of several verse poems as well as the analysis of a prose essay that informs these textual analyses. The first part of the chapter centres on the relation among women, love, and living death in 'Le Flacon', 'Une charogne, and 'Une martyre', among other works. The second part turns to Paris and its generation of living death. This section explores the effects of Haussmann's modernization, which creates a space of living death, to which the poet responds with his establishment of a community of the living-dead. Here poems include 'À une passante', 'Le Cygne', 'Le Squelette laboureur', and ideas from the essay 'Le Peintre de la vie moderne'. The final segment turns to a more theoretical context: the relation of the figure of living death to the important element in Baudelaire's work, allegory, which he relates to a kind of living death.

Chapter 3, on Zola, begins with the first book of the *Rougon-Macquart* series, which starts significantly in a cemetery and our Dide mentioned above, that originary mother of the series called by the narrator 'cette morte', from whom the remaining characters in this family descend. For Zola, the figure of living death merges with his theories of heredity from this mother, most visibly here in the character of Jacques Lantier in *La Bête humaine*. Contained within this chapter on several novels in the Rougon-Macquart family, the early novel, *Thérèse Raquin*, introduces the theme of consumer culture as it represents a love affair that takes place in a store, a perfect conjunction between love, gender, living death, and shopping.

In the next section, living death in *La Curée* stems not so much from heredity but rather from the social and political milieu of the Second Empire and the influence of this environment, which, along with heredity, forms the basis of Zola's naturalism. Renée represents the rich woman of this period, who has been 'sold' to her husband, and whose sole identity consists in appearing beautiful for others. She exemplifies the reified woman, an object to be seen rather than an individual, a living dead being. Her seduction into this form of life parallels the development of the spectacular new Paris of Haussmann and is specifically linked to phantasmagorical street life.

The final section, on *Au Bonheur des Dames*, investigates the evolution from the old-style shop, such as the one that belonged to the Raquin family, to the new world of modern shopping in the large department stores of Paris. Living death in this novel appears in both the old shop of Denise's uncle and the giant new building in which she works. Her outsider perspective as someone newly arrived from the provinces allows Zola to highlight the living death that has permeated Paris as Denise adapts herself to it.

The Conclusion, through the commonalities that emerge from these analyses, outlines how nearly all the fictional characters, and several of the individuals represented in Baudelaire's poems, are either widows or orphans, who exist on the margins of secure social life, similar in a social way to what Giorgio Agamben describes as political 'bare life'.[12] As these authors represent their new modern world, its central features come into clearer view through their marginalized characters, who are separated from it and exiled into a state of living death: social and/or economic bare-life. I also look at the way in which each author represents his contemporary society as fostering consumerism and the reign of money, which is beginning to contaminate all with the living death of the human.

Notes to the Introduction

1. Émile Zola, *La Fortune des Rougon*, RM, I, 5–315 (p. 135).
2. David Harvey, *Paris: Capital of Modernity* (New York: Routledge, 2006), p. 10. Further references to this book are given in the text.
3. François Loyer, in *Paris Nineteenth Century: Architecture and Urbanism*, trans. by Charles Lynn Clark (New York: Abbeville Press, 1988), also details architectural projects partially developed in pre-Haussmann Paris as far back as the eighteenth century, whose ideas were taken over by Haussmann.
4. Fulgence Marion, *L'Optique* (Paris: Hachette, 1867), pp. 275–76.
5. Walter Benjamin, *The Arcades Project*, ed. by Rolf Tiedemann, trans. by Howard Eiland and Kevin McLaughlin (Cambridge, MA: Harvard University Press, 1999), p. 11.
6. Ibid., pp. 14–15.
7. Ibid., pp. 181–82. Margaret Cohen elucidates this use of Marx by Rühle and Benjamin in her excellent book chapter, 'Benjamin's Phantasmagoria: *The Arcades Project*,' in *The Cambridge Companion to Walter Benjamin*, ed. by David S. Ferris (Cambridge: Cambridge University Press, 2004), pp. 199–220 (p. 6).
8. The subject of nineteenth-century prostitution has been widely studied; here we explore this only in relation to the images of living death associated with prostitution.
9. Debarati Sanyal reviews this notion of trauma in her introduction to *The Violence of Modernity: Baudelaire, Irony, and the Politics of Form* (Baltimore, MD: Johns Hopkins University Press, 2006), pp. 1–7.
10. Richard Terdiman, *Present Past: Modernity and the Memory Crisis* (Ithaca, NY: Cornell University Press, 1993).
11. Pierre Bourdieu, *Le Sens pratique* (Paris: Minuit, 1980), p. 91.
12. Giorgio Agamben, *Homo Sacer: Sovereign Power and Bare Life*, trans. by Daniel Heller-Roazen (Stanford, CA: Meridian, 1998).

CHAPTER 1

Balzac and the Living Death of Modernity

'Le défunt arriva donc voituré dans un cabriolet fort propre' [The deceased thus arrived in a very proper cabriolet]: this dead man who arrives in a socially acceptable vehicle represents the main aspect of living death in Balzac.[1] Chabert is not dead; he is alive and well, although drastically changed by a near-death experience and a bout of amnesia. His 'death' is a social death inflicted on him by the world around him, which marks him as dead, which names him, and defines his identity. In Balzac's world, living death is this social death that results from various crises in the social and political world, which have as a result the symbolic demise of a character. Symbolic death also moves out beyond characters to a variety of incarnations in places, things, and buildings. And it frequently relates to the transition from a world of the past, represented as a period in which honour and character mattered, to a world dominated by money and ambition, resulting in the death of honour.

Two early, historically oriented Balzac texts provide a fruitful introduction to living death in his works. In both *Adieu* (1830) and the aforementioned *Le Colonel Chabert* (1832), some of the main characters are described as enduring this death in life, in the sense that this character continues constantly to die. Philippe in *Adieu* claims, 'je meurs tous les jours, à tous les instants!' [I die every day, at every moment!].[2] Chabert's wife says to him, and this ends up being true, 'vous donneriez votre vie tous les jours' [you would be giving your life everyday] (*CH*, III, 365). Pierre Gascar notes that both stories are 'des histoires de morts vivants, de revenants' [stories of the living dead, of revenants].[3] This theme of a living death permeates both stories, which hover between the fantastic and the realist genres, in a threshold state and space typical of a number of Balzac's texts, as we shall see. Both texts also emphasize *place* as an important element in the characters' relation to the past, in a more generalized concept of 'lieux de mémoire' [realms of memory].[4] Most important, this threshold state straddles the oppositions of life and death in two different ways, the first exemplified by *Adieu*, and the second by *Le Colonel Chabert*.

The Ghostly Present: Balzac's *Adieu*

In Balzac's *Adieu*, life is haunted by the ghost of the past, here specifically the ghost of history, of war, which manifests itself in multiple ways in the text's representation of war's traumatic effects. This ghostly past is embodied symbolically in the character of Stéphanie, introduced in the text as a mysterious 'fantôme' (*CH*, x, 978) belonging more to 'la nature des ombres qu'au monde des vivants' [the nature of ghosts rather than to the world of the living] (p. 979).[5] The reader later learns her history as a victim of war trauma: she has forgotten who she is, what we would describe today as a repression of the traumatic past. She has lost her human identity (she doesn't seem to be a 'créature humaine', p. 981), and she can no longer speak except for one word senselessly repeated: *adieu*. The trauma and the resulting death of her humanity make of her someone who is both living and dead, as Philippe, her former lover, says: 'morte et vivante' [dead and alive] (p. 983).[6] In desperation, Philippe tries to cure her, to make her return to consciousness and memory by restaging the scene of her trauma, and he succeeds for a moment, after which Stéphanie dies.

Philippe displays symptoms similar to, but less extreme than Stéphanie's: he, too, cannot *speak*, as Sprenger notes, specifically of his past, as he says to d'Albon: '"Un jour, mon ami," lui dit Philippe [...] "je te raconterai ma vie. Aujourd'hui, je ne saurais"' ['One day, my friend,' Philip said to him [...] 'I will tell you my life story. Today, I would not know how'] (p. 976).[7] Balzac uses the word 'refouler' [to repress] for Philippe's repression of emotions that could never be expressed in words: 'il savait refouler ses émotions au fond de son cœur, et trouvait peut-être, comme beaucoup de caractères purs, une sorte d'impudeur à dévoiler ses peines quand aucune parole humaine n'en peut rendre la profondeur' [he knew how to repress his emotions in the bottom of his heart, and perhaps found, like many pure characters, a kind of indiscretion in the disclosure of his suffering, when no human words can express its depth] (p. 976).[8] Philippe's friend, d'Albon, after accusing Philippe of never having loved, realizes that he has touched 'une plaie qui probablement n'était pas cicatrisée' [a wound that had probably not healed] (p. 976), a kind of psychological wound that 'has cut' and keeps one from representing it in meaningful words, like Stéphanie's psychological 'war wounds'.[9] However, if Philippe does not speak of the past when he visits Stéphanie in her disabled state, he lives it daily, both the good and the bad, and it is in this context that he claims he dies every day, hovering on the threshold between present and past, life and death.

The past remains present in Philippe's memories, but for Stéphanie, the past is dead to her consciousness in her madness, which is her own type of living death. However, Balzac's representation of her condition and her actions shows that she, while not consciously remembering the past, actually continues living its trauma in the present. This situation is produced in the narration when Stéphanie's actions and state, her symptoms we might say, repeat and express what happened to her and the others on the banks of the Beresina river and after her crossing of it, in a kind of repetition compulsion prescient of Freud's description of traumatic neuroses and the death instinct.[10] As we shall see, for Stéphanie, the past of trauma and loss (war, her husband and lover, her humanity, her language) exists in the present and in that recurring word *adieu*, which repeats loss, as well as death, as Janet Beizer has observed.[11] One could consider Stéphanie to be living in the dead past of history.

It is through many different kinds of repetition that Balzac represents this continued presence of the past. In the first type, a number of descriptions and events from the past war story (which forms the centre of the text), are repeated in the frame story of Stéphanie's present state and actions. For instance, the mass of stragglers at the Beresina war scene 'n'avaient rien d'humain' [had nothing human about them] (p. 987); as we have seen, Stéphanie seems not to be human in the present frame story, not to be a 'créature humaine' (p. 981).[12] The army stragglers of the past are living and dead, called 'cadavres ambulants' [walking cadavers] (p. 986) and a 'masse de cadavres' [mass of cadavers] (p. 989); Stéphanie, as we saw above, is a living dead 'fantôme' in the present. In the war story, Philippe must save Stéphanie, 'Sauvons-la malgré elle!' [Let's save her in spite of herself!] (p. 994), and the general must save the mass of living-dead humans, '"Sauvons tout cela," dit le général' ['Let's save all that,' said the general] (p. 987). In the frame story Philippe then repeats this attempt at saving, when he confronts Stéphanie with the simulacrum of the Beresina site (another kind of repetition). In this attempt to save her, he forces her to return to the past in a kind of physical way, to bring the place of the dead past into the present and to relive it when he rebuilds the Beresina war zone in his property.

In fact, the narrative in a sense makes its own 'past' return by means of similar repeated details. After the Beresina crossing, the authorities had hunted Stéphanie, who was 'chassée comme un animal' [hunted like an animal] (p. 1001). In the present frame story, Philippe arrives at the Bons-Hommes (a former monastery where Stéphanie's uncle cares for her) as a lost *hunter*, who then 'hunts down' Stéphanie, essentially unwittingly killing her by forcing her back to conscious memory. In another example, in the war story, Philippe and the stragglers destroy 'le matériel de l'armée pour se construire des cabanes' (p. 986) and Philippe specifically destroys part of a hut to give the bark as food to his horse (p. 988). In a similar way, Stéphanie in the frame story destroys things in her house (curtains and vases) and a bird that she catches (pp. 985, 1008–09).[13] Thus Balzac 'retells', repeats elements of the war story in the present of the frame story, and this repetition narratively pulls the past into the present.

Balzac also provides a kind of symbolic structural similarity between Stéphanie's living-dead identity and the natural setting that encloses her uncle's property at the very beginning of the story. This is not a repetition between the past and the present, but a liminality shared by the space where Philippe and d'Albon stop before they see Stéphanie, and Stéphanie's liminal state between the opposites of life and death. In this scene, the narrator presents a visual tableau of a 'poésie ravissante' [ravishing poetry] (p. 978), where Philippe and d'Albon, who are lost, find themselves between two sets of trees: between the edge of the forest trees in nature, 'une lisière de la forêt' [an edge of the forest] (p. 973), and the protective ring of oak trees that encircles Stéphanie's home, 'un cercle immense autour de cette habitation' [an immense circle around this dwelling] (p. 977).[14] The two men are thus lost in a threshold between two spaces, as Stéphanie is lost in her liminal state between life and death. Furthermore, the time of year is a hot September day, the threshold month between summer and autumn, at five in the afternoon, the threshold time between day and evening (the autumn being the path to death in winter, and dusk the path to the death of day). This threshold setting thus presents in symbolic form Stéphanie's in-between state of living death.

Inside the oak tree circle, the property itself is in a limbic state, its buildings described as 'ruines' (p. 977), half destroyed.[15] Broken stairs, rusty railings, demolished terraces, unhinged doors: like Stéphanie, the buildings are in part destroyed, in part surviving. Like her (but for her one senseless word), the forest around the property is 'silencieuse', as the birds and insects are 'muets' [silent] (p. 974), and the bell has no ringer (p. 980).

Finally, a description of changes in the sky as Philippe and d'Albon approach creates a kind of allegory of the moment of Stéphanie's later 'cure', a symbolic representation of what is to come:

> En ce moment, quelques *rayons de soleil* se firent jour à travers les crevasses des nuages, illuminèrent par des jets de mille *couleurs* cette scène à demi sauvage. Les tuiles brunes resplendirent, les mousses brillèrent, des ombres fantastiques s'agitèrent sur les prés, sous les arbres; *des couleurs mortes se réveillèrent*, des oppositions piquantes se combattirent, les feuillages se découpèrent dans la clarté. Tout à coup, la *lumière disparut*. Ce paysage qui *semblait avoir parlé, se tut*, et redevint *sombre*. (*CH*, x, 978, my emphasis)
>
> [At that moment, several *rays of sunlight* appeared through the breaks in the clouds and illuminated with bursts of a thousand *colours* this half-savage scene. The brown tiles shone, the moss gleamed, fantastic shadows flitted on the meadows under the trees; *dead colours awoke*, intriguing contrasts clashed with each other, the foliage stood out in the brightness. Suddenly, *the sunlight disappeared*. This landscape that *seemed to have spoken, fell silent*, and became *dark* again.]

Here the rays of light symbolize enlightenment, the return of Stéphanie's intelligence in the later simulated Beresina scene. Dead colours awaken just as Stéphanie's face takes on colour before her death: 'Le beau visage de Stéphanie se colora' [the lovely face of Stephanie took on colour] (p. 1012). Nature seems to speak, 'semblait avoir parlé' (p. 978), just as God 'déliait [...] cette langue morte' [untied [...] this dead tongue] when she recognizes Philippe and speaks to him (p. 1013). This momentary awakening then ends, and the landscape and Stéphanie return to the silence, death, and darkness from which they had, for a moment, emerged. Here Balzac tells the story of the text twice, once poetically in the nature scene, and once literally in Stéphanie's awakening from madness in the later false Beresina scene. The story itself seems repeatedly to bring back its own 'history'.

The last two repetitions of past events represent two different kinds of the representation of the past, as excellent articles by Rachel Shuh and Maurice Samuels have shown.[16] The first is the story of the war that Stéphanie's uncle relates to d'Albon (and through him to the reader), which is, as Shuh notes, a wide overview of the battle scene combined with a third person narration of Philippe's story from his point of view, a narrative structure that rivals the genre of history writing.[17] The second is Philippe's spectacular, physical re-presentation of the scene, reminiscent of popular theatrical productions about Napoleon staged at the time, which, as Samuels shows, criticize this theatrical representation of the past.

This spectacular illusion created by Philippe is a 'fausse Russie' [false Russia] which Stéphanie seems to take as reality, as truth, as an 'épouvantable' and 'affreuse vérité' [a dreadful and atrocious truth] (p. 1011). This artificial representation of the past has been constructed from memory and seems to come alive, to become a 'souvenir vivant' [living memory] (p. 1012). The past appears to have returned in its physical and visual presence, but this is, of course, an illusion, a simulacrum whose seeming reality nevertheless has real results as it becomes fatal to Stéphanie.

There is one more twist to this artificial reconstruction of the past. It is significant that, when we return to the original description of the banks of the Beresina, Balzac describes it as being already an artificial reconstruction, a representation of the original town of the past:

> Mourant de faim, de soif, de fatigue et de sommeil, ces infortunés arrivaient sur une plage où ils apercevaient du bois, des feux, des vivres, d'innombrables équipages abandonnés, des bivouacs, enfin toute une ville improvisée. Le village de Studzianka avait été entièrement dépecé, partagé, transporté des hauteurs dans la plaine. Quelque *dolente* et périlleuse que fût cette cité, ses misères et ses dangers souriaient à des gens qui ne voyaient devant eux que les épouvantables déserts de la Russie. (*CH*, x, 986)

> [Dying of hunger, thirst, fatigue, and lack of sleep, these wretches reached a shore where they saw wood, fires, provisions, innumerable abandoned pieces of equipment, bivouacs, in effect a whole improvised town. The village of Studzianka had been entirely taken apart, divided, transported from the high elevation to the plain. However *doleful* and perilous was this town, its miseries and its dangers looked pleasing to these people who saw before them only the dreadful wastelands of Russia.]

That both towns, this false Studzianka and Philippe's false battlefield, are improvisations, artificial constructions, provides a different manner in which the text shows the dangers of the return of the past.[18] The first improvised Studzianka of the past could be said to play the symbolic role of a memory, in the sense that it is already an artificial reconstruction made from the debris of the past (it is not the original, real town of Sudzianka). It is dangerous to linger in this artificial town, this symbolic 'memory'; however, the stragglers care only about the food and shelter available there and not the perils of the imminent attack in which many will die. In a sense, they linger in this memory. Stéphanie in the frame story then experiences the false 'souvenir vivant' of the second artificial town, which for her is fatal as well. The text seems to represent the dangers of living in the memory of the past, which can be fatal, but which perhaps cannot be avoided.

Finally, Balzac creates a peculiar representation of the present. As we saw above, Stéphanie lives the past, she is a 'fantôme' whose body exists in the present but whose unconscious actions keep repeating the dead past. And, as we saw, this present past affects Philippe too, who 'dies' by it every day. The message this living death conveys is perhaps that we are the past. It remains ghostly in this text, both living and dead like Stéphanie, never wholly present in its multiple representations, nor wholly absent. Balzac's nuanced depictions of the past — from its poetic symbolization in nature and dwellings in the text's present, through the conventional historical narrative of the Beresina, to the real, physical re-creation of a past battle — provide a rich panoply that diversifies memory and history and their weighty presence in the present moment. When Philippe, after Stéphanie's death, states that he is never alone (p. 1013), implying that he is haunted by his memories of her, memory is still his ghostly present.

What does Stéphanie's story tell us about Balzac's representation of the historical relation of the past to the present? Philippe desires to recover the Stéphanie that he knew in the past, the Stéphanie who was significantly 'la reine des bals parisiens' [the queen of Parisian balls] (p. 993), *reine* being a word that one must take figuratively to mean the 'queen' of her social world, but that also contains within it a reference to the greatness of the *Ancien Régime* which, like Stéphanie's greatness, has been lost in Balzac's view. To do this, Philippe takes her back to the past in the false Beresina scene, trying to recover the Stéphanie who existed before the trauma. The death of the 'queen' of Parisian balls signifies that the desire to return to the past state of affairs cannot work, either personally or politically. Balzac who mourns the values and order of the monarchy of the past, seems to be showing metaphorically that 'la reine', the monarchy and its order, cannot be restored in its past form, even though this form has created the present, even though it exists in a ghostly form in the present Restoration, which itself disappears to haunt the reign of Louis-Philippe in the year listed by Balzac as the date of the writing of *Adieu* (1830).

The rather odd ending of the story underscores this impossibility of returning to the past. It contains the only representation of contemporary society in the text. The bulk of the action takes place in that other, symbolic domain of the odd and different society of Geneviève, Stéphanie, and her uncle, joined by Philippe and d'Albon, or in the past of the war. The social scene at the end appears to take place in 'le monde' [upper-class society] at a social gathering, and it displays the elements that Balzac bemoaned (but which also fascinated him) in his contemporary society. A woman there compliments Philippe on his fine qualities and asks him why he doesn't marry, and the narrator provides the detail that she has several daughters to marry. Her interest in him is thus self-serving: he is 'riche, titré, de noblesse ancienne' [rich, titled, of ancient nobility] (p. 1014) and thus an ideal catch in the marriage market. Significantly, this social group cannot understand Philippe's suicide and gossips about it afterwards, speculating that it must be some kind of moral lapse: gambling, love, ambition, secret immorality.[19] If Philippe's story is about love and tragic faithfulness, the end represents the crass forms of greed, ambition, and pettiness of the new bourgeois society. Balzac refers to the actions of God twice in the story: first it is God who loosens Stéphanie's tongue; however in the second instance, when Philippe is represented in his contemporary society, it is God who has withdrawn himself, and Philippe succumbs.[20] This creates a subtle reference to a society in which self-interest and money have replaced God and moral values. As Balzac shows so often in his texts, the ideals of the past haunt and create the present but cannot be restored in a changed and changing world.

Le Colonel Chabert: Buried in the Present

Both Stéphanie in *Adieu* and Chabert in *Le Colonel Chabert* suffer from amnesia and as a result enter the world of the living dead. Chabert regains his memory, as does Stéphanie; however, if Stéphanie dies immediately, Chabert exists in a symbolic state of living death because he rejects his identity.[21] His body is physically present, as is Stéphanie's, but he lacks the ability, and later the desire, to reclaim his name and is thus dead socially. As we saw above, Philippe dies 'tous les jours, à tous les instants!' [every day, at every moment!] (*CH*, x, 1009); Chabert is subject to the same fate, as his wife predicts, when he contemplates renouncing his identity, as we saw above, 'vous donneriez votre vie tous les jours!' [you would be giving your life every day!] (*CH*, III, 365). Although a number of critics have made wonderful and enlightening readings of this story, an analysis of it from the point of view of living death may give us a somewhat different take on this rich text and will complete the foundation of our analysis of living death in Balzac, before we turn to the topic in the longer novels and their relation to nascent 'modernity'.

Enterrer, ensevelir, and *anéantir* [bury, inter, and annihilate]. These three words recur in different contexts in this text and act as anchors to draw together three major aspects of living death, which we pursue in the following order: physical descriptions of Chabert and his space, the power of the law and the social order to turn people into the living dead, and the living death of the increasing artificiality of 'modern' life.

Chabert first 'died' when he was thought dead and was thrown unconscious into a common grave with other soldiers, as he says, 'J'ai été enterré sous des morts' [I was buried under the dead] (*CH*, III, 328). When he awakens, Balzac creates an ambiguous, fantastic space of living death, as Chabert thinks he hears voices from the dead soldiers around him: 'J'entendis, ou crus entendre, je ne veux rien affirmer, des gémissements poussés par le monde de cadavres au milieu duquel je gisais' [I heard, or thought I heard, I do not want to affirm anything, moans emitted by this society of cadavers in the midst of which I was buried (p. 325). 'Ci-gît' [Here lies] Chabert in the 'monde de cadavres', the word 'monde' suggesting a 'world of the dead', who seem to be living, like him. After he emerges from this tomb with the help of a dead man's arm, he hovers on the medical threshold between life and death, 'Je suis resté pendant six mois entre la vie et la mort' [I remained for six months between life and death] (p. 326).

Since in Balzac's world, humans are physically changed and influenced by their milieu (the best-known example being Madame Vauquer and her pension, which mutually shape each other),[22] Chabert's sojourn in the world of the dead changes him physically into someone who looks dead: his face 'semblait mort' [seemed dead] (p. 321), and he has a 'physionomie cadavéreuse' [cadaverous physiognomy] (p. 621), 'une face de requiem' [a deathly look] (p. 330).[23] These changes have made him unrecognizable to his good friend, Boutin, and only a shared story, known by Boutin and Chabert alone, can convince Boutin of his identity. Chabert's misfortunes 'l'ont à la longue défiguré' [have, over time, disfigured him] (p. 322), literally changing his *figure*, his face and appearance. While he was ill and absent from Paris, the city itself changed its 'face'. His house was demolished to make way for the new, and the street name was changed, paralleling the disappearance of Chabert, who had to disown his own name in order to be declared sane when he was in Germany. He comes back to a Paris that has demolished the place where he lived, his physical attachment to his social space.

His new, temporary abode, where his fellow soldier, Vergniaud, gives him a room, oddly resembles Stéphanie's dilapidated and 'half-dead' monastery. If Stéphanie's abode is a ruin from the past, Chabert's is a new construction that seems about to fall into ruin, 'Quoique récemment construite, cette maison semblait près de tomber en ruine' [Although recently constructed, this house seemed ready to fall to ruins] (p. 337). Significantly, it was also built from the 'ruins' left over from demolitions in Paris: 'Aucun des matériaux n'y avait eu sa vraie destination, ils provenaient tous des démolitions qui se font journellement dans Paris' [None of the materials there were used for their real purpose, they came from all the demolitions that take place daily in Paris] (p. 337).[24] It is thus a kind of threshold space, newly made from old materials, between old and new, blending 'dead' buildings into a newly formed structure. One of the building materials used there aptly and ironically symbolizes this odd space: 'Derville lut sur un volet fait avec les planches d'un enseigne: *Magasin de nouveautés*' [Derville read on a shutter that was made from the planks of a sign: *Novelty Shop*] (p. 337); a shop that sells 'new' things provides its old sign to form a new building. To round out the temporal hybridity of this home and the way it represents living death, we find 'deux murs bâtis avec des ossements' [two walls built with bones] and bedrooms that are '*enterrés* par une éminence' [*buried* by an incline] (pp. 336, 337, my emphasis). This new-from-old, half-buried construction built with the bones of dead beings, could be taken as a metaphor for the return of the monarchy in the Restoration, the period when Chabert returns to Paris: one constructs a new state by reusing the elements of the dead monarchy of the past. Indeed, Petrey reads the Restoration as the return of the dead: Chabert 'cannot (re)make his own history because the circumstances he encounters have brought a dead generation back to life, have produced a Restoration of the past'.[25] Chabert now tries to restore his own 'dead' identity, which a living-dead monarchy tries to rebury.

Although the Restoration seems to be built on firm ground, 'assise sur des bases en apparence inébranlables' [established on seemingly unshakeable foundations] (p. 349), those with stakes in the new Restoration society need to make Chabert go back to the grave, as Derville says, there are 'des gens qui vont avoir intérêt à nier votre existence' [people who will have an interest in denying your existence] (p. 340), and this activity applies to governmental bureaus as well. As shown in the use of one of our three words, the bureaus want to 'anéantir' [annihilate] (p. 343) those left over from the Empire.[26] This official annihilation reflects in part what has been called the 'politics of *oubli*', of forgetting: the political effort to repress the memory of the revolutionary period. As Sheryl Kroen summarizes, 'In keeping with the Article 11 of the Charter of 1814, the First Restoration government (in power until the Hundred Days) was guided by a spirit of *oubli* — oblivion, disregard, or forgetting — with regard to the past'.[27] According to Matthijs M. Lok, this attitude or policy continued beyond this initial period: 'Nonetheless, even under Charles X, the French Restoration regime showed itself remarkably consistent and steadfast in its striving to forget the revolutionary episode'.[28] Cathy Caruth links this 'politique de l'oubli' directly to Chabert in her study of the law in the text, which, as she notes, 'makes of forgetting itself a legal function'.[29]

This deliberate and enforced *oubli* accompanies the desire to bury one's personal past in the case of Chabert's wife. Significantly one of our three words, *ensevelir*, is used for her campaign to efface her past life as a prostitute. When Chabert in anger reveals this past in front of Derville, she later asks Chabert, 'Ce secret ne devait-il pas rester enseveli dans nos cœurs?' [Shouldn't this secret have remained buried in our hearts?] (p. 359), just as she wishes Chabert would remain buried. She also gains the secret loyalty of Delbecq (her husband Ferraud's secretary), whose talents make her so wealthy that her husband must hesitate to annul their marriage, but she again hides this to protect her social 'life': 'La comtesse avait enseveli les secrets de sa conduite au fond de son cœur. Là était des secrets de vie et de mort pour elle' [The countess had buried the secrets of her conduct deep in her heart. In that place existed secrets of life and death for her] (p. 349). Balzac broadens the scope of this secrecy to describe that of the majority of Parisian families, thus of the family system in general, when the perspicacious Derville is able to see through cover-ups to 'les mensonges sous lesquels la plupart des familles parisiennes cachent leur existence' [the lies under which most Parisian families hide their existence] (p. 351).

This public and private 'politique de l'oubli' creates an image of this society as one that represses the past and thereby projects an incomplete, false, and artificial image of the present. The goal is to bolster legitimacy, both of the Restoration and of private 'morality' (of Chabert's wife, for instance), but also to benefit financially those who promote it (in political terms, the noble families who would regain properties confiscated during the Revolutionary period, which is the subject of the law petition in the first scene of the novel). The politics of forgetting aims to enact a kind of performative construction of a new reality through the repression of the past and of people like Chabert, what Petrey, in an analysis of ideology in the text, describes as 'the performative nature of social representation'.[30]

This performative construction of identity in Balzac's works can be seen in the importance that he gives to clothing. In his 'Physiologie de la toilette' he writes, part humorously, part seriously, that 'par la cravate on peut juger celui qui la porte, et [...] pour connaître un homme, il suffit de jeter un coup d'œil sur cette partie de lui-même qui unit la tête à la poitrine' [by his tie, one can judge the man who wears it, and [...] in order to know a man, it suffices to cast a glance at that part of him that unites the head to the chest].[31] Balzac, while outlining the image one projects by the cut of one's tie, gives his readers the 'tie-code' for the intelligence and heart of the human being that one might want to be and that one could imitate.[32]

This importance of clothing for determining identity explains in part why Chabert cannot break into this social world: he doesn't look like Chabert, not only in his facial disfigurement, but also in his clothing, the artificial covering of a human body, which in this text is more important than that body itself. Many critics have noted that the first name given to Chabert is 'vieux carrick', the old overcoat he wears that identifies him as a poor, unstylish man. Even though Boucard, the master clerk, says that, no matter how poor a client is, he is still a man, this story puts that assertion into question. Money is required for clothing, and since Chabert has none, he is a shabby old coat. Indeed, when he appears later in Derville's office dressed appropriately, he seems to have reversed the trend and reconstructed his old identity:

> En reprenant les habitudes de l'aisance, il avait retrouvé son ancienne élégance martiale. Il se tenait droit. Sa figure, grave et mystérieuse, où se peignaient le bonheur et toutes ses espérances, paraissait être rajeunie et plus grasse [...]. Il ne ressemblait pas plus au Chabert en vieux carrick, qu'un gros sou ne ressemble à une pièce de quarante francs nouvellement frappée. (*CH*, III, 354–55)
>
> [Having resumed his affluent habits, he had found once again his former martial elegance. He held himself straight. His face, grave and mysterious, where could be seen happiness and all of his hopes, seemed rejuvenated and fleshier [...] He no more resembled the Chabert in the old overcoat than an old sou resembles a newly minted forty-franc coin.]

That Balzac compares him to a shiny new coin is not insignificant: money buys the clothes that can (re)make the man. As Prendergast notes, Balzac compares clothes to 'papier-monnaie' [paper money], because the fine clothes that were formerly available only to the aristocratic few before the Revolution are now buyable and thus are 'no longer reliable markers of social identity'.[33]

Indeed, it is also money that Chabert needs in order to get not just clothes but also the documents from Germany that could help him prove his identity. As is well known, money has, in Balzac's eyes, become the universal value, having replaced moral virtue and religion (as in the final scene of *Adieu* discussed above). Chabert represents one of the few characters in the *Comédie humaine* who actually values honour and affection above money, as he says, 'il vaut mieux avoir du luxe dans ses sentiments que sur ses habits' [it is better to have luxury in one's sentiments than in one's clothes] (p. 371). And it is because he no longer wants to live in a world that has lost what he values, that he decides to remain in a state of living death, with a number for a name.[34] Thus in their artificial nature, documents go hand in hand with money in the text. Money is an artificial value that can be exchanged for just about anything in Balzac's world. And documents create identities artificially on paper.

This is the crux of Chabert's difference from his wife. She wants to keep his money, and to do this she wants him to *sign* that he is not Chabert: in order to keep her artificial identity (she is not the 'femme comme il faut' [proper woman] that she pretends to be), she wants him to sign a document, a piece of paper, which this time would deny rather than prove his identity. Chabert's new world seems into be moving to a paper, representational mode, just as physical coins were being replaced by paper representations of monetary value.[35] Chabert, however, wants simply to *state* his promise that he will disappear, and he claims that his word should be enough for his wife.[36] Chabert believes in honour and in the word that is attached to the person in a promise. He believes that his case is simple: he is physically there in his body, as he says, 'me voilà' [here I am] (p. 340). However, his failure to 'be there' would seem to suggest that the notion of honour that relies on the meaning of a promise does not exist: there are only artificial documents and paper money. Chabert's failure shows that paper identity has more power than a physical body's presence.

Documents and money thus join with the performance of identity and the 'politique de l'oubli' to construct what Balzac depicts as a new and artificial social sphere of representation.[37] Identity is itself in a state of living death in a certain sense. Like Chabert's wife, one has an identity that has been added as a cover-up over one's past that has been erased, and thus one is and is not one's social 'identity'.[38] The strength of this social identity seeps into the narrative voice itself when it claims that Chabert is dead, which we saw in our opening quotation: 'Le *défunt* arriva donc voituré dans un cabriolet fort propre' (p. 354, my emphasis). Chabert himself even speaks of his death: 'ma mort est un fait historique' [my death is a historical fact] (p. 323), 'l'événement qu'il faut bien appeler ma mort' [the event that one must call my death] (p. 324). Balzac's society seems to have moved into the nether realm of living death in the social order. This artificial nature of social identity appears in the texts of Baudelaire and Zola as well. Its relation to paper becomes the subject of the last section of this chapter on *Illusions perdues* and *Splendeurs et misères des courtisanes*.

La Peau de chagrin: Shopping, Phantasmagorias, and Veils[39]

An early Paris novel by Balzac, *La Peau de chagrin* (1831), creates a remarkable threshold space between past and present, death and life.[40] Its first page situates the action in October 1830, itself a transition period just after the July Revolution, when civil unrest continued in the shift between Bourbon and Orléans rule.[41] The autumn season, of course, also symbolizes, as we saw in *Adieu*, the transition between summer and winter, life and death.

In addition to the specific date of the events of the novel, Balzac provides a very specific locale in Paris:

> Vers la fin du mois d'octobre dernier, un jeune homme entra dans le Palais-Royal au moment où les maisons de jeu s'ouvraient, conformément à la loi qui protégé une passion essentiellement imposable. Sans trop hésiter, il monta l'escalier du tripot désigné sous le nom de numéro 36.[42]

> [Near the end of last October, a young man entered the Palais-Royal at the moment when the gambling houses opened, which conformed to the law that protects a passion taxable by its nature. With little hesitation, he went up the stairs of the gambling den designated by the number 36.]

The Palais-Royal and the area around it appear in several other Balzac novels, which we investigate below. It was a place of gambling, prostitution, bookshops, *magasins de nouveautés* [novelty shops], and more: in other words, it was a place to spend money, a place to 'shop' for various things.

Indeed, these first few pages of the novel portray what we now think of as indices of modernization in this pre-Haussmannian novel. We see this, for instance, when Raphaël must surrender his hat, and the narrator poses a number of questions about the reason behind this procedure. He speculates first that it might be an infernal contract accepted with the gambling establishment, in which the hat is a kind of security deposit: this idea of contracts and financial agreements opens the question of pacts, exchanges, credit, and money — central concerns of modernity and of this text (particularly the pact with the *peau de chagrin* [the wild ass's skin]). The narrator also asks if the police are behind this un-hatting in order to learn the owner's name or the name of his hatter from the inscription on the inside; the increasing need of information on the part of the police is also an effect of the increasingly anonymous nature of the growing modern city. Finally, anonymity is reflected in the name of the gambling house, which is in fact a number and not a name (this number that 'names' suggests the 'modern' and current numbering system of Parisian buildings begun under Bonaparte).[43] Similarly, Raphaël, still an anonymous 'jeune homme' [young man] in the text, in surrendering his hat, receives a number in return, as if he were himself becoming an anonymous number. In fact, the narrator claims that a gambler is not dispossessed simply of his hat but also of himself: 'Mais, sachez-le bien, à peine avez-vous fait un pas vers le tapis vert, déjà votre chapeau ne vous appartient pas plus que vous ne vous appartenez à vous-même: vous êtes au jeu' [However, heed well, scarcely have you taken a step towards the gambling table, already your hat no longer belongs to you just as you no longer belong to yourself: you are at play] (*CH*, x, 58). Raphaël defiantly assumes this anonymous identity when he plans to leave a 'cadavre indéchiffrable' [an indecipherable cadaver] (p. 66) by drowning himself. These quasi-modern themes, some involving the loss or death of what one thinks of as one's identity, set the stage for the problematic of living death in the text, as the old regime of things meets the new.[44]

The main opposition in Raphaël's gambling trip is that between life and death, which can be read on his face when he enters the establishment: 'Les ténèbres et la lumière, le néant et l'existence s'y combattaient' [Shadows and light, nothingness and existence fought there] (p. 62). The only thing that keeps him from dying is, significantly, money (a gold coin), an idea that Balzac gleans in part from Rousseau: 'Oui, je conçois qu'un homme aille au Jeu; mais c'est lorsque entre lui et la mort il ne reste plus que son dernier écu' [Yes, I understand that a man might gamble; however it is when, between him and death, there is nothing left but his last écu] (p. 59). Just as the Palais-Royal was a place of unofficial speculation away from the Bourse, Raphaël's gambling is also a kind of speculation: risk money to make money (and as Gerard Cohen-Vrignaud points out, Raphaël's father made poor speculations in land and logging, and lost his and Raphaël's money, thus leading to the need for Raphaël's gambling speculation).[45] When Raphaël loses his bet, he reflects on his 'worth' as a human being and his value as a thing: alive he is worth nothing, but dead, an inanimate object, he is worth fifty francs (p. 66). Later he complains that his signature was worth 3000 francs, but he himself was not (p. 199). Balzac here introduces one of his preferred critiques of the society of his time:

all is reduced to money; people can be bought and sold in various ways and are exchangeable objects.

Once Raphaël loses and decides to commit suicide, Balzac traces the specific spatial path, a kind of map, that he takes on his distracted stroll through the Tuileries and across the Seine: this creates a strange kind of space-time of living death, a threshold state in which he hopes to 'tuer le temps'[kill time] (p. 66) as he postpones his suicide by walking through the city.[46] Balzac describes this state on the edge of life and death several times: Raphaël is 'cet homme presque mort' [this almost-dead man], 'le mourant' [the dying man] (p. 67), and 'ivre de la vie, ou peut-être de la mort' [drunk with life, or perhaps with death] (p. 68). He is now himself in a state between life and death, in a sense, in a state of living death.[47]

What links Raphaël's stroll most tightly to the modernity of his experience is that the way he kills time is to go shopping. Having decided to wait until night to commit suicide, and assuming 'la démarche indolente d'un désœuvré' [the indolent stride of an idler] (p. 66), an early version of a *flâneur* perhaps, he sees the sellers of used books by the Pont Royal and the Quai de Voltaire and becomes interested in doing some bargaining. An odd scene ensues, when he first smiles at himself for wanting to bargain for something when he has no money, then having shoved his hands into his pockets, he inexplicably hears money jingling there: 'il entendit avec surprise quelques pièces retentir d'une manière véritablement fantastique au fond de sa poche' [he heard with surprise several coins jingling in a truly fantastic way at the bottom of his pocket] (p. 66). This fantastic sound of money occurs several times in the text,[48] as coins take on an almost magical power, later allegorized by the *peau de chagrin*, which seems supernaturally to provide money to Raphaël (and to fulfill his desires).[49] Coins in their materiality as gold or metal objects embody a kind of religious fetish (as magic object that can fulfill wishes). The fantastic nature and fetishism of the coins here connect with the phantasmagorical in Benjamin's sense, as we shall see below.[50]

The scene continues as Raphaël tosses away these newly-found coins, expressed by the word 'jeta' [tossed] (which is used also for the toss of his gold coin in his gambling bet), when he realizes that they amount only to three sous, so he throws them to beggars. If in gambling he tossed money to gain money, here he tosses money and gains the highly charged but dubious wish for the granting of long life proffered to him by the beggars (a wish that is ironic, because when he makes the pact with the *peau*, his life will grow shorter with each wish): 'Nous prierons Dieu pour la conservation de vos jours' [We will pray to God for the conservation of your days] (p. 67). This repetition of tossing money is the first in a repeated back and forth action between finding/conserving and spending money (and energy), an alternation between opposite states, which continues throughout the text.

Raphaël's next time-killing shopping stop is at the shop window of a print seller, where he looks in to watch a beautiful and well-off woman bargaining with the shopkeeper (a scene of woman shopping that will recur in Zola), and then *to cast* ('lancer') an intense glance at her, a glance that we shall take up later in Baudelaire's 'À une passante': 'le jeune homme [...] échangea vivement avec la belle inconnue l'œillade la plus perçante que puisse *lancer* un homme' [the young man [...] intensely made eyes at the beautiful stranger with the most piercing glance that a young man could cast] (p. 67, my emphasis).[51] However, once again an exchange, here throwing a glance to receive a glance (a variation of giving a coin to gain coins), is a gamble lost by Raphaël when she remains indifferent.

After Raphaël continues 'window-shopping' for a time, he enters a shop even though he has no money, and thus engages in what we might consider to be a more modern form of shopping experience: as Rachel Bowlby terms it in her book title, he is 'just looking'.[52] In 1830, most shops were still speciality shops that one entered only if one were going to buy something.[53] There were also at that time the *magasins de nouveautés* (novelty shops, an intermediary form between old shops and department stores), which offered a variety of items, some of which even had a *prix fixe*, such as Au Chateau d'Eau, (whose owner M. Raimbaut was a 'marchand de nouveautés à prix fixe' [a novelty-shop merchant using fixed prices]), a shop mentioned in the *Petit Dictionnaire critique et anecdotique des enseignes de Paris par un batteur de pavé*, published in 1826 by Balzac's own press (which was not a financial success).[54] The shop that Raphaël decides to explore is an antique shop, significantly a type of shop that displays objects from the (dead) past.[55]

When Raphaël enters the shop, he is already in a vague, dream-like state. Balzac describes its cause in a quasi-medical way as a liquefaction of his organism caused by his dying state, his 'agonie', and, as a result, he sees the world through an artificial fog: 'Les tourmentes de cette agonie lui imprimaient un mouvement semblable à celui des vagues, et lui faisaient voir les bâtiments, les hommes, à travers un brouillard où tout ondoyait' [The torments of his death throes instilled in him a movement similar to that of waves, and that made him see buildings, people, through a fog in which everything was undulating] (p. 68). Once he enters the antique shop, this becomes a state between waking and dreaming, between what is real and what is illusion, an interesting variation on what Bowlby describes as the experience of commodities as of being real and unreal at the same time.[56] What he sees and experiences, called a 'rêve' [dream] (p. 71), a 'songe' [dream or illusion] (p. 73), a 'rêverie' [daydream] (p. 76), and a state of 'somnolence' (p. 77), is a threshold state often repeated in Balzac's works: 'le rapide intervalle qui sépara sa vie somnambulique de sa vie réelle' [the rapid interval that separated his somnambulistic life from his real life] (p. 77).

Although this dreamy condition is attributed to his living-dead state, it is also his experience of shopping, which in the space of the shop becomes an experience of illusion and fascination, and I would like to examine this as a representation of the shopping experience generally in a kind of allegory, as well as specifically in relation to the concept of living death.[57] The antique shop is quite large, composed of two stories packed with heterogeneous items from the entirety of human history: 'Cet océan de meubles, d'inventions, de modes, d'œuvres, de ruines' [This ocean of furnishings, of inventions, of fashions, of works, of ruins] (p. 71). Since it contains objects from the past, it seems to be the negative opposite of a 'magasin de nouveautés', which, like the antique shop, contains somewhat heterogeneous products, but which by contrast are 'nouveaux'.[58] Balzac calls it a 'vaste bazar' (p. 73), the word 'bazaar' conjuring up exotic environments as well as an early example of a large store, Le Bazar de l'Industrie, built in 1827 and enlarged in 1830.[59]

When Raphaël enters the shop and tells the shop boy that he wants to look around to see if anything catches his fancy, the first items the young man mentions to him are mummies.[60] This is the initial example in a list of dead but preserved humans and creatures that are for sale in the shop. Another type of preserved human is an 'enfant en cire, sauvé du cabinet de Ruysch' [a waxen child, saved from the office of Ruysch] (p. 72) which the Gallimard edition explains as: 'Cadavres en réalité dont la décomposition était ralentie par une série d'injections que l'anatomiste hollandais Frederik Ruysch [1638–1731] présentait dans son cabinet' [Cadavers, in fact, whose decomposition was slowed by a series of injections, and which the Dutch anatomist, Frederik Ruysch [1638–1731] displayed in his office].[61] Here we have again examples of dead humans for sale. The shop also contains stuffed animals: 'Des crocodiles, des singes, des boas empaillés' [Stuffed crocodiles, monkeys, boa constrictors] (p. 69). The *peau de chagrin* is itself one of these preserved creatures. Thus, Balzac begins Raphaël's shopping tour of the shop with humans and animals, now dead, but which continue to exist in what one might call a condition of suspended death, and which are commodities in the marketplace.

The second type of living dead commodity consists of creatures that are dead but which, for Raphaël in his current dreamy state, seem to come back to life. A skeleton 'pencha dubitativement son crâne de droite à gauche, comme pour lui dire: "Les morts ne veulent pas encore de toi!"' [tilted its head sceptically from right to left as if to say to him: 'The dead don't want you yet!'] (p. 76). He sees briefly in the twilight 'les fantômes par lesquels il était entouré' [the phantoms that surrounded him] (p. 77) and it seems as though 'l'Inde et ses religions *revivaient* dans une idole' [India and its religions *revived* in an idol] (p. 71, my emphasis).[62] The narrator's discussion of Cuvier's findings highlights the scientist's abilities to bring fossilized dinosaurs back to life: 'la mort se vivifie, le monde se déroule!' [death is revivified, the world unfolds!] (p. 75). Thus, the shop sells not only dead humans and animals, it contains dead beings that seem to come back to life. This threshold state of living death, created by Balzac who is situated on the threshold of modernity, parallels Benjamin's description of 'products [...] on the point of entering the market as commodities. But they linger on the threshold'.[63] The antique shop is not yet the department store, but it straddles the space between old shop and new store.

The antique dealer is himself a living being who hovers on the threshold of death.[64] Raphaël, asleep or daydreaming, wakes to see 'ce personnage qui semblait être sorti d'un sarcophage voisin. La singulière jeunesse qui animait les yeux immobiles de cette espèce de fantôme empêchait l'inconnu de croire à des effets surnaturels' [this person who seemed to have emerged from a nearby sarcophagus. The singular youth that animated the immobile eyes of this kind of phantom prevented the stranger from believing in supernatural effects] (p. 77). It is in this description of the antique dealer and of the general experience of living death in this shop that we come across several uses of the word *fantasmagorie*. Here the text builds on the visual experience of 'spectacle' in Raphaël's visual experience of 'just looking' in the shop, as well as on its origin in the visual, illusory ghosts of phantasmagorical spectacles: Raphaël experiences the antique dealer as something 'magical' and as a phantom, an apparition, both living and dead (*CH* X, 77). The word *fantasmagorique* appears just as Raphaël snaps out of the dream illusion when he sees a painting of Christ (in Balzac's world, something worthy of belief): 'À l'aspect de cette immortelle création, il oublia les fantaisies du magasin, les caprices de son sommeil, redevint homme, reconnut dans le vieillard une créature de chair, bien vivante, nullement fantasmagorique, et revécut dans le monde réel' [At the sight of this immortal creation, he forgot the fantasies of the shop, the caprices of his sleep, he became a man again, recognized in the old man a creature of flesh and blood, quite alive, not at all phantasmagorical, and he returned to life in the real world] (p. 79). As Benjamin reads the phantasmagorical as related to nineteenth-century commodity culture, so Balzac represents the relation of the ghostly phantasmagorias of spectacle to the dreamlike world of shopping.

In addition to the return to life of dead animals and humans, we also find inanimate objects that come to life in the shop, and in this context the word *fantasmagorie* appears again. Here the works of art for sale in the shop come to life before Raphaël's eyes:

> Il souhaita plus vivement que jamais de mourir, et tomba sur une chaise curule en laissant errer ses regards à travers les fantasmagories de ce panorama du passé. Les tableaux s'illuminèrent, les têtes de vierge lui sourirent, et les statues se colorèrent d'une vie trompeuse. À la faveur de l'ombre, et mises en danse par la fiévreuse tourmente qui fermentait dans son cerveau brisé, ces œuvres s'agitèrent et tourbillonnèrent devant lui; chaque magot lui jeta sa grimace, les paupières des personnages représentés dans les tableaux s'abaissèrent sur leurs yeux pour les rafraichir. (*CH*, x, 76)

> [He wished more than ever to die, and fell onto a curule chair, letting his eyes wander over the phantasmagorias of this panorama of the past. Paintings lit up, heads of the Virgin Mary smiled at him, statues took on the colours of a false life. Thanks to the low light, and set to dancing by the torment that fermented in his shattered mind, these works moved and swirled before him; each magot grimaced at him, the eyelids of the individuals represented in these paintings lowered over their eyes in order to refresh them.]

Commodities (here works of art for sale) that represent human beings come to life, become like humans in a phantasmagorical panorama, again the idea of spectacle, here two different kinds.[65] Cohen's study of Benjamin mentioned in the Introduction is useful for advancing our understanding of the phantasmagoria here as she provides the following convolute of Benjamin in its description of the ghostly commodity:

> Once escaped from the hand of the producer and divested of its real particularity, it ceases to be a product and to be ruled over by human beings. It has acquired a 'ghostly objectivity' and leads a life of its own [...]. Things have attained autonomy, and they take on human features.[66]

Objects become like people; Raphaël's dreamlike experience seems to reveal the unconscious underside of commodity culture, in a world where, as we saw above, anything can be bought and sold. Indeed, when Raphaël accepts the pact with the skin, he trades his life for the ability to acquire things, he essentially 'sells' himself (in the sense that the price he is willing to pay for the skin is his life).

The text makes explicit that Raphaël is just like the things in the antique shop in their shared state of living death, on the threshold between thing and human, object and subject: 'doutant de son existence, il était comme ces objets curieux, ni tout à fait mort, ni tout à fait vivant' [doubting his existence, he was like these curious objects, neither completely dead nor completely alive] (p. 73). In fact, in his past, he himself made a kind of commodity of his own mother when he 'sold' her, in the sense that he sold the island on which her body was buried, and he significantly thought he saw her ghost when he completed the sale: 'Il me semblait entendre la voix de ma mère et voir son ombre' [It seemed to me that I heard my mother's voice and saw her shade] (p. 201).[67] This fills out the picture of the commodification of human beings mentioned above, when anything, people included, can be bought and sold in Balzac's representation of his contemporary society. As Raphaël himself says to his friend Émile after Raphaël has accepted the skin, he will become the representative of his society, which consumes everything, even people: 'Je ne m'amuserai pas à dissiper de vils écus, j'imiterai, je résumerai mon époque en consommant des vies humaines, et des intelligences, des âmes [...]. Tu es à moi, si je veux' [I won't be amusing myself with spending worthless écus, I will imitate, I will summarize my era by consuming human lives, and minds, souls [...]. You are mine, if I wish] (p. 203). To summarize, Balzac represents the commodification of his culture in Raphaël's shopping trip, a phantasmagorical spectacle where humans and things, ready for sale, meld in a condition of living death.[68]

This human-like quality of things appears in other commodities in the text (if we take 'commodities' to mean generally objects to be sold in the marketplace), and they become enmeshed in the identities of their possessors. Raphaël's hat, for instance, which took his place in the gambling den, is later deformed by the rain, and as Raphaël explains, it resembles him: 'Pour comble de malheur, la pluie déformait mon chapeau [...] il était blessé, déjeté, fini, véritable haillon, digne représentant de son maître' [To make matters worse, the rain had deformed my hat [...] it was wounded, deformed, finished, a veritable rag, worthy representative of its master] (pp. 159–60). In this example, an object of clothing becomes closely linked to the identity of the owner, and indeed, this recalls the topos of Balzac's world we saw above: clothes make the man. One cannot attain a high social standing without the appropriate costume, and Raphaël, when he is poor, does not have it: 'j'avais un habit râpé, des souliers mal faits, une cravate de cocher et des gants déjà portés' [I had a worn frock coat, poorly-made shoes, a coachman's tie, and gloves that had already been worn] (p. 122). Success depends on displaying the proper clothing, which serves as a signifier of wealth and class. Money allows one to buy a distinguished identity, in a sense, and the skin represents the ultimate spending power. Thus, clothing harbours deeper meanings in its very surface covering.

This deeper meaning links clothing to living death through the idea of the fetish. Raphaël claims that he loves cloth itself, 'Certes, je me suis cent fois trouvé ridicule d'aimer quelques aunes de blonde, du velours, de fines batistes' [To be sure, I had found myself ridiculous a hundred times for loving a few feet of lace, of velvet, of fine batistes] (p. 143). A woman must be covered by this artificial surface of expensive clothing in order for her to be attractive, thus desire itself blends with clothing as commodity, when human desirability merges into the cloth.[69] Here Raphaël needs cloth in order to desire, thus the commodity regulates the (sexual) relation between people, who also define themselves and others through the clothing that they wear. In describing the effect that a veil of lace has on him, Raphaël reveals its fantastic qualities: 'Des yeux brûlants, cachés par un voile de dentelle que les regards percent comme la flamme déchire la fumée du canon, m'offrent de fantastiques attraits' [Fiery eyes, hidden by a veil of lace and that pierce it like a flame rips through canon smoke, offer me fantastic attractions] (p. 142). The fetish object of desire creates a phantasmagorical effect as human relationships become a ghostly presence hidden in the veil of the purchasable object.

This veil brings us back to the idea of the dreamlike state of Raphaël in the antique shop. We learn from the narrator that this dream state is like a 'voile étendu sur sa vie et sur son entendement par ses méditations' [a veil spread over life and over his comprehension because of his meditations] (p. 79), another kind of veil that obscures reality, so that he sees even the antique dealer as being 'fantasmagorique' (p. 79). However, as we saw above, he awakens from this dream and the veil drops when he is faced with the old 'world' of faith, represented in the image of Christ (p. 79).

Other instances of this somnambulistic state occur in the text, as when Raphaël explains his life of debauchery to Émile, saying that intoxication can produce the same phantasmagorical dream state, 'L'ivresse vous plonge en des rêves dont les fantasmagories sont aussi curieuses que peuvent l'être celles de l'extase' [Intoxication plunges you into dreams whose phantasmagorias are as curious as can be those of ecstasy] (p. 197). Raphaël even describes himself as trying to believe in this type of illusory dream when he manages to spend time alone with Fœdora and to kiss her hand, 'j'étais alors si voluptueusement enfoncé dans l'illusion à laquelle j'essayais de croire, que mon âme se fondit et s'épancha dans ce baiser' [I was then so voluptuously steeped in the illusion that I was trying to believe to be true, that my soul melted and poured out into that kiss] (pp. 186–87). The illusion is so desirable that he wishes to remain in it.

Near the end of the novel when Raphaël rests in a mountain resort, the same image of an illusory 'voile étendu sur sa vie' appears, which in this case is a veil that covers social reality itself. Raphaël has been living in his own world, ignoring at his peril the social group that surrounds him. This group joins forces in their desire to show their power, and Raphaël suddenly sees through their hypocritically polite behaviour to the truth that lies beneath as he sees this power of the social group and the reality of human morality: 'Pris de pitié d'abord à cette vue du monde, il frémit bientôt en pensant à la souple puissance qui lui soulevait ainsi le voile de chair sous lequel est ensevelie la nature morale' [Seized at first by pity at the sight of this society, he soon trembled at the thought of the supple power that raised the veil of flesh for him, under which is buried our moral nature] (p. 265).

The metaphor used by Balzac to express this revelation is an extremely odd one, in which Raphaël's brain becomes 'animated', and the past of his behaviour is resurrected, when it is compared to a cadaver injected with a scientist's concoction, which reveals the tiniest of veins — again *animer* in the following quotation suggests that the dead person's veins seem to come to life:

> Soudain un rapide mouvement anima son cerveau, le passé lui apparut dans une vision distincte où les causes du sentiment qu'il inspirait saillirent en relief comme les veines d'un cadavre chez lequel, par quelque savante injection, les naturalistes colorent les moindres ramifications. (*CH*, x, 264)
>
> [Suddenly a rapid fluctuation animated his brain, the past appeared to him in a distinct vision in which the reasons for the feeling he inspired in these people stood out in relief like the veins of a cadaver into which, by some clever injection, naturalists colour the tiniest of ramifications].

The veil, the *vernis* [varnish] (p. 265) of human courtesy, is stripped away and Raphaël sees the 'ramifications' of his actions and the pettiness and reality that lie beneath the false, phantasmagorical surface. However, unlike his awakening when he sees the painting of Christ in the antique shop, here he wishes no longer to see reality, closes his eyes, and lets the veil (here curtain) fall back in place: 'il [...] ferma les yeux comme pour ne plus rien voir. Tout à coup un rideau noir fut tiré sur cette sinistre fantasmagorie de vérité' [he [...] closed his eyes as if to see no more. Suddenly a black curtain was drawn on this sinister phantasmagoria of the truth] (p. 265).[70] These veils of illusion, analogous to the cloth necessary for Raphaël's desire, unite the phantasmagoria of merchandise with the desire to ignore reality, and reveal the living death of Balzac's nascent modernity.

Illusion perdues and Splendeurs et misères des courtisanes

Raphaël de Valentin makes an interesting counterpart to Lucien (Chardon) de Rubempré, one of the main characters in *Illusions perdues* (1837) and *Splendeurs et misères des courtisanes* (1838). Both come from noble lineage, at least in part in Lucien's case; their families, although distinguished, are not wealthy; and they both, on the verge of suicide, are reborn into a new, symbolically 'post-mortem' life by 'selling' themselves, only to commit suicide in the end.[71] Thus they both, because they had decided to die, symbolically return from the dead when their first suicide attempt is prevented. As Lucien puts it in his letter to his sister: 'Au lieu de me tuer, j'ai vendu ma vie. Je ne m'appartiens plus' [Instead of killing myself, I sold my life. I no longer belong to myself.[72] Esther, too, returns from a first unsuccessful suicide attempt only to kill herself later. Finally, Vautrin undergoes a kind of symbolic death near the end of *Splendeurs et misères des courtisanes* when Lucien dies, after which he returns for his last metamorphosis and a new life in the police.[73]

A final significant similarity joins three of these characters. Raphaël and Lucien both make a pact in which they 'sell' their lives: Raphaël makes a pact with the *peau* and exchanges his life for the granting of wishes; Lucien makes a pact with Vautrin and sells himself (*CH*, v, 708–09). Esther has lived a life as a prostitute, and thus has literally sold herself. Again, in these two texts, the issue of the 'sale' or exchange of human beings arises in relation to the symbolic or real 'death' of a character.

Loss of illusions, loss of life: the title, *Illusions perdues*, introduces the important theme of the 'death' of youth and innocence that is the subject matter of this novel. However, if Lucien loses his youthful illusions in Paris, it is only to be reborn to new, modern illusions, as D. A. Miller notes.[74] Thus the title also contains within it another sense of the word 'illusions', which we saw in the phantasmagorical spectacle of Raphaël's shopping trip in *La Peau de chagrin*: the illusions created by the dreamlike world of modern Parisian life, along with the veils that this world places over reality. This dream world is figured by the word 'splendeurs', surface splendours that cover over the material 'misères' that lie beneath the illusion. At stake in the loss of illusion in these works, lost illusions being the death of a character's beliefs, is the question of the possibility of human beings to change.

The Living Death of the Provinces

Before we explore how these texts represent the new illusions of Paris that seem to turn people into the living dead, we must briefly examine the original illusions generated for Lucien in Angoulême, illusions that he loses in Paris. As we have seen in *Adieu*, *Le Colonel Chabert*, and *La Peau de chagrin*, Balzac links living death to the material environment, and in *Illusions perdues* he locates the beginning of the story in Angoulême, the place of Lucien's origin. The old part of this city, where the aristocratic families reside, represents the ghostly remains of an aristocracy that no longer has life and viability. It is a city section composed literally of the ruins of the past, of the remains of a fortress and its walls, which prevent it from moving into the modernity of financial commerce:

> L'importance qu'avait cette ville au temps des guerres religieuses est attestée par ses remparts, par ses portes et par les restes d'une forteresse assise sur le piton du rocher. Sa situation en faisait jadis un point stratégique également précieux aux catholiques et aux calvinistes; mais sa force d'autrefois constitue sa faiblesse aujourd'hui: en l'empêchant de s'étaler sur la Charente, ses remparts et la pente trop rapide du rocher l'ont condamnée à la plus funeste immobilité [...] le Commerce avait pris les devants ailleurs. (*CH*, v, 150)
>
> [The importance that this city had at the time of the Wars of Religion is witnessed by its ramparts, by its city gates, and by the remains of a fortress set on the peak of a rocky cliff. Its location made of it in the past a strategic point valuable equally to Catholics and Calvinists; but its former power constitutes its weakness today: by preventing it from spreading out on the Charente, its ramparts and the steep slope of the rock cliff condemned it to the deadliest immobility [...] Commerce had taken its first moves elsewhere.]

The deathly immobility of this aristocratic quarter represents the lag in the modernization of the provinces, where, as Séchard claims to his son David, things do not change: 'les habitudes des gens de province étaient si fortement enracinées, qu'il essaierait en vain de leur donner de plus belles choses' [the habits of provincial people were so deeply rooted that he would try in vain to give them more beautiful things] (p. 133).

Lucien, well-educated but poor, in a liminal state as half-aristocratic through his mother, straddles Angoulême's two quarters, aristocratic and commercial. His hybrid state and location combine with what Balzac calls the mobile nature of his mind (p. 146), a mobility crucial to the representation of his identity in the novel (and which contrasts with the immobility of aristocratic Angoulême). Because of his quasi-aristocratic status, he is able to achieve some small success in the old city as a poet when he is mentored by Mme Louise de Bargeton. She and Lucien share the same provincial illusion: that Lucien's literary talent will naturally find favour in Paris, where they think he is certain to succeed and where they can be together. The narrator at one point states that the imaginary pedestal on which those around Lucien have placed him creates 'une atmosphère pleine de mirages' [an atmosphere full of mirages] (p. 230). This first illusory mirage accompanies the couple to Paris.

Living Death in Paris: Selling Books, Selling Bodies

Of course, this mirage dissipates quickly when Lucien and Louise encounter the wildly different social structures of Paris and lose the illusions they had about themselves: 'Il se préparait chez Mme de Bargeton et chez Lucien un désenchantement sur eux-mêmes dont la cause était Paris' [For Mme de Bargeton and Lucien, a disenchantment with themselves was being prepared, the cause of which was Paris] (*CH*, v, 266). However, as this disenchantment takes place, new, more modern enchantments overtake Lucien. At first it is the seduction of theatre advertising that lures him when he strolls around Paris, where he 'se trouva sans force contre les séductions des affiches de spectacle' [found himself powerless to resist the seductions of the theatre posters] (p. 299). Balzac gives us a kind of social history of this new type of advertising, 'création neuve et originale' [a new and original creation] (p. 300) and later predicts, through Finot, the subordination of journalism itself to advertising, and thus to a kind of prostitution, which, as so many have noted, is perhaps *the* main theme of the text (p. 403). After being seduced by these advertisements, the theatre itself seduces Lucien, where the dreamy 'féerie'[75] of the scene and the drug-like intoxication it provides give way to reveal, just as this novel itself, the misery that lies beneath in a kind of warning or prefiguration:[76]

> Pour Lucien, ces deux heures passées au théâtre furent comme un rêve. [...] Ce fut comme un narcotique pour Lucien, et Coralie acheva de le plonger dans une ivresse joyeuse. Le lustre s'éteignit. [...] À la féerie de la scène, au spectacle des loges pleines de jolies femmes, aux étourdissantes lumières, à la splendide magie des décorations et des costumes neufs succédaient le froid, l'horreur, l'obscurité, le vide. Ce fut hideux. (*CH*, v, 391)

> [For Lucien, those two hours spent in the theatre were like a dream. [...] It was like a narcotic for Lucien, and Coralie finished by plunging him into joyous intoxication. The chandelier was extinguished. [...] The *féerie* of the scene, the spectacle of the boxes filled with pretty women, the astonishing lights, the splendid magic of the decor and new costumes were followed by the cold, the horror, the darkness, the void. It was hideous.]

This shiny, yet artificial surface appearance comprises one of the main illusions of Balzac's vision of nineteenth-century Parisian life, under which lies horror and emptiness.[77] As artifice and fiction, it represents a kind of death of reality in its dreamlike state.

This same image of living in a dreamy illusion appears later in Lucien's impression of Parisian luxury, where magic and dreams seem to have overtaken reality:

> Vers huit heures, au feu des lustres allumés, les meubles, les tentures, les fleurs de ce logis prirent cet air de fête qui prête au luxe parisien l'apparence d'un rêve. [...] il ne s'expliquait plus ni comment ni par qui ce coup de baguette avait été frappé. Florine et Coralie, mises avec la folle recherche et la magnificence artiste des actrices, souriaient au poète de province comme deux anges chargés de lui ouvrir les portes du palais des Songes. Lucien songeait presque. [...] il lui prenait des inquiétudes comme aux gens qui, tout en rêvant, se savent endormis. (*CH*, v, 471)

> [Around eight o'clock, under the flame of the chandeliers, the furnishings, the wallpaper, the flowers of this dwelling created the air of a party, which imparts to Parisian luxury the appearance of a dream. [...] he did not seek to know how nor by whom this magic wand had been waved. Florine and Coralie, dressed with the fanatic meticulousness and the artistic magnificence of actresses, smiled to the provincial poet like two angels charged with opening the doors for him to the palace of dreams. Lucien seemed almost to be dreaming. [...] he felt apprehensive, like those who, while dreaming, know they are asleep.]

Disenchantment, as Lucien moves away from the moribund life in Angoulême, thus leads to D. A. Miller's new seductions and illusions in the 'modern' world of Paris, where Lucien moves into the alluring, artificial 'phantasmagoria' of Parisian culture.

Given that the composition of the two novels, *Illusions perdues* and *Splendeurs et misères des courtisanes*, was not linear but rather somewhat piecemeal, the earliest depiction of the city of Paris in these two novels, in terms of the date of writing, might well be the one that appears in the beginning of *Splendeurs*.[78] This is the odd and somewhat fantastic description of the neighbourhood of the rue de Langlade where Esther lives, a neighbourhood of prostitution, where humans are literally sold (even though Esther at this point has given up prostitution to be pure for Lucien). At night, the nearby bright, well-lit, and popular district of the Palais-Royal, where 'reluisent les chefs-d'œuvre de l'Industrie, de la Mode et des Arts' [gleam the masterpieces of Industry, Fashion, and the Arts], is encircled by this dark and frightening neighbourhood.[79] In this 'red light district,' people seem literally to have become things, whereas inanimate things come alive. Half-nude human forms seem like furnishings that line the walls of buildings, darkness and shadow are alive, clothing walks and speaks, doors laugh:

> Des formes à demi nues et blanches meublent les murs, l'ombre est animée. Il se coule entre la muraille et le passant des toilettes qui marchent et qui parlent. Certaines portes entrebâillées se mettent à rire aux éclats [...]. Cet ensemble de choses donne le vertige [...]. [C]ette nature étrange offre toujours le même spectacle: le monde fantastique d'Hoffmann le Berlinois est là. Le caissier le plus mathématique n'y trouve rien de réel. (*CH*, vi, 447)

[Half-nude, white forms line the walls, the darkness is alive. Between the wall and the passerby slip dresses that walk and speak. Certain half-open doors begin to laugh heartily [...]. This collection of things makes one dizzy [...]. This strange nature always offers the same spectacle: the fantastic world of Hoffman of Berlin is there. The most mathematical clerk finds nothing real there.]

The human for sale has disappeared and remains only in its ghostly, fantastic or phantasmagorical 'forme'. This dark underside of Paris lurks on the edges of the shiny surface of the Paris of fashion, shopping, and the products of industry and art, similar to the description of the theatre above, when the illusory production has ended to show the shabby reality beneath. Balzac cannily introduces, through this literal reification of women prostitutes, the underlying problem that he sees as the growing prostitution of society itself, the death of human dignity.

Life in this Paris changes how people view their own worth, here Lucien, in *Illusions perdues*: 'cet homme d'imagination éprouva comme une immense diminution de lui-même' [this man of imagination felt a kind of immense diminution of his being] as those who were respected in the provinces are subjected to a 'perte totale et subite de leur valeur [...] une espèce d'anéantissement' [complete and sudden loss of their value [...] a kind of annihilation] (*CH*, v, 264). Mme de Bargeton undergoes a different kind of change, that of her appearance: 'Louise de Nègrepelisse ne se ressemblait pas à elle-même' [Louise de Nègrepelisse did not resemble herself] (p. 655). Indeed, Paris actually creates people, as Balzac claims for Samanon, significantly a shopkeeper. The narrator in *Illusions perdues* notes that characters from the works of Scott and Hoffmann cannot compare with what 'la nature sociale et parisienne s'était permis de créer en cet homme' [social and Parisian nature managed to create in this man] (p. 507). This question of identity and the possibility of its transformation by Paris lies at the heart these two novels, which explicitly explore the nature of human identity and the influence of social and environmental change on it, an influence that at times leads to living death, or simply to death itself.

If Esther's neighbourhood allegorizes the reification of Parisian society and the symbolic death of the human in prostitution, another Parisian space highlights prostitution in several forms, first literally: 'les Galeries de Bois étaient pour la prostitution un terrain public' [The Galeries de Bois were public terrain for prostitution] (p. 360). Balzac describes them as a veritable spectacle, somewhat like the seductive theatre, that 'tout Paris' comes to see, and he goes into great detail about the prostitutes' dresses and their elaborate hats and hairstyles created to draw the eye. So many people come to this public spectacle that walking is reduced to a crawl, but the slow pace, as Balzac puts it, only enhances one's ability to look, 'servait à l'examen' [aided observation] (p. 360). Balzac calls the Galeries a 'bazar' (p. 360), the word used in *La Peau de chagrin* for the antique shop, and here, in the Galeries, as in the antique shop, one finds heterogeneous objects, both people and things, for sale. It is interesting that some of these objects are other types of entertaining spectacles for which one must pay, most of which involve an illusion of one kind or another. There are ventriloquists, Cosmoramas, and automatons that play chess (p. 359): illusions themselves are for sale.

Also for sale in the Galeries are books (literature itself might be thought of as an illusion for sale), specifically those in Dauriat's bookshop. Balzac emphasizes the enormous profits that could be made at the time of the narrative, before there were 'cabinets de lecture' [reading rooms] (p. 360), when to read a book one had to buy it. Lucien learns that books have lost their aura in that 'les livres étaient comme des bonnets de coton pour des bonnetiers, une marchandise à vendre cher, à acheter bon marché' [books were like cotton hats, merchandise to be sold at a high price, to buy at a low price'] (p. 303). As many have noted, Balzac accompanies Esther's literal prostitution with that of the selling of books and also with the more symbolic selling of a writer's ideas, which themselves become objects of commerce when they acquire value, not because of their quality or veracity, but rather because they can be used for profit, particularly in journalism. As Michel Chrestien explains to Lucien, any author who enters the game becomes a kind of prostitute who must 'trafiquer de son âme, de son esprit et de sa pensée' [traffic in his soul, in his mind, and in his thought] (p. 328).[80]

Again, just as Raphaël trades his life for the fulfilment of his desires in his pact with the skin, writers sell their soul and mind for money, which is the death of their integrity. Balzac makes the link between prostitution and the book/newspaper sphere crystal clear:

> À l'aspect d'un poète éminent y prostituant la muse à un journaliste, y humiliant l'Art, comme la Femme était humiliée, prostituée sous ces galeries ignobles, le grand homme de province [Lucien] recevait des enseignements terribles. L'argent! était le mot de toute énigme. (*CH*, v, 365)
>
> [At the sight of an eminent poet prostituting his muse to a journalist, humiliating Art, just as Woman was humiliated, prostituted in these ignoble galleries, the great man of the provinces [Lucien] received some terrible lessons. Money! That was the solution to every enigma.]

To complete the image of living death that this prostitution brings at a symbolic level, Balzac informs us that the Galeries themselves are, at the time of the text's writing, 'dead', and he resurrects them for the reader. The narrator explains that they had been torn down before the novel was written, and he claims that, for the younger generation, this description of the Galeries is actually unbelievable (p. 355).

The final aspects of the Galeries of note here are the fashion shops, particularly hat shops (and we recall the symbolic value of hats in *La Peau de chagrin*), important in Balzac's world because, as with Chabert's *carrick*, 'clothes make the man' (we shall look at Lucien's multiple shopping trips below). In the Galeries, wild hats, books, and clothes are sold side by side, emphasizing again the commercial foundation of literature: 'Les libraires et les marchandes de modes vivaient en bonne intelligence' [the booksellers and the fashion merchants got along well with each other] (p. 359). The beginning of the section of the text that describes this bazaar involves one of the strangest descriptions in Balzac's works: it is the liminal space that separates the Galeries' buildings from the outside public space. The metaphors in this passage create a remarkable allegory that reveals the artificiality of the dream world of shopping and literature. This allegory is created by mixing the imagery of natural flowers with the artificial creations of fashion and literature and by placing them in a dirty and fetid area.

Balzac writes that, in the Galeries, literature itself 'flowers': "Là fleurissaient les nouvelles et les livres' [There flowered novellas and books] (p. 358). Outside the Galeries exists the odd space next to the building's walls, a border 'infâme et nauséabonde' [vile and putrid], two or three feet wide (p. 356), where one finds decidedly odd plants, and here I build on Prendergast's cogent reading of the 'tenuous distinction between the genuine and the fake' in this scene.[81] The words that describe the growing plants are used for both natural and artificial products in this border 'où végétaient les produits les plus bizarres d'une botanique inconnue à la science, mêlés à ceux de diverses industries non moins florissantes' [where vegetated the most bizarre products of a botany unknown to science, mixed with products of diverse industries no less blooming] (p. 356). Here the difference between natural plant and artificial industry has been blurred, and this ambiguity continues. A blotting paper, used in the making of printed material, displays words that are 'fleurs de rhétorique' [flowers of rhetoric] (p. 356). This rhetorical paper flower 'coiffait' — capped, in the sense of covering like one of the hats sold in the Galeries — a natural rosebush of decaying flowers ('fleurs avortées', p. 356), which give scent to the artificial paper flower.

The mixing of natural and artificial — of hats and flowers and print copy — continues when leaflets advertising literature along with discarded hair ribbons also 'flower' ('fleurissaient') in the greenery (p. 356). Significantly, discarded fashion items suffocate, 'kill' natural vegetation ('Les débris de modes étouffaient la végétation', p. 356), symbolic of both the powerful artifice of fashion, and the superficial, shiny surface of Parisian life that overpowers and suffocates the natural and the real. The potent illusion of artifice itself is brought home in the passage when in the description of how people are suddenly disappointed as they admire a dahlia in this garden and discover that it is in reality a satin bow. One might think of this disillusionment as one of the meanings of the title and of the text itself, as Balzac draws aside the false surface to show what is not alive beneath.

The description of this small space in Paris thus turns into an allegory of the sordid and empty, illusory dream created by modern Paris, and Balzac compares this fetid border to a fairytale dragon guarding a desired princess, the desired fantastic 'illusions' of beauty inside the 'palais fantasque' [fantastic palace] of the Galeries (p. 356). He notes that, like the hero in a fairy tale, the public's desire is unimpeded by this dirty dragon's lair, and people brave the sordid space to enter the dream world.[82] The flowery examples resonate with Lucien's particular destiny, first because of their shared hybridity (his noble and bourgeois lineage), but also because his book of poems, *Les Marguerites*, is a collection of sonnets, each on a particular flower, which he has come to the Galeries to try to sell. And he ends up selling himself, entering the ghostly world of the human commodity, which d'Arthez predicts will be his symbolic death: 'Là serait la tombe du beau, du suave Lucien que nous aimons et connaissons' [There would be the tomb of the handsome, of the suave Lucien that we love and know] (p. 327). His sister, Ève, confirms the result of this symbolic death sentence when she claims that 'j'aime mon frère, comme on aime le corps d'un être qui n'est plus' [I love my brother, like I love the body of a being who is no more] (p. 642).

In this Paris of outer glamour and dark depth, clothing as the surface that covers the human body creates that person's identity for others, as we saw in Chabert, no matter what the reality that lies beneath might be. The two provincials who arrive in Paris together, Mme de Bargeton and Lucien, immediately observe that their own fashion style is woefully inadequate and understand that fashion items are paradoxically 'superfluités nécessaires' [necessary superfluities] (p. 270). Both quickly go shopping (one is reminded of Raphaël's limbic shopping trip). Significantly, when Lucien goes to Louise's rooms to find her, she is out shopping and she won't be 'in' for him much longer, as she will refuse to see him. Louise has some luck with her choices because Châtelet gives her crucial information, which Balzac passes along in detail, about where to buy each garment (p. 262), although de Marsay still finds that she resembles, significantly, a mummy (p. 282). Lucien has no such guide and rushes out to the Palais-Royal to spend his meagre money on clothes that make him appear to be a best man at a wedding (p. 272) and a dressed mannequin at the door of a tailor's shop (p. 280). He eventually goes to Staub, *the* tailor in Balzac's Paris, is later dressed by Coralie, his mistress, learns the ropes, and becomes a dandy (pp. 454, 479).

Once again, however, Balzac gives an odd description of the underside of this surface elegance of fashion, in a scene that links fashion to prostitution. It is first necessary to take a detour through *Splendeurs et misères des courtisanes*, where Nucingen goes to a used clothing shop to haggle about, 'marchander', the fee he will pay for Esther. Here, the selling of clothes and the selling of women go hand-in-hand: Asie is there 'prête à vendre le contenu, tant elle a l'habitude d'acheter le contenant, la robe sans la femme ou la femme sans la robe!' [ready to sell the contents, so familiar is she with buying the container, the dress without the woman or the woman without the dress!] (p. 571). Just as one sees in Esther's neighborhood outfits that walk and talk, so in the shop where Esther's sale is being arranged, articles of clothing eerily seem to emit the sounds and sights of those who have died in them, and the dead seem to live: 'On y voit des défroques que la mort y a jetées de sa main décharnée, et on entend alors le râle d'une phtisie sous un châle, comme on y devine l'agonie de la misère sous une robe lamée d'or' [One sees there tattered old clothes that death tossed there with its fleshless hand, and one then hears the death rattle of a consumptive under a shawl, just as one detects the death throes of misery under a gold lamé dress] (p. 571). The clothes that walk in the rue de Langlade find an echo in this shop, where one can almost physically see the face of the former owner in the turban that she used to wear for sale there: 'On y retrouve la physionomie d'une reine sous un turban à plumes dont la pose actuelle rappelle et rétablit presque la figure absente' [One finds there the physiognomy of a queen under a feathered turban, whose present pose recalls and almost restores the absent face] (p. 571).[83] Balzac remarkably again links prostitution and clothing to living death in this shopping boutique.[84] Thus in these symbolic passages in the two novels, clothes not only represent the surface illusion that creates an artificial but functioning identity, they also reveal the death of human integrity that becomes lost in selling oneself and in surface artifice. What is left are the remains of a living person whose identity has 'died', a symbolic counterpart to Chabert.

Power, Change, and Living Death

In this Paris where individuals are confronted with the changes that accompany modernity, the three main characters of *Splendeurs et misères des courtisanes* attempt to reshape their own identities, and their success or failure in this enterprise grounds the plot of the text. In a sense, they must try to 'kill' their former selves and emerge into a new identity and a new life. Lucien aims to erase his bourgeois past and to establish his aristocratic identity while accumulating money in order to marry a wealthy, aristocratic young woman. Esther Van Gobseck tries to erase her past identity as the prostitute, La Torpille, in order to purify herself and her love for Lucien. And Vautrin, Jacques Collin/Carlos Herrera, continues to assume multiple identities and literally has tried to erase the proof of his past criminal identity by burning scars into his flesh to cover over the letters TF branded on his shoulder. Thus, Balzac explores the possibility of effecting a radical change in one's identity, in a sense a way of erasing the past, of killing the past of one's identity. Behind these deliberate efforts aimed at change lies the more general question: Can humans deliberately change? Is identity physical, in the blood, impossible to destroy? Or can one shape it as it is shaped by society and circumstances? Or both? The answers to these questions posed by Balzac, as well as by the science of his time, play themselves out through these three characters as they negotiate a world in the process of becoming our modernity.

Balzac provides much more detail about the nature and possibility of change in the case of Esther, even going into scientific explanations. At the beginning of *Splendeurs et misères des courtisanes*, Esther has already been trying to erase her life of prostitution, but she fails and consequently tries to commit suicide, the first of her brushes with death. Vautrin, who also loves Lucien and desires his happiness, tells her she must kill this past completely and change from courtesan to proper lady if she wants to continue to see Lucien and to help him succeed. Vautrin couches the stakes of this change in terms of life and death: she was not yet strong enough to 'enterrer la fille de joie' [bury the prostitute] (*CH*, VI, 461), so in the future she must change entirely (p. 460). She must, in a sense, commit a kind of social 'suicide' in order to be reborn in a new identity.

For Esther, the heart of the problem lies in the milieu, which Balzac had already famously explored in the case of Madame Vauquer, who is in fine harmony with her pension. The narrator anchors Esther's Jewish 'type' in what he terms the 'race' and the place of her origin — 'les races venues des déserts' [the races that come from deserts] — which reveal themselves in her eyes (p. 464). Thus, her identity lies in some way in the milieu of her family. The narrator then poses the main question about the reasons for this interdependence of identity and milieu: the question of nature or nurture. He asks: did 'nature' (God, in this case for Balzac) create this quality of the eyes so that these humans could survive in the desert (p. 465)? Or, were these qualities formed over time as a result of the exposure of this people to the desert environment, in other words, 'nurture' (p. 465)?

The entire section of the text on Esther and race that follows these questions was extensively reworked by Balzac and is difficult to untangle. It involves the idea of instinct, which is really behaviour, of sheep as they graze: a particular sheep variety (which would correspond to race for Esther, who is from a Jewish family with origins in those desert environments) has specific instincts/behaviours that result from different 'necessities' of the environment inhabited by this variety. If the sheep are transferred to a different environment, they at first retain their old behaviour; yet they change this behaviour over time as they adapt to the new environment. That means that nurture, transformation by the environment, trumps nature; however, this kind of change happens very slowly. Balzac then throws a wrench into this argument by saying that, after many years, the old 'instincts' will sometimes reappear in one refractory sheep that has not changed: this wayward sheep is Esther with her desert eyes that reappear, after an absence of 1800 years, in the city of Paris in the nineteenth century (p. 465). In this case we have the idea of the distant past that returns to haunt the present, a situation that we shall find again in Chapter 3 on Jacques Lantier in Zola's *La Bête humaine*. Thus, it would seem that some, but not all sheep and persons can change, and that at times the dead past of ancestry returns in the present.

This ambiguity concerning the nature and possibility of change is then played out in Esther's social context.[85] She converts to Catholicism and undergoes what appears to be a 'complete' transformation through her education: 'Le changement devint si complet que [...] Herrera fut surpris, lui que rien au monde ne paraissait devoir surprendre' [The change became so complete that [...] Herrera was surprised, he whom nothing in the world seemed to surprise] (p. 466). However, her past has actually not been erased so completely because she has physical needs that remain and that were formed by her milieu of prostitution: 'elle ne pouvait vaincre les instincts développés par la débauche' [she could not vanquish the instincts developed by debauchery'] (p. 467). These 'instincts' that she developed as a prostitute prevent her from being able to live the life of the virtuous Catholic maiden. She describes this as a conflict between two fanaticisms: her love for purity and her love for Lucien, and she becomes ill and nearly dies — her second brush with death. In a heady mixture of metaphors of life and death, Vautrin then lets her know that she will be able to be with Lucien and remain 'pure' in her faithfulness to him, and this allows her to come back from the edge of death [elle ressuscita] [(p. 472). After this, Vautrin lets Lucien know that her former self is dead, 'La Torpille n'existe plus' [La Torpille no longer exists] (p. 478), and she remains faithful to Lucien for six years (p. 597); her previous identity appears indeed to be dead. She has been transformed by her education and her love for Lucien: 'Esther avait complètement oublié son ancienne vie' [Esther had completely forgotten her former life] (p. 596).

However, it is her social role, specifically the role of courtesan, which is resurrected by Vautrin in order to finance Lucien's social success (and not her race or her ingrained instincts of prostitution), that combines with her purified love for Lucien and prevents her from continuing in this new identity. Should she choose not to submit to Nucingen, she would stand in the way of Lucien's goals of succeeding in society. So she decides to sacrifice her purity and her life when she gives herself to Nucingen and then finally succeeds in committing suicide. These are not, then, her physical instincts formed by the distant past that force her into this role, but rather the power of the social strictures around her that force her to act. She is not allowed to bury her past and, in her eyes, it must return. After she has made the decision to die for Lucien, she alludes in a veiled manner to her pure self as a friend who is already dead, and Esther the prostitute is waiting to follow that friend: 'J'avais une amie, une femme bien heureuse, elle est morte, je la suivrai... voilà tout' [I had a friend, a really happy woman, she is dead, I will follow her... that is all] (p. 684). In this interim period between purity and prostitution, the text calls her 'la mourante' as she is between life and death; her pure self is dead, her impure self lives. She joins the ranks of the living dead.

Thus, the social world prevents Esther from changing her social role as prostitute, which she is not permitted to quit. And it is this world that reduces her to a thing whose 'beauté passait à l'état de capital' [beauty was becoming capital] (p. 569).[86] In her suicide letter to Lucien, she describes herself as 'une morte' [a dead woman] (p. 762), anticipating his reading of the letter when she will be dead, but also describing the strange literal and figurative lives and deaths of her identities. In the final instance, change does not happen completely for Esther: her past life continues to haunt her present until she ends it.[87]

Vautrin would seem to be the character who changes the most, at least superficially, as he transforms his outward, social identity numerous times. Having escaped from prison, Vautrin, called a 'mort-civil' [dead person in terms of civil rights] because of his criminal identity as Jacques Collin, decides to turn himself into a priest in order to begin a solitary life without family entanglements and to live again (*revivre*) (p. 503). To do so, he murders the real Carlos Herrera and transforms himself physically by effacing most of the letters TF branded on his shoulder and by lugubriously scarring his face with chemicals in order to resemble the corpse of the dead priest: 'En se métamorphosant ainsi devant le cadavre du prêtre avant de l'anéantir, il put se donner quelque ressemblance avec son sosie' [By thus metamorphosing himself as he looked at the cadaver of the priest before destroying the dead body, he was able to give himself a certain resemblance to his double] (p. 503). Already 'civilly' dead, Vautrin takes on the identity of a dead man to begin a new life; he now turns himself in a more symbolic way into a dead man who lives.

Balzac compares this odd 'body snatching' to the story of the way in which a 'derviche a conquis le pouvoir d'entrer, lui vieux, dans un jeune corps par des paroles magiques' [dervish acquired the power to enter, as an old man, a young body by means of magic words] (p. 503). On a symbolic level, this description of his spirit entering another's body and taking it over accurately describes what Vautrin tries to do symbolically with Lucien. He aims to be Lucien, in a sense, and to be able to say, as in *Illusions perdues*, 'Ce beau jeune homme, c'est moi!' [This young man, that is I!] (*CH*, v, 708). Lucien has, in *Splendeurs et misères des courtisanes*, become his 'second lui-même' [second self] (*CH*, vi, 502).[88] He wants to accompany Lucien in his carriage (*CH*, v, 708), he dines at the Grandlieu's, slips into the chambers of great ladies, and vicariously loves Esther (*CH*, vi, 813). And through the dead priest's identity and Lucien's living body, Vautrin can live again: he 'revivait dans le corps élégant de Lucien, dont l'âme était devenue la sienne. Il se faisait représenter dans la vie sociale par ce poète, auquel il donnait sa consistance et sa volonté de fer' [came alive again in Lucien's elegant body, whose soul had become his own. He represented himself in social life by means of the poet, to whom he gave his force and his iron will] (*CH*, vi, 502).

It seems as though, after Lucien commits suicide, Vautrin does change, and the text links that change with death.[89] When he holds Lucien's cold, dead hand, the chill of death takes over Vautrin's life:

> La froideur se communique aux sources de la vie avec une rapidité mortelle. Mais l'effet de ce froid terrible, et agissant comme un poison, est à peine comparable à celui que produit sur l'âme la main roide et glacée d'un mort tenue ainsi, serrée ainsi. La Mort parle alors à la Vie, elle dit des secrets noirs et qui tuent bien des sentiments; car, en fait de sentiment, changer, n'est-ce pas mourir? (*CH*, vi, 818)

> [Cold communicates itself to the sources of life with a mortal rapidity. However, the effect of this terrible cold, acting like poison, is scarcely comparable to the one that generates in the soul the rigid and icy hand of a dead man held thus, gripped thus. Death then speaks to Life, it tells dark secrets that kill many feelings; for, in the case of feelings, to change, is it not to die?]

Vautrin says to Grandville twice that they are burying his own life with Lucien's body, most forcefully here: 'Jacques Collin est en ce moment enterré, monsieur de Grandville, avec Lucien, sur qui l'on jette actuellement de l'eau bénite et qui part pour le Père-Lachaise' [Jacques Collin is at this moment buried, monsieur de Grandville, with Lucien, on whom they are now sprinkling holy water and who is setting off for Père Lachaise] (p. 923).[90] Vautrin also uses a vestimentary metaphor (clothing being so important) to describe this death when he thinks of himself as 'un vêtement sans corps' [an item of clothing without a body] (p. 822), having lost his *raison d'être*, Lucien.

However, the text remains somewhat ambiguous concerning this deathly change. Although Vautrin claims that he wishes simply to join the forces of order by joining the police, in his discussion with Grandville he has a different end in sight, that of revenge. Although he convinces Grandville, and in part his reader, of his interest in order, the text also represents him as manipulating Grandville, playing a kind of game: 'Jacques Collin lut dans le cœur du procureur général et continua le même jeu' [Vautrin read the heart of the general prosecutor and continued the same game] (p. 925). In another example, the lack of transformation appears in his discussion with his aunt, Jacqueline, when he says that he lives to revenge Lucien's death and that joining the police is the way to accomplish this. According to Vautrin, outward social states (such as being a policeman) do not matter, only the idea that one lives by: 'Les états qu'on fait dans le monde ne sont que des apparences; la réalité, c'est l'idée!' [The professions that one has in society are only appearances; reality is the idea!] (p. 912). Vautrin may change his superficial identity, but he implies that there is a deeper level that does not change. The dead Lucien remains, in a sense, his *raison d'être*.

This change that is not really change corresponds to the conclusions of D. A. Miller in his important article. Miller shows that criminals and police are interchangeable, and they are in a sense, reflective of the general social milieu, because in this novel all submit to the same, inescapable and overarching Foucauldian and mechanizing social power.[91] Thus Esther, too, is forced back into prostitution against her will by the social forces surrounding her and Lucien. In this novel, this ubiquitous social force of nascent modernity represents perhaps the process of the reduction of all things to money and the resulting generalized prostitution. Balzac's text formulates this idea of power through Vautrin's words to Grandville, even though, as we have seen, Vautrin's motives are suspicious:

> Eh bien! j'ai vu, depuis vingt ans, le monde par son envers, dans ses caves, et j'ai reconnu qu'il y a dans la marche des choses une force [...]. Une seule [place] me convient, c'est de me faire le serviteur de cette puissance qui pèse sur nous, et quand cette pensée m'est venue, la force dont je vous parlais s'est manifestée clairement autour de moi. (*CH*, VI, 922–24)
>
> [Well then! I have seen, for the last twenty years, the underside of society, in its cellars, and I have realized that there is in the way of the world a force [...]. Only one [place] suits me: it is to make myself the servant of this power that weighs on us, and when this thought came to me, the force I spoke about to you showed itself clearly around me.]

Although Vautrin gives this force the name 'le hasard' [chance] (p. 922), and Grandville might call it God's work, it is a force that shapes human destiny and that results in the impossibility of resistance, of escape, of change.[92] Thus Vautrin's example in this text, through the representation of the reversibility of criminal and police, also shows that change is merely superficial. The 'force' of the new social order in a sense destroys, kills the possibility of human freedom, and all become puppets of this social power.

Finally Lucien's attempt to change becomes more generally symbolic, because his efforts to become a member of the Parisian nobility allegorize the state of the monarchy and the problematic definition of nobility itself. At first, Lucien would seem to be the person most likely to change, because, as we saw above, the text several times describes his personality as mobile. His provincial mobility, when he moves between the aristocratic and more modern sections of Angoulême, becomes his social mobility in Paris as he moves among many different social circles there.[93] Between noble and bourgeois, between provincial and Parisian, between the worlds of literature and journalism, he reflects the liminal, transitional space of Paris itself that we saw above. *Splendeurs et misères des courtisanes* tells the tale of this liminal state of Lucien, which is represented as a kind of living death after his first decision to commit suicide, a kind of life after accepting to die; as he himself says to Mlle des Touches, the success of his book upon his return to Paris is a 'succès posthume' [posthumous success] (p. 488). This post-mortem state would seem to represent his decision to sell himself to Vautrin and to plunge wholeheartedly into a culture dominated by money, as he writes to his sister, Ève, as we saw above, 'Au lieu de me tuer, j'ai vendu ma vie. Je ne m'appartiens plus'.

However, Lucien's second decision to kill himself reveals that he has not, in fact, been able to change and adapt himself to this new world. His failure involves Vautrin's idea of power: here this power is given shape in the battle waged between, on the one hand, the unified couple Lucien/Vautrin as they struggle to create a future, and on the other, Camusot, the judge assigned to get to the bottom of Esther's death and her missing money. Vautrin's support and fidelity represent for Lucien the old-fashioned honour involved in the 'loi de solidarité' [law of solidarity] (p. 774); Lucien should not speak, should not give up his associate, Vautrin, to the police (p. 774). However, Lucien is tricked into revealing Vautrin's identity by the judge Camusot, the representative of the new social power of the law and the police. Camusot represents a force that no longer rests in the hands of the king, but that has become more diffuse.[94] The narrator bemoans the fact that someone like Camusot represents the loss of power of the monarchy and its transfer to the machine of the judiciary. No human, not even the king, can interfere with Camusot's inquiry: 'Aucune puissance humaine, ni le Roi, ni le garde des Sceaux, ni le premier ministre ne peuvent empiéter sur le pouvoir d'un juge d'instruction' [No human power, not the King, not the Keeper of the Seals, not the prime minister, can impinge on the power of an examining magistrate] (p. 718).

In this novel, this shift from the old judicial order to the new is disastrous because members of the judiciary are now paid public servants. In the past, judges were independently wealthy and thus independent: they were not slaves to ambition and money, and their rulings were based on the ideas of justice and honour. In Lucien's time, money reigns: 'Aujourd'hui le magistrat, [est] payé comme un fonctionnaire, pauvre pour la plupart du temps [...]. Là gît le vice de l'institution actuelle [...]. [O]n pourrait relever la magistrature en exigent d'elle de grandes fortunes' [Today the magistrate [is] paid like a civil servant, poor for the most part [...]. There lies the flaw in the current institution [...]. One could elevate the magistrature by requiring of it large fortunes] (pp. 718–19). Driven by the desire for money, ambition prevails:

> Le traitement payé par l'État fait du prêtre et du magistrat des employés. Les grades à gagner développent l'ambition; l'ambition engendre une complaisance envers le pouvoir [...]. Ainsi, les deux colonnes de tout ordre social, la Religion et la Justice, se sont amoindries. (*CH*, VI, 801–02)
>
> [The salary paid by the State makes employees of the priest and the magistrate. The ranks to be earned develop ambition; ambition engenders complacency towards power [...]. In this way, the two pillars of every social order, Religion and Justice, are diminished.]

And Camusot fits the bill as an ambitious man; when he pries out from Lucien the identity of Vautrin, he feels he has triumphed and will now be considered 'l'un des plus habiles juges d'instruction' [one of the cleverest examining magistrates] (p.

774). Here the narrator states once again one of the major 'lessons' of the novel: in this new world, 'on fait de l'argent la garantie sociale universelle' [one makes money the universal social guarantee] (p. 801), as even justice is beholden to financial considerations.

Lucien then reveals his basic 'nobility' in his decision to end his life, even though he has now partially fulfilled his dreams. It is ironically Camusot who informs Lucien that he is extremely rich because of his inheritance from Esther, and that all he has worked for has come to pass: he finally seems to possess what he needs to take part in the new world where money reigns, and he has obtained his official aristocratic name. However, Lucien now realizes that this success means nothing because he betrayed his duty in his obligation to Vautrin when he succumbed to Camusot's wiles. Lucien's acceptance of his own guilt reveals that he remains faithful, in a sense, to that more ancient and general law from the past, that 'loi de solidarité' [law of solidarity] that we saw above. When Lucien realizes the wrong he did to Vautrin, his decision to retract his statements and to die reveals that he has not been transformed by the new order of money and instead remains formed by the 'noble' past, both in his aristocratic, ancestral name and in his adherence to what the narrator regards as more noble laws, rather than those variable contemporary social edicts that reign with the likes of Camusot. Lucien thus does not change and his past 'kills' him.[95] This shows perhaps the contradictions involved in Lucien's desire to be noble and at the same time succeed in a world based on money: in the end 'nobility' can no longer exist in his contemporary society, and he is a relic of the past, like Chabert.[96]

Balzac allegorizes Lucien's situation in the material and materialistic world of Paris in the remarkable and moving description of his final moments as he looks out at the Conciergerie. This building links his noble identity to the history of royalty in France, symbolized by the Conciergerie prison and the Palais de Justice, because Lucien and these buildings have something in common: a half-effaced noble past. Lucien tries to resurrect his maternal nobility and to reinstate that part of his past in the present. The past of the Conciergerie and the Palais de Justice was its identity as the Palais des rois [Palace of kings] and of Saint Louis in particular. However, their royal history lies submerged beneath the present structure, and we find again the idea of fossils from *La Peau de chagrin*, the dead that continue to exist in the present:

> Ce palais de nos rois, sur lequel vous marchez quand vous arpentez l'immense Salle des Pas-Perdus, était une merveille d'architecture [...]. Aujourd'hui bien des plaies affectent ce gigantesque monument, enfoui sous le palais [de justice] et sous le quai, comme un de ces animaux antédiluviens dans les plâtres de Montmartre. (*CH*, VI, 708–09)
>
> [This palace of our kings, on which you walk when you traverse the immense Salle des Pas-Perdus, was an architectural marvel [...]. Today, many wounds affect this gigantic monument, buried under the courthouse and the quay, like one of those antediluvian animals in the gypsum of Montmartre.]

Balzac goes to great lengths to describe the architecture and history of the Conciergerie and the narrator criticizes the newer construction that has scarred the surface of this admirable royal past. The crime of this remodelling is described with a word very important in the text — prostitution:

> L'un des côtés du préau [...] présente aux regards une enfilade de colonnes gothiques entre lesquelles les architectes de je ne sais quelle époque ont pratiqué deux étages de cabanons pour loger le plus d'accusés possible, en empâtant de plâtre, de grilles et de scellements les chapiteaux, les ogives et les fûts de cette galerie magnifique [...]. Cette prostitution des plus grands souvenirs de la France est d'un effet hideux. (*CH*, VI, 793)

> [One of the sides of the inner courtyard [...] presents to one's gaze a succession of gothic columns, between which architects, from who knows what era, added two stories of prison cells in order to house as many accused as possible, by filling with plaster, prison bars, and sealants the column heads, the ogives, and the columns of this magnificent gallery [...]. This prostitution of the greatest memories of France has a hideous effect.]

Lucien, imprisoned in the Conciergerie, and just about to hang himself in his cell, looks out at this gallery, and his suicide is once more postponed: 'son suicide fut retardé par son admiration' [his suicide was delayed by his admiration] (p. 793). Having sold himself to Vautrin and then having betrayed him, Lucien looks out at this architectural prostitution, which symbolizes his own, and he hallucinates its beautiful restoration, the return of its past beauty:

> Lucien vit le Palais dans toute sa beauté primitive. La colonnade fut svelte, jeune, fraîche. La demeure de saint Louis reparut telle qu'elle fut, il en admirait les proportions babyloniennes et les fantaisies orientales. Il accepta cette vue sublime comme un poétique adieu de la création civilisée. (*CH*, VI, 794)

> [Lucien saw the Palace in all of its original beauty. The colonnade was slender, young, fresh. The dwelling of Saint Louis reappeared just as it was; he admired its Babylonian proportions and oriental fantasies. He accepted this sublime view as a poetic adieu from the creations of civilization.]

This hallucination, the fictional dream of restoring the Conciergerie to its splendid previous state, represents a return to the past that differs from the dreamy modern illusions of the theatre and the luxuries of rich Parisian society inhabited by Lucien before, which he calls in his suicide letter 'les enchantements d'un rêve' [the enchantments of a dream] (p. 790). This vision of the palace pays homage to the aesthetic beauty created by past 'civilized' society, an aesthetic that has turned in Lucien's current time to the prostitution of profit in the bookselling trade and in the degradation of the palace.[97] In one symbolic sentence, Balzac tells us that a stone that served Saint Louis for the distribution of alms serves in the current structure as a table where food is sold to the prisoners — royal charity has turned to capitalist commerce (p. 823). Here perhaps, in the beauty of this vision of the old palace, we see the beauty in Lucien's own desire to restore his noble past, which actually emerges, past his own weakness and prostitution, in the noble honour of his final, fatal actions. Indeed, here, in this new illusion, both the Conciergerie and Lucien's noble past are symbolically restored, but the Conciergerie remains marred and Lucien is destroyed. This return is described as the dead who have come back to life, if just for a moment, in the splendour of this different kind of hallucination: 'Alors apparaissent les spectres, les fantômes, alors les rêves prennent du corps, les choses détruites revivent alors dans leurs conditions premières' [Then appear the spectres, the ghosts, then dreams take physical form, things destroyed then revive in their original conditions] (p. 793).

In sum, then, on the one hand, the attempt by Lucien to restore the pure past in his current reality fails in the real world, just as the Conciergerie has been irrevocably scarred by new construction.[98] Is this perhaps a statement about the monarchy, which simply can never be repaired or restored because of the weight of history, the weight of changes that have happened over too long a period, like those sheep, whose instincts eventually are transformed by time spent in the new milieu? Lucien dies, significantly, around the time of the July Revolution.

On the other hand, the attempts by Vautrin and Esther to erase the past also fail; one cannot eradicate the past in the present. Balzac seems to be showing some kind of resignation to the power of a present that he sees as a time of contamination, where the past can neither be restored nor erased, a kind of impasse. The power of an individual in the past (the king) has now become invisible and diffused throughout the social order itself, making it impossible to counter. Thus, any attempt to change brings defeat at the hands of the 'power' of the social order, and a living death to the royal past: as the narrator says: 'changer n'est-ce pas mourir?' [To change, is it not to die?] (p. 818).[99]

Change is a major structural element of Balzac's interrogation of his society. The figure of living death in his works shows a past in the process of disappearing, a past that acts as a ghostly presence in a new world of living death that is being ushered in. In the representations of our characters, we see how they are formed by the changing social world around them, how they are defined by it, and how that change makes of them the living dead. The formation might occur because of the trauma that transforms them in a society that wages war. It might be the necessity in their culture to obtain the superficial signs of wealth, which become more important than a person's character. And it might be the emergence of a society where all is for sale. The Galeries de Bois embody the latter by revealing that hats, books, and people can be bought and sold there. Humans themselves agree to sell out to the new world and to destroy their former honour, becoming commodities aptly represented by the human mummies that are for sale in the antique shop.

This honour that marks the past in Balzac's world still exists in some characters, however they have difficulty surviving in the new, changing world. Those who insist on living in the past or in following the codes of the past cannot succeed, or they decide to leave, for example Derville, who decides to flee life in Paris at the end of *Le Colonel Chabert,* or Lucien who decides to seek real death. Yet even though the past is disappearing, its ghostly remnants remain to haunt and potentially disrupt the new world by reminding society of these changes, just as Chabert's existence threatens his wife's standing. This spectral residue of the past also appears in threshold spaces in the new present: Stephanie's ruined lodging and symbolic milieu; Chabert's temporary house, built from ruins; Esther's neighbourhood of ghostly talking outfits. Balzac's texts themselves serve as a testament of this transformation and make us ask ourselves about the nature of our own society and the choices that it gives us.

Notes to Chapter 1

1. Honoré de Balzac, *Le Colonel Chabert*, CH, III, 311–73 (p. 354). All further references are to this edition unless otherwise noted.
2. Honoré de Balzac, *Adieu*, CH, X, 973–1014 (p. 1009). All further references are to this edition unless otherwise noted.
3. Pierre Gascar, 'Préface', in Honoré de Balzac, *Le Colonel Chabert, suivi de El Verdugo, Adieu, Le Réquisitionnaire*, ed. by Patrick Berthier (Paris: Gallimard, 1974), pp. 7–8. Gascar sees this as a desire to push this past back where it belongs, however I look rather at the impossibility of accomplishing this.
4. *Les Lieux de mémoire: La République, La Nation, Les France 1*, ed. by Pierre Nora (Paris: Gallimard, 2004); *Realms of Memory*, trans. by Lawrence D. Kritzman (New York: Columbia University Press, 1998).
5. Ghosts appear somewhat frequently in Balzac's works, although nearly always symbolically, as Andrew Watts has noted: 'Les Spectres muets: l'adaptation de Balzac dans *Narayana* et *The Conquering Power*', *L'Année Balzacienne*, 13.1 (2012), 213–29 (p. 217). In this fascinating article about silent films, Watts notes that early filmmakers often featured ghosts and made films based on several of Balzac works, one of which is *La Peau de chagrin*, analyzed below. Watts finds that both film and the Balzacian novel exploit 'la nature spectrale de leur pratique esthétique' [the spectral nature of their aesthetic practice] (p. 218), Balzac's spectre for Watts being the Gothic novel, which Balzac and the filmmakers who resurrect his works use and innovate (p. 215).
6. Scott Sprenger interprets this living death historically: if Stéphanie is 'symboliquement "morte"' [symbolically 'dead'] it is because she belongs to the pre-revolutionary world: 'Quand "je" est un autre pays: archéologie, folie et espace identitaire dans *Adieu* de Balzac', in *Balzac voyageur: parcours, déplacement, mutations*, ed. by Nicole Mozet and Paule Petitier (Tours: Université François Rabelais, 2004), pp. 151–71 (p. 157).
7. Sprenger, 'Quand "je" est un autre pays', p. 163. Scott Lee, in his investigation of presence and realism in *Adieu*, also notes Philippe's refusal to narrate the past: 'Le Réalisme au risque de Balzac: témoignage et récit dans "Adieu"', *Études françaises*, 37.2 (2001), 181–202.
8. See Sprenger for an analysis of Philippe's madness and repression: 'Quand "je" est un autre pays', p. 158.
9. Janet Beizer reads this cutting that makes scars and wounds as representative of the division in meaning: 'Encore "Adieu": de la repetition à la mort', *L'Année Balzacienne*, 7.1 (2006), 55–66 (pp. 61–66).
10. Stéphane Vachon makes an interesting connection between the Beresina river and the myth of the river Styx, which relates to living death: 'En traversant la Bérésina, la comtesse, désespérée d'abandonner au royaume des morts son amant, franchit le Styx. Franchissant ce fleuve de l'oubli qui charrie des milliers de morts, elle quitte de fait le monde des vivants où son amant espérait la rejoindre'; 'Le Désir de l'homme est le désir de l'autre: *Adieu* d'Honoré de Balzac', in *Balzac, pater familias: études réunies par Claudie Bernard et Franc Schuerewegen* (Amsterdam: Rodopi, 2001), pp. 85–94 (p. 90).
11. Beizer, 'Encore "Adieu"', p. 57.
12. Madeleine Borgomano reads this as the shared madness and animality occasioned by war: '*Adieu*, ou l'écriture aux prises avec l'histoire', *Romantisme*, 76 (1992), 77–86 (p. 83); Véronique Cnockaert shows similarly the blurred boundaries between the animal and the human in the text: 'L'Empire de l'ensauvagement: *Adieu* de Balzac', *Romantisme*, 145.3 (2009), 37–49 (p. 38). In another direction, Dominique Jullien looks at animality in *Adieu* through the lens of psychiatry and philosophy: 'Entre psychiatrie et philosophie: la folie dans *Adieu* de Balzac', *Littérature*, 162 (June 2011), 24–35.

13. Lucienne Frappier-Mazur has also noted this particular similarity, which she, using the text's temporality, describes as anticipating the war description. Frappier-Mazur goes on to interpret Stéphanie's killing of the bird also as a kind of symptom, what she calls an ' "acting out" des violences subies' ['acting out' of the violence endured]: 'Violence et répétition dans *Adieu* de Balzac', in *Pratiques de l'écriture: mélanges de poétique et d'histoire littéraire offerts à Jean Gaudon*, ed. by Jean Gaudon and Pierre Laforgue (Paris: Klincksieck, 1996), pp. 157–66 (pp. 160, 162).
14. Shoshana Felman's groundbreaking article on this story begins its analysis with the loss of identification and localization in this odd place: 'Women and Madness: The Critical Phallacy', *Diacritics*, 5.4 (Winter 1975), 2–10.
15. These are the ruins of a monastery, which perhaps symbolize the ravages wrought by the Revolution on the Catholic Church (and, significantly, a doctor replaces the monks). Jeannine Guichardet reads in this ruined landscape the images of the battlefield and the storm of war in a kind of repetition: 'Errance et folie dans *Adieu*', in *Balzac mosaïque*, Cahiers romantiques, 12 (Clermont-Ferrand: Presses universitaires Blaise Pascal, 2007), pp. 205–15 (pp. 205–06). Michel Butor sees these ruins as the destruction wrought by time in the dilapidated state of the grounds: *Le Marchand et le génie: improvisations sur Balzac I* (Paris: La Différence, 1998), p. 218.
16. Rachel Shuh, 'Madness and Military History in Balzac's *Adieu*', *French Forum*, 26.1 (Winter 2001), 39–51. Maurice Samuels, 'Realizing the Past: History and Spectacle in Balzac's *Adieu*', *Representations*, 79.1 (Summer 2002), 82–99.
17. Shuh, 'Madness and Military History in Balzac's *Adieu*', p. 39. Borgomano in '*Adieu* ou l'écriture aux prises avec l'histoire' explains that the original teller of this story is actually Fleuriot (who was with Stéphanie when she was separated from her husband and lover), who is dead at the moment of this historical retelling, making it a 'récit d'outre-tombe' [tale from beyond the grave] (p. 78).
18. Beizer in 'Encore *Adieu*' reads this double improvisation as the lack of origin (p. 62).
19. Shuh in 'Madness and Military History in Balzac's *Adieu*' notes this social ending and sees it as turning to a present 'ignorant of the historical causes of current events' (p. 50).
20. Miranda Gill discusses these two references to God in her article 'Psychomachia and the Limits of Masculine Agency in Balzac's *Adieu*', *MLR*, 110.4 (October 2015), 1027–44 (pp. 1037, 1041).
21. See Michael D. Garval's article on the *état civil* and its link to names and identity in this text: 'Balzac's *La Comédie humaine*: The Archival Rival', *NCFS*, 25.1–2 (Fall-Winter 1996–97), 30–40.
22. 'L'embonpoint blafard de cette petite femme est le produit de cette vie, comme le typhus est la conséquence des exhalaisons d'un hôpital' [the pasty stoutness of this little woman is the product of this life, just as typhus is the result of the exhalations of a hospital] (*CH*, III, 55).
23. Jean-Marie Roulin and Colette Windish discuss the idea of *habitus* (in Mauss's sense), the social formation of an individual's identity, in its relation to the masking of that identity of Chabert: 'The Return of the Undead: The Body Politic in *Le Colonel Chabert*', *South Central Review*, 29.3 (Fall 2012), 20–35 (pp. 22, 27).
24. This use of old materials that have been taken apart and transported to build a new place reminds us of the first reconstruction of Studzianka by the freezing soldiers in *Adieu*.
25. Sandy Petrey, 'The Reality of Representation: Between Marx and Balzac', *Critical Inquiry*, 14.3 (Spring 1988), 448–68 (p. 450).
26. Gascar, in his preface to the story, writes about the time of the Revolution and the Empire, when 'Balzac [...] s'emploie à exorciser les mânes de ce proche passé, comme pour en protéger le monde nouveau qu'il s'apprête à décrire' [Balzac [...] works to exorcise the manes of the recent past, as if to protect the new world, which he prepares to describe, from them]. I agree that Balzac echoes this attempt by his society, but that he also reveals that this exorcism is not complete: 'Préface', in *Le Colonel Chabert*, p. 7. I am thus more in line with Marcelle Marini, who claims that 'le passé qu'on voulait oublier, s'impose à la mémoire des hommes comme événement ineffaçable et réclame sa place dans l'Histoire' [the past that one wanted to forget imposes itself on the memory of men as an inerasable event and it reclaims its place in History]: 'Chabert mort ou vif', *Littérature*, 13 (February 1974), 92–112 (p. 94).
27. Sheryl Kroen, *Politics and Theater: The Crisis of Legitimacy in Restoration France, 1815–1830* (Berkeley: University of California Press, 2000), p. 41.

28. Matthijs M. Lok, '"Un oubli total du passé"? The Political and Social Construction of Silence in Restoration Europe (1813–1830)', *History and Memory*, 26.2 (Fall-Winter 2014), 40–75 (p. 48).
29. Cathy Caruth, 'The Claims of the Dead: History, Haunted Property, and the Law', in *Literature in the Ashes of History* (Baltimore, MD: Johns Hopkins University Press, 2013), pp. 18–39 (p. 21). Maxime Goergen also looks at this in terms of the 'effacement' of the Napoleonic epic in relation to Chabert's story in 'Les Noms du *Colonel Chabert*: langage et pouvoir après Napoléon', *Romance Notes*, 54.3 (2014), 353–68.
30. Petrey, 'The Reality of Representation', p. 466. This false surface that hides the truth is reinforced by numerous references to theatricality; a concept expertly explored by Maurice Samuels in his analysis of the spectacular, dramatic nature of the representations of history in the text, which make reality 'indistinguishable from its counterfeit'. Indeed, as Samuels notes, Chabert's wife is described several times as an actress in the role she plays: *The Spectacular Past: Popular History and the Novel in Nineteenth-century France* (Ithaca, NY: Cornell University Press, 2004), p. 229. Thus, the social world has become an artificial performance, a simulacrum of a reality that remains hidden. And, as Sandy Petrey shows in another article, the simulacrum can be more effective in its production of meaning and truth than reality itself: 'Balzac's Empire: History, Insanity, and the Realist Text', in *Historical Criticism and the Challenge of Theory*, ed. by Janet Levarie Smarr (Urbana: University of Illinois Press, 1993), pp. 25–41 (p. 36). Also taking an historical view, Jean-Luc Martine writes that 'la Bérézina charrie les tristes fantômes d'une humanité anéantie' [the Beresina transports the sad phantoms of an annihilated humanity] and that the river symbolizes 'la fin d'un monde, la fin d'un âge. En elle, le siècle à venir se dispose comme un arcane, celui d'une révolution rendue à ses énigmes, d'un Empire effondré et d'une restauration comme improbable retour du passé' [the end of a world, the end of an age. In it, the century to come poses itself as a mystery, that of a revolution given over to its enigmas, of a collapsed Empire, and of a restoration as an improbable return of the past]: *'Adieu!* de Balzac, un texte qui soigne ou un texte qui tue?' *Études épistémè*, 13 (2008), 121–41 (p. 29).
31. *Œuvres complètes de H. de Balzac*, 24 vols (Paris: Calman Lévy, 1869–79), xx, 462.
32. See Christopher Prendergast's insightful discussion of this 'code' in *The Order of Mimesis: Balzac, Stendhal, Nerval, Flaubert*, Cambridge Studies in French (Cambridge & New York: Cambridge University Press, 1986), pp. 94–95.
33. Ibid., p. 116.
34. Peter Brooks explores this idea of remaining 'buried' as the possibility that Chabert's story may remain buried: 'Narrative Transaction and Transference (Unburying *Le Colonel Chabert*), *Novel*, 15.2 (Winter 1982), 101–10 (p. 101).
35. See John Vernon, *Money and Fiction: Literary Realism in the Nineteenth and Early Twentieth Centuries* (Ithaca, NY: Cornell University Press, 1984).
36. Goergen also studies how Chabert resists insertion into the Restoration world by insisting on the importance of his word: 'Les Noms du *Colonel Chabert*', p. 367.
37. Prendergast notes that 'the problematics of clothes, language, and money converge, as interrelated terms of an unstable semiotic': *The Order of Mimesis*, p. 115.
38. Petrey goes so far as to say that for Chabert, there is a 'total destruction of identity': 'The Reality of Representation', p. 449.
39. Several observations in this section on *La Peau de chagrin* appeared in my article 'The Living Death of the Past: Body Parts, Money, and the Fetish in *La Peau de chagrin*', *Lingua Romana*, 8.1 (Fall 2009), no pagination. However, that essay deals with the different topic of language and the psychoanalytic interpretation of the novel. Samuel Weber also analyzes veils in his analysis of Raphaël as fetishist in *Unwrapping Balzac: A Reading of 'La Peau de chagrin'* (Toronto & Buffalo: University of Toronto Press, 1979), pp. 81–83.
40. Andrea Goulet studies the threshold state of the antique shop in her *Optiques: The Science of the Eye and the Birth of Modern French Fiction*, Critical Authors and Issues (Philadelphia: University of Pennsylvania Press, 2006), p. 54.
41. The transition was understandably not entirely smooth, as Pamela M. Pilbeam describes, 'The July Days were a mere incident in a long chain of unrest [...] market riots, protests against shipment of grain, strikes against wage reductions and so on': *The French Revolution of 1830* (New York: St Martin's Press, 1991), p. 174. Another problematic change was that censorship of the

press began to be reintroduced in October 1830, the date listed on the first page of this novel in which Raphaël will be tapped for a journalist role (ibid., p. 94). There were also violent demonstrations in Paris on 17, 18, and 19 October, 1830: William Fortescue, *France and 1848: The End of Monarchy* (London & New York: Routledge, 2005), p. 21.

42. Honoré de Balzac, *La Peau de chagrin*, *CH*, x, 57–294 (p. 57). All further references are to this edition unless otherwise noted.
43. Weber discusses these forms of control in *Unwrapping Balzac*, pp. 14–16.
44. One might also view the scientific scenes in the text as another inclusion of 'modern' ideas in the novel.
45. Gerard Cohen-Vrignaud, 'Capitalism's Wishful Thinking', *Modern Language Quarterly*, 76.2 (June 2015), 181–99 (pp. 190–92).
46. Patrick Bray reads the *peau de chagrin* as itself a kind of 'map' of Raphaël's life: *The Novel Map: Space and Subjectivity in Nineteenth-century French Fiction* (Evanston, IL: Northwestern University Press, 2013), pp. 3–5.
47. David Bell notes this liminal state in his essay 'Fantasy and Reality in *La Peau de chagrin*', in *The Cambridge Companion to Balzac*, ed. by Owen Heathcote and Andrew Watts (Cambridge: Cambridge University Press, 2017), pp. 52–66. Peter Brooks examines what he calls 'living a death-within-life in order to preserve life-within death' in his study of narrative desire and the death instinct in the text: 'Narrative Desire', *Style*, 18.3 (Summer 1984), 312–27 (p. 319).
48. 'Le son de l'or exerçait une éblouissante fascination sur ses sens' [the sound of money exerted a dazzling fascination on his senses] (*CH*, x, 58); 'L'ivoire fit rendre un bruit sec à la pièce' [The ivory gave a sharp sound to the coin] (p. 63); 'Il entendit sonner les écus' [He heard coins jingling] (p. 66); 'plusieurs pièces d'or étincelèrent et sonnèrent sur le comptoir' [several gold coins shone and clinked on the counter] (p. 67); 'J'entendais frétiller l'or' [I heard gold jangling] (p. 123).
49. Françoise Gaillard analyzes the *peau* as a material object fetishized like gold that has magic properties and is both gold and phallus, and which is the general equivalent of exchange: 'L'Effet peau de chagrin', in *Le Roman de Balzac: recherches critiques, méthodes, lectures*, ed. by Roland Le Huenen and Paul Perron (Montreal: Didier, 1980), pp. 213–30 (p. 222).
50. As a curious aside, Walter Benjamin describes *La Peau de chagrin* as his 'most exciting experience at an auction': *Selected Writings*, ed. by Michael W. Jennings, Howard Eiland, and Gary Smith, trans. by Rodney Livingstone and others, 4 vols (Cambridge, MA: Harvard University Press, 1996–2003), II, 490.
51. In this, the first of our analyses of living death and commodities, it is significant that Balzac links sexual desire to shopping here. This becomes a major theme of Zola later.
52. Rachel Bowlby, *Just Looking: Consumer Culture in Dreiser, Gissing and Zola* (New York: Methuen, 1985).
53. Michael B. Miller writes that 'The idea of "shopping" was, for all practical purposes, non-existent, as entry into a shop entailed an obligation to make a purchase': *The Bon Marché: Bourgeois Culture and the Department Store, 1869–1920* (Princeton, NJ: Princeton University Press, 1981), p. 24.
54. The engagement of Balzac in the production and marketing of books, his desire to sell, immersed him in the growing commodification of books in the nineteenth century; this historical development is outlined by Bowlby (*Just Looking*, p. 8) and others. *Petit Dictionnaire critique et anecdotique des enseignes de Paris par un batteur de pavé*, in *Œuvres complètes de H. Balzac*, XXI, 126.
55. For a detailed analysis of the objects in the shop see Nicole Cazauran, 'Le "Tableau" du magasin d'antiquités dans *La Peau de chagrin*', in *Mélanges de langue et de littérature française offerts à Pierre Larthomas*, ed. by Jean-Pierre Seguin (Paris: École normale supérieure de jeunes filles, 1985), pp. 87–98.
56. Bowlby, *Just Looking*, p. 2.
57. Balzac himself encourages an allegorical reading of the text in his Epilogue, in which the narrator invites an interlocutor, in a kind of fictional conversation, to interpret the meaning of the two female characters, Pauline and Fœdora.

58. The items in Rastignac's room seem almost to be a combination of the old of the antique shop and the *nouveautés*: a juxtaposition of objects old and new, expensive and worn (*CH*, x, 194).
59. Henri-Russell Hitchcock, *Architecture: Nineteenth and Twentieth Centuries* (New Haven, CT: Yale University Press, 1987), p. 176. Michael Stephen Smith notes that in the 1820s the bazaar was a place 'where dozens and even hundreds of dealers in housewares and clothing occupied adjoining stalls in a single building': *The Emergence of Modern Business Enterprise in France: 1800–1930* (Cambridge, MA: Harvard University Press, 2006), pp. 120–21.
60. Nicholas Daly has an interesting article on mummies in Victorian fiction: 'That Obscure Object of Desire: Victorian Commodity Culture and Fictions of the Mummy', *Novel*, 28.1 (Fall 1994), 24–51 (p. 24).
61. Honoré de Balzac, *La Peau de chagrin*, ed. by Guillaume Kichenin (Paris: Gallimard, 2003), p. 27, n. 1.
62. Watts describes the influence of these Balzacian phantoms on early cinema in his 'Les Spectres muets', p. 223.
63. Benjamin, *The Arcades Project*, p. 13.
64. Nicoletta Pireddu describes this threshold state in the text, which she analyzes in terms of Todorov's fantastic: 'Between *fantasque* and *fantasmagorique*: A Fantastic Reading of Balzac's *La Peau de chagrin*', *Paroles Gelées: UCLA French Studies*, 9 (January 1991), 33–47.
65. Arjun Appadurai mentions what he calls the biographical aspect of things (in his discussion of Kopytoff's theories) such as antiques, and one might view some of the descriptions of the owners of the various objects in the antique shop as an example of their biographical aspect, a different kind of humanization of the object. Raphaël himself can become the imagined previous owner of an object: 'Mais tout à coup, il devenait corsaire, et revêtait la terrible poésie empreinte dans le rôle de Lara, vivement inspiré par les couleurs nacrées de mille coquillages, exalté par la vue de quelques madrépores qui sentaient le varech' [Yet suddenly, he became a corsair, and took upon himself the horrifying poetry contained in the role of Lara, vividly inspired by the pearly colours of the a thousand seashells, as he was exalted by the sight of several Madrepora that smelled of seaweed] (*CH*, x, 72). Or he can imagine the 'biography' of the objects themselves through their owners and travels: 'Les plus coûteux caprices de dissipateurs morts sous des mansardes après avoir possédé plusieurs millions, étaient dans ce vaste bazar des folies humaines' [The costliest caprices of spendthrifts, who died in garrets after having possessed several millions, were in this vast bazaar of human follies] (p. 73). Arjun Appadurai, 'Introduction', in *The Social Life of Things: Commodities in Cultural Perspective*, ed. by Arjun Appadurai (Cambridge: Cambridge University Press, 2013), p. 13.
66. Benjamin, *The Arcades Project*, pp. 181–82.
67. He sells his mother's island to pay his debts, which he imagines in the form of a ghostly debt collector: 'Ce monsieur sera ma dette, ce sera ma lettre de change, un spectre qui flétrira ma joie' [This man will be my debt, he will be my bill of exchange, a spectre who will debase my joy] (*CH*, x, 200). In another scene, he thinks of selling the gold frame that holds the picture of his mother so that he has enough money to take Fœdora to, significantly, see an actor 'aux Funambules' (p. 176). This theatre produced *féeries* (among other things), a type of spectacle that will become important in relation to Zola in Chapter 3 and is a word used to describe the orgy in this text (p. 107), which itself seems to be peopled by the dead: 'jonchés de morts et de mourants' [scattered with dead and dying people] (p. 117). The animation of things occurs as well in his room when he is working on his two projects: 'Le bureau [...], mon lit, mon fauteuil, les bizarreries de mon papier de tenture, mes meubles, toutes ces choses s'animèrent et devinrent pour moi d'humbles amis. [...] À force de contempler les objets qui m'entouraient, je trouvais à chacun sa physionomie, son caractère; souvent ils me parlaient' [The desk [...], my bed, my armchair, the bizarreries of my wallpaper, my furniture, all of these things came alive and became humble friends for me. [...] By dint of gazing at these objects that surrounded me, I found in each one its own physiognomy, its character; often they spoke to me] (pp. 137–38). The city of Paris itself becomes animated; it is 'un désert pavé, un désert animé, pensant, vivant' [a paved desert, an animated desert, thinking, living] (p. 133). Raphaël called his room significantly a 'sépulcre aérien' [aerial sepulchre] (p. 137).

68. Robert Kopp notes that Benjamin was familiar with Balzac's *La Peau de chagrin* and adds that 'face aux débris de l'histoire, Benjamin se retrouve dans le rôle de l'antiquaire de *La Peau de chagrin*' [confronting the debris of history, Benjamin finds himself in the role of the antique dealer in *The Wild Ass's Skin*]: 'Le "Balzac" de Walter Benjamin', *L'Année Balzacienne*, 7 (1986), 339–48 (pp. 347–48).
69. I pursue the psychoanalytic meaning of this in 'The Living Death of the Past'.
70. Gérard Gengembre, in an interesting article, reads this 'fantasmagorie de vérité' [phantasmagoria of truth] as a representation of the post-1830 crises of time: 'Temps et argent ou la politique du temps fantastique dans *La Peau de chagrin*', *Otrante*, 9 (1997), 113–17.
71. Raphaël, knowing that his desire will kill him, embraces Pauline, acts on that desire — this thus can be considered a type of suicide.
72. Honoré de Balzac, *Illusions perdues*, CH, v, 123–732 (p. 724). All further references are to this edition unless otherwise noted.
73. I use the name 'Vautrin' for the character because it is most commonly employed in literary analysis, even though his name is mainly 'Carlos Herrera' in these two texts.
74. D. A. Miller writes, 'disillusionment is exposed as a mere phase: a psychological adjustment which permits the transition from one "illusion" to another': 'Balzac's Illusions Lost and Found', *Yale French Studies*, 67 (1984), 164–81 (p. 170). Adam Bresnick describes this in another way as 'the incessant return of the imaginary lure': 'The Paradox of Bildung: Balzac's *Illusions perdues*', *MLN*, 113.4 (September 1998), 823–50 (p. 836).
75. As noted above, the reference to this type of spectacular theatre production, with elaborate machinery and special effects, will be important in my discussion of Zola in Chapter 3.
76. Later, the dream turns to nightmare for Lucien: 'Pour Lucien, la vie était devenue un mauvais rêve' [For Lucien, life had become a bad dream] (*CH*, v, 540).
77. Sotirios Paraschas analyzes the action behind the scenes of the book trade and the theatre as being the subject of this novel 'about the backstage of both worlds': '*Illusions perdues*: Writers, Artists and the Reflexive Novel', in *The Cambridge Companion to Balzac*, ed. by Heathcote and Watts, pp. 97–110 (p. 101).
78. The first version of *Splendeurs et misères des courtisanes*, *La Torpille* (Esther's nickname), was ready in some form for publication in May 1836, but was not accepted. *La Torpille* was later published in September 1838, and this early version of the text is nearly identical to that of the current edition. The section of *Illusions perdues* that contains descriptions of Paris in *Un grand homme de province à Paris*, was written in 1839: Philippe Berthier, 'Histoire du texte', in Honoré de Balzac, *Splendeurs et misères des courtisanes*, ed. by Philippe Berthier (Paris: Garnier Flammarion, 2006), pp. 41–43 (p. 41).
79. Honoré de Balzac, *Splendeurs et misères des courtisanes*, CH, vi, 429–935 (p. 446). All further references are to this edition unless otherwise noted.
80. Prendergast describes this as the 'underbelly of the mercantilist ethic': *The Order of Mimesis*, p. 89.
81. Ibid., p. 90.
82. Jeannine Guichardet takes this metaphor further and describes the Galeries as the setting of an oriental tale with its own sultan and with Cinderella: '*Illusions perdues*: quelques itinéraires en pays parisien', in *Balzac, 'Illusions perdues': l'œuvre capitale dans l'œuvre*, ed. by Françoise van Rossum-Guyon (Groningen: University of Groningen, 1988), pp. 89–93 (pp. 90, 92).
83. One here thinks of Baudelaire's description of outdated fashion plates: 'Le passé, tout en gardant le piquant du fantôme, reprendra la lumière et le mouvement de la vie, et se fera présent' [The past, all the while retaining the piquant of the phantom, will take on again the light and movement of life, and will become present]: 'Le Peintre de la vie moderne' (*OC*, ii, 684).
84. It is not surprising, then, that as Lucien prepares his suicide, he dons his good Parisian clothes as a shroud: 'il s'était fait un linceul de ses habits parisiens' [he had made a shroud of his Parisian clothes] (*CH*, v, 688).
85. Owen Heathcote examines whether prostitutes can change in Balzac's works; he, too, notes the ambiguity of her state, 'it is supremely difficult to say whether prostitution is simply a position or an essence, whether it is a role or an ineradicable mode of being': 'Negative Equity? The Representation of Prostitution and the Prostitution of Representation in Balzac', *Forum for*

Modern Language Studies, 40.3 (2004), 279–90 (p. 282). Charles Bernheimer also discusses the 'liquidity of personal properties, their easily effaceable and interchangeable qualities', although this is at the surface level of appearance: *Figures of Ill Repute: Representing Prostitution in Nineteenth-century France* (Cambridge, MA: Harvard University Press, 1989), p. 63.

86. Maurice Samuels's article, 'Metaphors of Modernity: Prostitutes, Bankers, and Other Jews in Balzac's *Splendeurs et misères des courtisanes*', *Romanic Review*, 97.2 (2006), 169–84, on the representation of Esther and Jewishness, provides a rich interpretation of this capitalization and co-optation of her beauty and identity.

87. If Esther must make a choice between two impossible options, Diana Knight notes that the situation of an upright unmarried woman can be even worse in Balzac's world, as she simply, in a sense, stops existing socially — perhaps another kind of living death: 'Female celibates either marry or, in the conjugal economy described by Balzac, fall out of the picture altogether. At best, they exist in a state of alienation; at worse, in a state of dereliction, both social and linguistic: they are not even objects of exchange': 'Celibacy on Display in Two Texts by Balzac: *Le Cabinet des Antiques* and the Preface to *Pierrette*', *Dix-Neuf*, 2.1 (2004), 1–15 (p. 11).

88. Oddly enough, this is also the fantasy of Lucien's friend, David in *Illusions perdues*: 'Sois heureux, je jouirai de tes succès, tu seras un second moi-même' [Be happy, I will enjoy your success, you will be my second self] (*CH*, v, 184). Another similar curiosity: in *Splendeurs et misères des courtisanes* Lucien wishes he could combine Esther and Clotilde in one person (*CH*, vi, 518).

89. Balzac describes this change through the extended metaphor of metal that has weakened (*CH*, vi, 821–22). In a strange counterpart to this weakening of Vautrin's metal, Madame de Sérizy, in her panic to get to Lucien, breaks one of the metal bars of the Conciergerie with her bare hands (p. 795). Balzac adds the wonderful detail that the great event of that day for the employees of the prison was not Lucien's suicide but the metal broken by the delicate hands of a society lady (p. 809).

90. The other instance is, 'on enterre en ce moment ma vie, ma beauté, ma vertu, ma conscience, toute ma force!' [they are burying at this moment my life, my beauty, my virtue, my conscience, all my force!] (*CH*, vi, 899).

91. D. A. Miller, 'Balzac's Illusions', pp. 174–75, 178. Prendergast also notes the similarity not just between criminals and the police, but among all levels of society, 'Vautrin experiences no difficulty, undergoes no profound change, in "joining" society because the real values of that society are qualitatively no different from his own as a criminal': 'Melodrama and Totality in *Splendeurs et misères des courtisanes*', *Novel*, 6.2 (1973), 152–62 (p. 161).

92. Richard Terdiman discusses this inescapability as the generalized power of the semiotic system over people who seek power: 'Structures of Initiation: On Semiotic Education and its Contradictions in Balzac', *Yale French Studies*, 63 (1982), 198–226 (p. 216).

93. Prendergast casts this in a dark mode: 'Lucien's body thus circulates throughout the social organism like an insidious poison': 'Melodrama and Totality in *Splendeurs et misères des courtisanes*', p. 159. Bernheimer also notes in a different way, 'the mobile, transgressive, theatrical prostitute-courtesan seems to figure the creative impulse of Balzacian narrative': *Figures of Ill Repute*, p. 35.

94. See D. A. Miller on the diffusion of power: 'Balzac's Illusions', p. 177.

95. Terdiman comes to a similar conclusion from a different direction — Lucien's suicide 'means the failure of initiation to transform Lucien': 'Structures of Initiation', p. 219.

96. Lucien is similar to Chabert, who accepted a living death rather than joining forces with the new. Lawrence Schehr sees this as the illusory 'accession to an outdated aristocracy' related to the 'belief in the power of the printed word', of poetry: 'Fool's Gold: The Beginning of Balzac's *Illusions perdues*', *Symposium*, 36.2 (Summer 1982), 149–65 (p. 154).

97. Catherine Nesci's excellent article highlights this scene, as well as the scene in the antique shop in *La Peau de chagrin*, in terms of their 'point de vue de la mort' [point of view of death]: 'De l'histoire-panorama à l'histoire-mémoire: Balzac et la "fantasmagorie" du passé', in *Balzac dans l'histoire*, ed. by Nicole Mozet and Paule Petitier (Paris: SEDES, 2001), pp. 55–67 (p. 61).

98. Bresnick describes this as 'the aristocratic illusion has been permanently fractured in post-revolutionary France': 'The Paradox of Bildung', p. 846.

99. Esther is defeated by her imposed social role as prostitute, Lucien is defeated by his moral nobility that has no place in the current social order, and Vautrin submits to and enforces the social order (through the police) while retaining his goal of revenge.

CHAPTER 2

Baudelaire: Woman, the City, and Living Death

> La 2ᵉ édition des 'Fleurs'. Ici, un squelette arborescent.
> [The 2nd edition of the 'Flowers'. Here, an arborescent skeleton.]
> — CHARLES BAUDELAIRE[1]

'Lazare odorant déchirant son suaire' [Lazarus, odorous, tearing his shroud] (*OC*, I, 48) — this is the physical image of active living death in Baudelaire's works, here in the poem 'Le Flacon'.[2] The decaying smell that permeates the air, like perfume that expands, makes clear that Lazarus comes back to life not fresh and young, nor as a ghost, but as putrefying flesh, a dead person who yet moves and lives in physical space. This image of living death functions in the allegorical structure of 'Le Flacon' to represent the concrete invasion of the dead past into the present. In this chapter we review the remarkably extensive use of this image in Baudelaire's works and its meanings through close readings of several poems.[3]

In Benjamin's projected title for a book on Baudelaire, he encapsulates the conflicted stance that Baudelaire takes toward the dying past as he confronts the modern world. 'Charles Baudelaire: A Lyric Poet in the Era of High Capitalism' expresses, on the one hand, that part of Baudelaire that holds onto the past, in the formal aspect of the lyric poetry that is written in canonical structures: sonnets, alexandrines, rhyming verses. Yet in certain other formal aspects and in the content and vocabulary of his poems, Baudelaire turns away from the past to abandon its rules, and his work becomes a site of experimentation. As does Balzac, Baudelaire hovers on this threshold where a lost past survives in a present in which it no longer has a viable place: he uses, for instance, religious symbols and forms in a poetry that revolts against them; he evokes Andromache in a poem on modernized Paris; he doubles certain poems in verse and prose forms.

Baudelaire's use of the image of the living dead expresses this ambiguous state between what is and what is no more, yet it goes beyond the simple figuration of the continuation of the past in the present to unveil his understanding that his own state, as well as the general human condition in modernity, is that of a living death. He does this both in the lyric, interpersonal mode in his poetry on modern love and women, and in the monumental mode — in the sense of the buildings, dwellings, and physical spaces that surround and symbolize human activities — in his representations of Paris and society in the modern city. This study traces the image of living death in these two areas: the poetry on women and love, and the poetry on Paris. The figure of the living dead haunts both of these categories, and Baudelaire shows how it structures the society and culture in which he lives.

Memory, Love, and Poetry as Living Death: 'Le Flacon'

> Le passé, tout en gardant le piquant du fantôme, reprendra la lumière et le mouvement de la vie, et se fera présent.
>
> [The past, while retaining the piquant of the phantom, will again take on light and movement, and will make itself present.]
>
> — CHARLES BAUDELAIRE[4]

'Le Flacon' contains in exemplary form the four main aspects of the Baudelairean image of living death that structure our analyses of the love poems: the collapse of antithetical categories, in particular those of life and death; the inadequate covering or containment of death and dissolution; love's relation to death and memory; and the ambiguity of the lyric poet's identity and gender as they are staged in the poems. 'Le Flacon' exemplifies how the living death related to woman and love involves the male poet's own identity, which hovers in a liminal space as it is constructed and deconstructed in the poems. 'Le Flacon' serves as our introduction to this set of specific manifestations of living death in Baudelaire's *univers poétique*.

In its first two lines, 'Le Flacon' transgresses the limit between interior and exterior and erases the distinction between a material object and its surroundings by means of the image of a scent that can penetrate all matter: 'Il est de forts parfums pour qui toute matière | Est poreuse. On dirait qu'ils pénètrent le verre' [There are strong perfumes for which all matter | Is porous. One might say that they penetrate glass] (*OC*, I, 47). Scents in Baudelaire's works have received much critical attention as they generate numerous and powerful relays of meanings among the categories of memory, the woman's body, reverie, and the idea of infinite expansion. The strength of scent emphasized in 'Le Flacon' is this ability to penetrate matter, even matter such as glass that would seem impermeable. The enjambment of the first line, as it spills over into the next, formally repeats the transgressive action as it penetrates into the *vers* ('verse', the next line of poetry) as well as through the 'verre' as glass, thus creating a correspondence between the ability of scent to penetrate things and the action of the verses in this poem, which spill over formal poetic boundaries of verse lines through enjambment.[5] This symbolic ability of verse to penetrate suggests as well that the reader, 'taking in' the text as if inhaling a scent, will be invaded, 'penetrated' by the powerful action of these verses.[6]

As the poem progresses, scent and its symbolic equivalents cross more borders: those of past and present time, and the limits between life and death. The glass penetrated in the first two lines of the poem becomes the glass of the flask, the 'flacon', found in a decrepit state or milieu, which evokes the passage of time. From this bottle springs a revenant soul that comes back alive, just as Lazarus later in the poem comes back from the grave:

> En ouvrant un coffret venu de l'Orient
> Dont la serrure grince et rechigne en criant,
>
> Ou dans une maison déserte quelque armoire
> Pleine de l'âcre odeur des temps, poudreuse et noire,
> Parfois on trouve un vieux flacon qui se souvient,
> D'où jaillit toute vive une âme qui revient. (*OC*, I, 47–48)

[While opening a coffer that came from the Orient | Whose lock grates and objects by screeching, | Or in a deserted house some wardrobe | Full of the acrid odour of time, dusty and black, | Sometimes one finds an old flask that remembers, | From which leaps fully alive a soul who returns.]

This 'soul who returns' is identified later in the poem as an old love ('un vieil amour') that emerges from the flask, most logically in the sense that the perfume contained there evokes the memory of the poet's former lover and their 'old' love.[7] As Peter Broome has shown, perfume in Baudelaire's poetry represents something material that has become ethereal and intangible and that makes present in a physical way something that is no longer there.[8] It is a kind of materialization of memory, and its physicality seems to bring the lover back 'toute vive'.

By means of scent, the past thus appears to penetrate the barrier of time and returns, as in 'Un fantôme (II — Le Parfum)', where a woman's scent makes the past present, and the poet picks this scented flower/memory for his *Fleurs du mal* [Flowers of Evil]:

> Charme profond, magique, dont nous grise
> Dans le présent le passé restauré!
> Ainsi l'amant sur un corps adoré
> Du souvenir cueille la fleur exquise. (*OC*, I, 39)

[Charm, profound and magical, by which, | In the present, the past restored intoxicates us! | Hence the lover on an adored body | From memory picks the exquisite flower.]

Memory in this case then also takes on the sense of something that can be accessed physically, or in the case of 'Le Flacon', physically released: the flask contains the soul/memory/perfume that is freed, and it represents the poet himself as their coffin:

> Ainsi, quand je serai perdu dans la mémoire
> Des hommes, dans le coin d'une sinistre armoire
> Quand on m'aura jeté, vieux flacon désolé,
> Décrépit, poudreux, sale, abject, visqueux, fêlé,
> Je serai ton cercueil, aimable pestilence! (*OC*, I, 48)

[Thus, when I am lost to the memory | Of men, in the corner of some sinister armoire | When they have thrown me out, an old desolate flask | Decrepit, dusty, dirty, abject, viscous, cracked, | I will be your coffin, amiable pestilence!]

Like the poet, this flask remembers, 'un vieux flacon qui se souvient' [an old flask that remembers]: *souvenir* in this poem takes on the meaning of *sous-venir*, to come from below, as from the depths of memory and the unconscious, or from the abyss of the tomb the *gouffre* where Lazarus moves.⁹ The 'I' of the lyric poet becomes the symbolic flask/coffin that contains the memory of this dead love.

Just as the dead soul, the revenant, comes back to life in memory, emerging from the flask as perfume that fills the air, the poet's memories ('thoughts' here) associated with the lover/soul are transformed from a death-like state to life in the image of chrysalides that become butterflies (or moths in the armoire!), which fly out to fill the air:

> Mille pensers dormaient, chrysalides funèbres,
> Frémissant doucement dans les lourdes ténèbres,
> Qui dégagent leur aile et prennent leur essor,
> Teintés d'azur, glacés de rose, lamés d'or. (*OC*, I, 48)

[A thousand thoughts were sleeping, funereal chrysalides, | Quivering gently in the dark shadows, | They free their wing and take their flight, | Tinged with azure, glazed with pink, threaded with gold.]

The word 'funèbres' that describes the chrysalides lends to the process of metamorphosis the sense of a death that turns into life, so that the chrysalides, which are funereal as well as nascent (and which would have been originally and significantly *vers*, in this sense, both larvae [*vers* in French can mean 'larva'] and verse), are in a state of living death, a repetition of the concept of the revenant soul returning 'toute vive'.¹⁰ Richard D. E. Burton's term 'limbic', as the state in limbo between heaven and hell, will be used to describe this in-between state or location on the border between life and death, man and woman, and other oppositions that branch out from these.¹¹

The winged perfume and memories that have arisen in the air are beautiful and pleasurable in their blue, pink, and gold colours. Like the perfume that has jogged them, thoughts take wing and circulate in the air in the Baudelairean trope of the ideal, symbolized in the azure blue and the form of the wing-like letter 'v' (used by Mallarmé later in his swan poem, 'Le Vierge, le vivace et le bel aujourd'hui'), which in its upturned shape echoes the wings of their flight: 'Voilà le souvenir enivrant qui voltige' [There is the intoxicating memory that flutters].¹²

However, the brief, uplifting push of the three upper-case Vs (along with four lower-case) in stanza four, is transformed from there into only three lower-case letters in stanza five. In a downward decrease or fall caused by vertigo, beautiful thoughts/memories of the soul are pushed down to land in the reality of human decay, as pleasing scent becomes noxious miasma, human emanations coming from the grave (an unpleasant smell already introduced by the 'âcre odeur des temps' [acrid odour of time]):

> Voilà le souvenir enivrant qui voltige
> Dans l'air troublé; les yeux se ferment; le Vertige
> Saisit l'âme vaincue et la pousse à deux mains
> Vers un gouffre obscurci de miasmes humains;
>
> Il la terrasse au bord d'un gouffre séculaire,
> Où, Lazare odorant déchirant son suaire,
> Se meut dans son réveil le cadavre spectral

> D'un vieil amour ranci, charmant et sépulcral.
> (*OC*, I, 48, my emphasis)

> [There is the intoxicating memory that flutters | In the troubled air; the eyes close; Vertigo | Seizes the vanquished soul and pushes it with two hands | Towards an abyss obscured by human miasmas; | It forces the soul down to the edge of an ancient abyss, | Where, Lazarus, odorous, tearing his shroud, | Moves in its awakening the spectral cadaver | Of an old, rancid love, charming and sepulchral.]

Here it is clear that there has been no return to pure life of these memories of love, but an emergence into a state of living death.[13] The spectral corpse of rancid love, which lies at the bottom of the abyss (and in its delayed appearance as the subject of this part of the sentence, it lies awkwardly at the end, at the 'bottom' of the stanza), moves and awakens in parallel to Lazarus. This old love is sepulchral, from the tomb; spectral, like a revenant. Thus, once again it is a dead form that is alive: this cadaver is decayed, rancid, and in its decayed state, it moves. What is important and odd here, then, is that the love that is remembered is not ideal; those chrysalides that hatched into the flight of memory were already funereal, Lazarus returns not whole and new but rather odorous, love is rancid and sepulchral.[14] What is reborn is love that is already decayed, an idea similar to that of 'Une charogne', as we shall see. Rather than the typical Lamartinian topos of nostalgia for ideal love in 'Le Lac', 'ces moments d'ivresse, | Où l'amour à longs flots nous verse le Bonheur' [Those moments of intoxication | When love in great waves pours out for us Happiness], Baudelaire gives us instead decomposition.[15]

Indeed, this living death is what the poem/poet preserves for us in 'Le Flacon'. The poet looks to the future when he and his poem will be, as we saw above, that flask/coffin of a love that is not only itself an 'amour ranci', but that also makes the poet's heart both live and die:

> Je serai ton cercueil, aimable pestilence!
> Le témoin de ta force et de ta virulence,
> Cher poison préparé par les anges! liqueur
> Qui me ronge, ô la vie et la mort de mon cœur! (*OC*, I, 48)

> [I will be your coffin, amiable pestilence! | The witness to your force and to your virulence, | Dear poison prepared by the angels! Liqueur | That eats away at me, O the life and the death of my heart!]

The fragrant liquid contained in the poet/flask is here liquor (which echoes the 'souvenir enivrant', the intoxicating memory of past love). This liquor is a poison, similar to the 'miasmes humains', which conjure images of the spread of illness and death as they penetrate the bodies (as perfume penetrates flasks, and when inhaled, nose, and lungs) that breathe or drink its maleficent substance.

Thus, this pestilence creates the state of living death of the poet's heart, 'la vie et la mort de mon cœur', a heart that preserves the living-dead love as memory, through a kind of contagion of living death. In a repetition of the structure of the collapse of opposites in life and death, this poison has been prepared by angels, it is a limbic 'aimable pestilence', both pleasurable and fatal. If earlier the allegory of uplifting, beautiful thoughts in a first moment turned and fell in a second moment into decaying human miasmas, here the paradoxical state of the poet's heart combines the antithesis of life and death into something not temporal but simultaneous, life and death at once.[16] The poison liquor of a decayed love preserved, kept alive, creates both pleasure and pain as the poet envelops and safeguards the poison that continually corrodes his heart.

This state of the living death of the heart, mind, or being of the poet appears in a number of other poems, in particular the poems in and near the 'Spleen' series: the poet is a cemetery, his heart is a tomb, his bed is a tomb and he is a 'jeune squelette' [young skeleton], he is a 'cadavre hébété' [a stupefied cadaver], his corpse must continue to work after death, his mind and heart are wrapped in a shroud, and more.[17] 'Le Mauvais Moine' was originally titled 'Tombeau vivant'. An old poet has the sad voice of a 'fantôme frileux' [shivering phantom] in 'Spleen, pluviôse, irrité contre la ville entière'.[18] As Jackson, following Benjamin, puts it, death is for Baudelaire a point of view in the perception of the real.[19] And Dolf Oehler calls the *flâneur* Baudelaire a 'cadavre vivant' [living cadaver].[20]

If we return to the first stanza of the poem, we find that the poetic *vers* we have just read have become the glass 'flask' that contains the scents/memories, which penetrate the *verre/vers* [glass/verse] and reach us from the living dead (the poet Baudelaire himself who speaks to us).[21] The idea of the first two lines of the poem, which show poetry's ability to penetrate, now becomes the ability of this poem to affect and change us. As in other poems that we shall examine, Baudelaire sends us this message from and about the living dead to 'contaminate' us, his 'frères hypocrites' [hypocritical brothers], with its pestilential knowledge, to make us ask ourselves what this state of living death might be and if we, like our brother, share it.[22]

'Une charogne': Poetry and the Living Dead Woman

In 'Le Flacon', living death describes the poet's love and his memory of it, which poison him and condemn his heart to a death within life. The poet's lover, who generates this love, does not really appear specifically in that poem, except possibly as the configuration of the 'âme qui revient' [the soul who returns] in the poet's memories. However, the woman he loves, particularly her body, is specifically associated with living death a number of times in his poems and shows Baudelaire's debt to standard literary and cultural topoi, such as the *memento mori* in the poem 'Une charogne' [A Carcass]. Baudelaire goes beyond the traditional use of these topoi, however, by strengthening the link of the woman's body and death to poetry, as he ties living death directly to the poetry itself. In 'Le Flacon', the poem/poet is the body and coffin that holds living death and brings it to the reader; in 'Une charogne', as we shall see, the poem 'grows' its new life from the living dead body of the lover as carcass.[23]

'Une charogne' begins with what seems to be a standard poetic address to the woman as 'mon âme' [my soul], as the poet asks her with seeming affection if she remembers what they had seen one sweet summer morning. However, after the first two lines, affection reveals its dark underside as we read on:

> Rappelez-vous l'objet que nous vîmes, mon âme,
>   Ce beau matin d'été si doux:
> Au détour d'un sentier une charogne infâme
>   Sur un lit semé de cailloux,
>
> Les jambes en l'air, comme une femme lubrique,
>   Brûlante et suant les poisons,
> Ouvrait d'une façon nonchalante et cynique
>   Son ventre plein d'exhalaisons. (*OC*, I, 31)

[Recall the object that we saw, my soul, | That beautiful summer morning so sweet: | At the turn of a path a repugnant carcass | On a bed strewn with stones, | Its legs in the air, like a lubricious woman, | Burning and sweating poisons, | Opened in a nonchalant and cynical fashion | Its belly full of exhalations.]

As many have noted, here the woman is immediately identified with the animal carcass through images of sexuality: the carcass is on a 'lit' [bed], its legs in the air like those of a licentious woman, 'burning' with seeming passion, but also in a literal sense heated by the sun, as the carcass opens its 'ventre' to give life to the larvae that teem there.[24]

As with so many of Baudelaire's poems, the initial allegorical meaning seems clear enough. First, in the topos of *memento mori*, the carcass represents what the woman will become, as she will die and become rotting matter. However, as Pichois notes, this *memento mori* does not serve to seduce (*OC*, I, 889):

> Le soleil rayonnait sur cette pourriture,
>   Comme afin de la cuire à point,
> Et de rendre au centuple à la grande Nature
>   Tout ce qu'ensemble elle avait joint;
>
> Et le ciel regardait la carcasse superbe
>   Comme une fleur s'épanouir.
> La puanteur était si forte, que sur l'herbe
>   Vous crûtes vous évanouir. (*OC*, I, 31)

[The sun shone on this putrefaction | As if to cook it just right, | And to give back hundredfold to great Nature | All that she had joined together. | And the sky watched the superb carcass | Like a flower unfold. | The stench was so strong, that on the grass | You thought you would faint.]

The sun shines on the carcass that opens like a flower, not a trivial word in *Les Fleurs du mal*, and this undoing by death becomes the 'flowering' of the carcass.

The woman later in the poem takes the place of the sun, becoming the 'soleil de ma nature' [sun of my nature] for the poet. Just as here the sun shines down on the carcass and creates new and expanded life in the flowering armies of larvae it generates, so the image of the woman/carcass is the 'soleil' [sun] to the poet's 'nature', when she as future carcass generates the poem/flower in him, in which he (in this very poem) will keep alive the form of their love:

> — Et pourtant vous serez semblable à cette ordure,
> À cette horrible infection,
> Étoile de mes yeux, soleil da ma nature,
> Vous, mon ange et ma passion!
>
> Oui! telle vous serez ô la reine des grâces,
> Après les derniers sacrements,
> Quand vous irez, sous l'herbe et les floraisons grasses,
> Moisir parmi les ossements.
>
> Alors, ô ma beauté! dites à la vermine
> Qui vous mangera de baisers,
> Que j'ai gardé la forme et l'essence divine
> De mes amours décomposés! (*OC*, I, 32)

[— And yet you will resemble this foul matter, | This horrible infection | Star of my eyes, sun of my nature, | You, my angel and my passion! | Yes! Thus, you will be, O queen of graces, | After the last sacraments, | When you will go, under the grass and the lush flowerings, | To molder among the bones. | Then, O my beauty! Tell the vermin | That will devour you with kisses, | That I have preserved the form and the divine essence | Of my decomposed loves!]

Thus, birth comes from death: first from the dead 'ventre plein' of the carcass that 'flowers'; then here in the poet's future imagining, the dead woman's body gestates new life in the vermin and nourishes the flowers above her as well as nourishing the poem itself, which physically preserves the memory of the dead. Indeed, the carcass as a whole is, in a sense, both living in these vermin and dead, which Baudelaire emphasizes in the description of 'vivants haillons' of its body which seems to be alive. Similarly, the poet imagines the woman as dead and rotting, yet at the same time creating new life while she communicates (thus she is in a sense living) with the beings she creates ('dites à la vermine').

This link between the poem and the carcass/woman continues in the physical appearance of the verses themselves. The alternating length of the poem's lines mimics the irregular shreds of the carcass, as the lines of different length seem to drip from one verse to the next, similar to the black battalions of larvae that flow like liquid from the body, specifically as in the enjambment of the second line below, which spills over without punctuation into the next line:

> Les mouches bourdonnaient sur ce ventre putride,
> D'où sortaient de noirs bataillons
> De larves, qui coulaient comme un épais liquide
> Le long de ces vivants haillons.
>
> Tout cela descendait, montait comme une vague,
> Ou s'élançait en pétillant ;
> On eût dit que le corps, enflé d'un souffle vague,
> Vivait en se multipliant. (*OC*, I, 31)

[Flies buzzed on this putrid belly, | From which emerged black battalions | Of larvae, which flowed like a thick liquid | Along these living tatters. | All of that descended, rose up like a wave, | Or rushed out shimmering; | One might have said that the carcass, inflated with a vague breath | Lived as it reproduced.]

A similar image of the birth and growth of the poem emerges in the following stanzas from the musical sound of the work of nature as it transforms the carcass. This music becomes the poet's rhythmic words, the sounds of the 'grains' he 'winnows' in his writing, as it grows into the flower of his poem:

> Et ce monde rendait une étrange musique,
> Comme l'eau courante et le vent,
> Ou le grain qu'un vanneur d'un mouvement rythmique
> Agite et tourne dans son van. (OC, 1, 31)

> [And this world gave out a strange music, | Like water running and the wind, | Or the grain that a winnower with a rhythmic movement | Shakes and turns in his basket.][25]

The sound of the buzzing 'mouches' echoes the sounds of the words we read, and the black flies and 'noirs bataillons' of larvae resemble the black letters of words on the white page.[26]

The rhythm of the carcass is also in this first instance of the word 'vague', meaning here a 'wave' that rises as if the carcass were breathing, which provides the 'souffle' [breath] of inspiration for the poem, as the 'souffle vague' [vague breath] in the second sense of 'vague'. 'Une charogne' represents its own creation and physical form through these images of inspiration (respiration), music, rhythm, and visual colour and shape, which all derive from the living dead carcass.[27]

Moreover, the poem contains images of eating: just as the poet uses the inspiration of the corpse/woman to 'nourish' his poem, the female dog waits for the couple to leave before continuing to sustain its own life from the carcass that nature, the sun, succeeds, so to speak, in cooking to perfection. Eating is further linked with the poet when vermin, like the poet lover, would consume his lover with kisses. The living and dead woman/carcass therefore gives inspiration as sustenance to the poet and becomes the 'body' of the poem itself.

Thus, as in 'Le Flacon', it is not memory of wholeness and life that forms the basis of this poem and its main metaphors, but rather the memory of a dead body that 'lives on' through other forms: the carcass lives on in the new life it sustains, and the future dead woman 'lives on' in memory and in the poem.[28] This living death expands its metatexual role to include the genesis of art more generally. The decaying form of the body of the carcass is compared to a form sketched by an artist:

> Les formes s'effaçaient et n'étaient plus qu'un rêve,
> Une ébauche lente à venir
> Sur la toile oubliée, et que l'artiste achève
> Seulement par le souvenir. (OC, 1, 32)

> [The forms faded and were but a dream, | A sketch slow to come forth | On the forgotten canvas, and that the artist finishes | Only from memory.]

As the animal decays, its form is erased and no longer has unity. It becomes ghostly, vague, limbic, and its separation from its physical exterior has been effaced as insects from the outside nourish themselves from the inside of the body. This vagueness of form becomes that of the sketch/poem that an artist completes, not from a present fullness of life, but from the fragmented form of the carcass as from fragmented memory.[29] Thus it is not the living, beautiful woman who is sketched as the poet/artist sees her when he speaks with her, but the decayed woman/carcass whose form the poet/artist preserves. Indeed, what he keeps is not his love but his decomposed love, 'mes amours décomposés'. Once again, this emphasis is not on the plenitude of love or presence but on the death that is life, so to speak, and, as we shall see, the living death in the artist's sketch is linked here to Baudelaire's aesthetic theories.[30]

Chambers, in his superb analysis of Baudelaire's *Le Peintre de la vie moderne*, a collection of essays about the artist Contantin Guys, shows that Baudelaire insists on 'loss of presence' as an expression of literature. Baudelaire first emphasizes that Guys's work (like that of the artist of 'Une charogne') is executed not from life but from memory: 'Il dessine de mémoire, et non d'après le modèle [...]. En fait, tous les bons et vrais dessinateurs dessinent d'après l'image écrite dans leur cerveau, et non d'après la nature' [He draws from memory, and not from the model [...]. In fact, all good and true artists draw from the image written on their brain, and not from nature] (*OC*, II, 698). Chambers, after noting this, goes on to analyze Baudelaire's meditation on memory in the work of Guys:

> He works feverishly, not in loiterly fashion, and his instrument isn't the eye, the instrument of supposedly unmediated vision, but a hand guided by memory — and this belatedness with respect to the immediate sensations of the flâneur, while it is short term, nevertheless signals the specificity of his task. He doesn't *reproduce* the erstwhile objects of flâneur vision, but *extracts* from them, by a process that Baudelaire calls translation and refers to also as a 'mnemotechnics of the beautiful', the beauty that lay concealed beneath [...]. [Baudelaire] presents the subject of his case study, Guys, as obliged to work fast, in order not to lose something — he calls it a phantom, in a way that's reminiscent of the haunted city Baudelaire's own poetry describes [...] the phantom must be captured.[31]

For Baudelaire it is the phantom, the ghost or living dead presence, that is caught and not the thing itself. In *Le peintre de la vie moderne*, he also uses the Lazarus figure, which we discussed in 'Le Flacon' above, to represent this living-dead presence in the works of Guys:

> Ainsi, dans l'exécution de M. G. se montrent deux choses: l'une, une contention de mémoire résurrectionniste, évocatrice, une mémoire qui dit à chaque chose: 'Lazare, lève-toi!'; l'autre, un feu, une ivresse de crayon, de pinceau, ressemblant presque à une fureur. C'est la peur de n'aller pas assez vite, de laisser échapper le fantôme avant que la synthèse n'en soit extraite et saisie. (*OC*, II, 699)[32]

> [Thus, in M.G.'s practice two things can be seen: first, an effort of memory that is resurrectionist, evocatory, memory that says to each thing: 'Lazarus, rise!'; the other, an ardour, an intoxication of the pencil, of the brush, almost resembling furore. It is the fear of not going fast enough, of letting the phantom escape before the synthesis has been extracted and seized.]

The result of Guys's phantom tactic is an *ébauche*, like the 'ébauche lente à venir' [sketch slow to come forth] of 'Une charogne', which represents the poem itself: 'Elle a cet incomparable avantage, qu'à n'importe quel point de son progrès, chaque dessin a l'air suffisamment fini; vous nommerez cela une ébauche si vous voulez, mais ébauche parfaite' [It has this incomparable advantage that, at any point in its progress, each drawing has a sufficiently finished look; you could name that a sketch if you want, but a perfect sketch] (OC, II, 700). Thus, the living dead, the sketch, the phantom, represent the essence of art, which is not to express plenitude, but to capture the phantom, sketchy form of life that is already 'dead', as it is registered in memory.

In these poems, woman and the poet's love for her are the living dead 'phantoms' that the poet attempts to sketch in his poetry.[33] So it is not surprising that women in the poems are frequently identified specifically as phantoms, ghosts, and the living dead at times.[34] And we must not forget that his muse Jeanne Duval at the time of the writing of a poem such as 'Un fantôme' was an invalid, in whose living yet ill body Baudelaire perhaps saw the death of the younger Jeanne (OC, I, 901).

Fetish and Androgyny: The Poet's Relation with Woman

In a number of poems, the relationship between the poet and his lover generates the trope of living death. In 'Le Léthé', the poet flees reality and seeks a forgetting explicitly generated by his sexual relations with the woman, as he kisses the polished, shiny surface of her body:

> Je veux dormir! dormir plutôt que vivre!
> Dans un sommeil aussi doux que la mort,
> J'étalerai mes baisers sans remords
> Sur ton beau corps poli comme le cuivre. (OC, I, 156)

[I want to sleep! to sleep rather than to live! | In a slumber as soothing as death, | I will spread my kisses without remorse | Over your beautiful body polished like copper.]

Being lost in love as in sleep might permit the poet to forget, to flee the painful past that makes him sob:

> Pour engloutir mes sanglots apaisés
> Rien ne me vaut l'abîme de ta couche;
> L'oubli puissant habite sur ta bouche,
> Et le Léthé coule dans tes baisers. (OC, I, 156)

[To engulf my appeased sobs | Nothing can match the abyss of your bed; | Powerful oblivion dwells on your mouth, | And the Lethe flows in your kisses.]

However, this sleep is like death, a kind of living death from the poisonous hemlock that he drinks from her breasts:

> Je sucerai, pour noyer ma rancœur,
> Le népenthès et la bonne ciguë
> Aux bouts charmants de cette gorge aiguë. (OC, I, 156)

[I will suck, to drown my rancor, | Nepenthes and good hemlock | From the charming tips of these pointed breasts.]

In a similar way, in 'Le Flacon' one could consider the integrity of the poet's 'self' to be undermined and put into question by the paradoxical condition of living death caused by the ingestion of the poisonous liquor of rancid love.[35] Thus the very union of love that joins the amorous couple produces the state of living death for the poet.

In other poems, the woman is related to living death in a different way. Indeed, some of the most powerful and shocking moments in Baudelaire's poetry are those in which the beautiful surface of the woman's body no longer succeeds in providing forgetfulness, when it stops functioning as beautiful carapace and reveals what lies beneath.[36] Several clear examples include the poem 'Le Masque', which represents the shock experienced when one sees the troubled and troubling woman's face behind the smiling mask of Christophe's statue. In 'Les Métamorphoses du vampire', the poet turns to what was seemingly a beautiful living woman beside him to find that her body has changed into the horrific form of the debris of a skeleton.

In 'Danse macabre', a female skeleton has dressed herself coquettishly in an attempt to appear beautiful on the surface (she resembles the living dead of 'Une charogne' as she is a 'vivante carcasse' [living carcass]). Her ruffle should hide her funereal charms; however, her rocklike, fleshless collarbone hints at the skeletal form below:

> La ruche qui se joue au bord des clavicules,
> Comme un ruisseau lascif qui se frotte au rocher,
> Défend pudiquement des lazzi ridicules
> Les funèbres appas qu'elle tient à cacher. (*OC*, I, 97)

[The frill that plays around her clavicles, | Like a lascivious stream that rubs up against a boulder, | Discreetly protects from ridiculous taunts | The funereal charms that she wants to hide.]

The poet asks her to speak and to inform the living that they, too, harbour death beneath their make-up, beneath their artificial surface:

> Bayadère sans nez, irrésistible gouge,
> Dis donc à ces danseurs qui font les offusqués:
> 'Fiers mignons, malgré l'art des poudres et du rouge
> Vous sentez tous la mort! Ô squelettes musqués [...].'
> (*OC*, I, 98)

[Bayadère without a nose, irresistible wench, | Say to these dancers who act offended: | 'Proud darlings, despite the art of powder and rouge | You all smell of death! O musky skeletons']

The beautiful surface covers over death and loss, and thus the skeletal woman here embodies the limbic structure of living death itself as this woman lives, moves, and speaks, but she is dead.[37] She also says that she is not alone in living death, as the living, too, are the living dead, living skeletons, and this provides the symbolic aspect of the poem. As we shall see below, this structure of the surface that covers death resembles the structural role of the fetish in a number of ways, an important concept in the second half of this chapter on the city poems.[38]

The poem 'Une martyre' resonates with previous poems in both semantic and thematic ways. First, its very words repeat those of 'Le Flacon' (*lamés-lamées* [lamé], *verre* [glass], *or* [gold], *rose-rosâtre* [pink-pinkish], *flacon(s)* [flask(s)], *parfum(ées)* [perfume(d)], *cercueil* [coffin]) and repeat a few words of 'Une charogne' (*forme* [form], *vague* [wave/vague]). This is as well a poem of limbic states, particularly in its exchange between natural and artificial, which has been much discussed by critics, and particularly well in Sanyal's analysis of the poem.[39] Part of this mixing of artificial and natural lies in the exchange between the 'natural' dead woman and the 'artificial' painting in her room, between life and art. The artificial painting relates to her life, because it reveals truths about her love:

> Le singulier aspect de cette solitude
>   Et d'un grand portrait langoureux,
> Aux yeux provocateurs comme son attitude,
>   Révèle un amour ténébreux. (*OC*, I, 112)

> [The singular aspect of this solitude | And of a large, languorous portrait | With eyes provocative like her attitude, | Reveal a dark love.]

Just as her love and life are revealed in the marks on the surface of the portrait, on the 'toile' [canvas] (or the ink on the page of the poem), the other 'toile' [cloth] of her pillow is marked by her real, living blood: 'Un sang rouge et vivant, dont la toile s'abreuve' [A blood red and living, from which the cloth drinks].[40] The strange word 'vivant' brings in our notion of living death, in the paradoxical idea of the living blood of a dead woman.[41] One again, through the poem's metatextual references to art, this living blood spilled on the metaphorical 'toile' [canvas] of her pillow, ties her living death to artistic creation.

In another metatexual reference to poetry, the woman's severed head is compared to a flower (and this poem appears in the very section named 'Fleurs du mal'):

> La tête, avec l'amas de sa crinière sombre
>   Et de ses bijoux précieux,
> Sur la table de nuit, comme une renoncule,
>   Repose [...]. (*OC*, I, 112)

> [The head, with its mass of dark hair | And its precious jewels, | On the night table, like a ranunculus, | Reposes [...].]

This comparison links the metaphorical flower/head to the real dying flowers, 'des bouquets mourants', of the second stanza, as both are situated:

> Dans une chambre tiède où, comme en une serre,
>   L'air est dangereux et fatal,
> Où des bouquets mourants dans leurs cercueils de verre
>   Exhalent leur soupir final. (*OC*, I, 112)

> [In a warm room where, as in a greenhouse, | The air is dangerous and fatal, | Where bouquets dying in their caskets of glass | Exhale their final sigh.]

The 'sigh' of these flowers, in a state between life and death, combines with the warmth of the room to contaminate the air with deadly vapours, an air 'dangereux et fatal'. Like the perfume that escapes from the *verre* in 'Le Flacon', the exhalations of the deathly flowers here escape from their 'cercueils de verre' [caskets of glass], and from the *vers* of this poem, to reach the reader. These lugubrious flowers are dangerous *Fleurs du mal*, and act, as the poem 'Le Flacon', to spread living death metaphorically.

In a reversal of 'Une charogne', where the poet guards 'la forme et l'essence divine' [the form and divine essence] of his love, in 'Une martyre' it is the ghost of the dead woman whose 'forme immortelle' keeps guard over her spouse when he sleeps. She is one of Baudelaire's living-dead women in her haunting presence:

> Ton époux court le monde, et ta forme immortelle
> Veille près de lui quand il dort;
> Autant que toi sans doute il te sera fidèle,
> Et constant jusques à la mort. (OC, I, 113)

[Your spouse travels the world, and your immortal form | Keeps watch over him when he sleeps; | Just as you, he will doubtless be faithful to you, | And constant until death.]

The dead woman is faithful to her spouse as she remains at his side, a haunting that stands for the memory that he has of her, perhaps in his dreams of her ('quand il dort'), as he too is faithful. The tenacious ghost thus represents memory that cannot be erased, yet is not present either: it is like the phantom/sketch of 'Une charogne', like the poetry of 'Le Flacon' that preserves the decayed form of past love. An unforgettable image or memory, the woman's head is also compared to pale visions which, like ghosts born from darkness, would rivet our eyes, mesmerize us in a sense: 'Semblable aux visions pales qu'enfante l'ombre | Et qui nous enchaînent les yeux' [Similar to the pale visions to which darkness gives birth | And that chain our eyes].

A further evocation of the living dead appears when the poet asks the dead woman to answer his questions, demanding that in death she speak to reveal what the man did after her murder: 'Réponds, cadavre impur!' [Answer, impure cadaver!] (similarly, we recall that the poet in 'Danse macabre' tells the dressed-up skeleton to speak to the living, and the poet asks the dead woman in 'Une charogne' to speak to the insects who will devour her). Barbara Johnson in her article on apostrophe explains that this trope, 'by means of the silvery voice of rhetoric, calls up and animates the absent, the lost, and the dead', thus the poet's voice itself calls back this living dead woman and attempts to make her speak.[42]

'Une martyre' manifests androgynous limbic structures as well. The dead body appears to be that of a woman, described as someone with jewels, a stocking and garter, a mane of hair, and the poem's title is in the feminine form. However, initially she lacks subjectivity: we have only a body and its parts — 'un cadavre', 'la tête', 'des yeux', 'le tronc', 'la jambe', 'l'épaule', 'la hanche' [a cadaver, the head, the eyes, the torso, the leg, the shoulder, the hip]. There is actually no gendered article, adjective, or pronoun after the title that would reveal her gender until the eleventh stanza, which finally begins, 'Elle' [She]. A small doubt thus begins to arise before we reach that *elle*, particularly when we read that the body is not that of a voluptuous woman, for her shoulder is skinny and angular, the hip is pointy:

> [...] la maigreur élégante
> De l'épaule au contour heurté,
> La hanche un peu pointue et la taille fringante
> Ainsi qu'un reptile irrité' [...]. (OC, I, 112)

[the elegant thinness | Of the shoulder with an abrupt contour, | The hip a little sharp and the waist supple | Like an irritated reptile.]

This young, non-fleshy body conjures up the 'buste d'un imberbe' [chest of a beardless youth] of 'Les Bijoux'. In that poem, the question of androgyny is raised when the poet thinks he sees in his lover both man and woman:[43]

> Je croyais voir unis par un nouveau dessin
> Les hanches de l'Antiope au buste d'un imberbe,
> Tant sa taille faisait ressortir son bassin.
> Sur ce teint fauve et brun, le fard était superbe! (OC, I, 158)

[I thought I saw united in a new drawing | The hips of Antiope to the chest of a beardless youth, | So much did her waist make her hips stand out. | On this skin tawny and brown, the makeup was superb!]

In the first part of 'Les Bijoux', the mixed passive and active, male and female states that alternate become specific gendered mixing in the androgynous lover, in the bust of a beardless young male joined to the hips of the Amazon woman. This androgynous image thus erases the distinction between male and female in their simultaneous presence in the woman, which in its questioning of traditional differences, also undermines the poet's gender in 'Les Bijoux', as noted by a number of critics.[44]

In 'Une martyre', an additional limbic element that destabilizes traditional categories of gender and sexuality is that Baudelaire had originally intended to place it before the three lesbian poems, thus creating an interesting metonymical relation among the four poems.[45] Pichois further suggests that 'Une martyre' was influenced by Balzac's 'La Fille aux yeux d'or', a story that represents lesbian love and in which genders and sexualities blur.[46] Thus to the unsettling of traditional gender categories is added a suggestion of the unsettling of normative, heterosexual love, through this masculinized martyr in a relationship with a man. Dominique Fisher relates the lesbian theme in Baudelaire's poetry not simply to the destabilization of masculine identity but also to Baudelaire's poetic theories: 'not only is the lesbian a recurrent motif that contextualizes Baudelaire's misogyny within the framework of the destabilization of the masculine subject, but she is also at the core of both his aesthetics and his poetics'.[47] This unsettling of masculine identity thus results in 'Une martyre' from androgyny and from the poem's metonymic relation with homosexuality through Balzac, through the original plan for its placement near the lesbian poems, and through the woman's masculine body.

Indeed, the image of the ghost itself is related to lesbianism, as Terry Castle has noted in *The Apparitional Lesbian*.[48] There she shows that homosexuality is often a phantom presence in dominant culture, and lesbians in literature are often rhetorically associated with ghosts. Diana Fuss has also linked ghostliness to the perception of homosexuality in heterosexual culture; as she writes on homo and hetero: 'Each is haunted by the other, but here again it is the other who comes to stand in metonymically for the very occurrence of haunting and ghostly visitations'.[49] Thus in 'Une martyre' the ghostly presence of this poem's initial lesbian association (in its initial placement in the 1857 collection next to the lesbian poems) finds an echo in the suggestion of non-normative sexuality in the ghostly haunting by the androgynous martyr when she visits her male lover after her death.[50]

At the end of 'Les Bijoux' the firelight on the skin of the lover looks like blood, a violent but symbolic image, which in 'Une martyre' is real blood. Bersani claims that the violence at the end of 'Les Bijoux' is a silencing of the ambiguities raised by the androgynous exchanges in the main part of the poem.[51] Here in 'Une martyre', the androgynous woman has literally been killed. Thus, the poem remains suspended between conflicting needs: the need both to silence the ambiguity of the androgynous body (in death) and to make that body speak, 'réponds cadavre impur!' [answer, impure cadaver!].

Most importantly, in this poem we also find once again the structure of the polished skin of the poem 'Le Léthé' in the description of the dazzling surface of the martyr's headless body in its nudity:

> Sur le lit, le tronc nu sans scrupules étale
>   Dans le plus complet abandon
> La secrète splendeur et la beauté fatale
>   Dont la nature lui fit don. (OC, I, 112)

[On the bed, the naked, shameless torso displayed | In the most complete abandon | The secret splendour and the fatal beauty | That nature gave it.]

Splendeur in French carries the same connotations as 'splendour' in English, of radiance and light, here that of her bare skin. In addition to this nude skin, in the next stanza we find a kind of second skin, this time in a 'bas rosâtre' [pinkish stocking], held in place by a jewelled garter, which has remained on the leg 'comme un souvenir' [like a memory]. Here a direct link develops between a fetishistic object (this isolated body part, the leg, covered by the stocking with a shiny jewel) and memory, 'un souvenir'. In terms of the fetish, memory would point to the hidden underside, the repressed memory of loss that the fetish commemorates, a loss embodied in the decapitated head and the symbolism of the isolated body parts. However, in this stanza, a kind of protection against loss, as Freud analyzed it in 'Medusa's Head', appears in the multiplication of symbolic eyes.[52] In addition to the 'yeux révulsés' [eyes rolled back] of the dead martyr, the artificial 'eye' of the garter, the shiny jewel, darts and gleams as if alive:

> Un bas rosâtre, orné de coins d'or, à la jambe,
>   Comme un souvenir est resté;
> La jarretière, ainsi qu'un œil secret qui flambe,
>   Darde un regard diamanté. (OC, I, 112)

[A pinkish stocking, decorated with gold thread, on the leg, | Like a memory remained; | The garter, like a secret eye that blazes, | Darts a diamond gaze.]

Here the fetish, the artificial eye (of the jewelled garter) seems to live and look, while the woman's natural eye is literally dead; the two together present the limbic state between presence and loss (the fetish as reassurance and mortal memorial) in the co-presence and exchange of life and death.[53]

The next eyes are our own, 'nos yeux', as this head is similar to those pale visions that rivet our eyes in a kind of paralysis, similar to the effect of Medusa's head.[54] The martyr's head, which, as a strange fetish object, is both beautiful as flower ('une renoncule') and frightful ('effrayante'), pleases in its beauty while memorializing death and loss.

In the final two stanzas of the poem, a mechanism of distancing is at work, which is similar to that of the end of 'Les Bijoux', which moves away from the amorous couple to the fire and lamp. Here, distancing can be seen when the woman's corpse is no longer displayed before our eyes but is invited to sleep (and thereby still live, in a certain sense) far away from curious gazes in its quiet grave. Multiplication, as we saw with the eyes, is introduced with the repetition of the words 'loin' [far away] and 'dors en paix' [sleep in peace], as if the poet were conjuring the woman away:

> — Loin du monde railleur, loin de la foule impure,
>   Loin des magistrats curieux,
> Dors en paix, dors en paix, étrange créature,
>   Dans ton tombeau mystérieux. (OC, I, 113)

[— Far from the mocking crowd, far from the impure throngs, | Far from curious magistrates, | Sleep in peace, sleep in peace, strange creature, | In your mysterious tomb.]

There is however, at the same time, a tenderness of tone here that suggests an identification of the poet with the dead woman, a kind of empathy for her and desire for her peace, a reversal of the violent context at the end of 'Les Bijoux'.

The change of attitude toward the martyr begins with that word 'Elle' in stanza eleven, as the description of disconnected, fetishized, and objectified body parts turns into a female subject, and as the poet turns from third person description of her body to direct address to her as 'tu' in the familiar form. As the poet addresses her and asks her to speak, he gives her subjectivity, and then moves her away from objectification and from the gaze of others, to place her in her peaceful tomb. This can be read in two ways: both as a protective gesture, to preserve her integrity as she becomes humanized, but also as a gesture that would 'forget' the act of objectification by silencing her, covering up her decapitated body, and burying it in its enclosed and reassuring carapace of the 'tombeau mystérieux'.[55] In the end, however, her ghost escapes, as if the attempt to keep her hidden beneath the surface cannot succeed.

To understand what is at stake in the ambiguous stance in 'Une martyre', we turn to the concept of phantasmagoria and living death, which combines our theme of the living dead with the concept of the fetish (in its meanings of assurance against, as well as memorial to loss) and to our second domain, the poems on Paris and commodity fetishism in modernity. Here Benjamin's crucial analysis of Baudelaire's writings informs our investigation of the structure of the fetish and its relation to the living dead. Although Benjamin does not analyze this poem in any depth, he does begin the second section of 'Louis Philippe, or the Interior' with lines from this poem that describe the martyr's head as it sits on a table.[56]

As we saw above, in its initial description in 'Une martyre', the woman's body is object-like and consists of a list of body parts without human subjectivity. Her head, the symbolic locus of human identity and thought, sits on a table, a position that equates it with the other commodity objects in the room: flasks, expensive fabrics, plush furniture, marble statues, paintings, perfumed dresses, and the flowers in their vases.[57] Thus, Benjamin places the martyr's head at the 'head' of one section of his 'Exposé of 1939'. He analyzes the collection of objects in the bourgeois interior as a way for humans to invest their humanity in things: 'the traces of its inhabitant are molded into the interior', as he reads the equivalence between things and humans as a symptom of the rise of commodity culture.[58]

Of significance here is the shiny quality of the martyr's torso that we saw above, a quality she shares with the sparkling jewel on her garter. Indeed, this idea of shininess belongs to the commodity fetish for Benjamin: 'A profane glimmer [Schein] makes the commodity phosphorescent', with 'its glitter of distractions'.[59] And, of course, Benjamin highlights the woman's link with the commodity: 'Under the dominion of the commodity fetish, the sex appeal of the woman is more or less tinged with the appeal of the commodity'.[60] For Benjamin, make-up establishes the woman (specifically the prostitute) as a mass-produced item: 'In the form taken by prostitution in the big cities, the woman appears not only as commodity but, in a precise sense, as mass-produced article. This is indicated by the masking of individual expression in favour of a professional appearance, such as makeup provides'.[61] And the commodification of the female body appears in both Baudelaire's work (particularly in 'Le Peintre de la vie moderne' and his writing on makeup and on prostitutes) and Benjamin's writings on prostitution.

For us here, it is more specifically Benjamin's notion of phantasmagoria that is important for the concept of the living dead in the city of Paris: 'The crowd is the veil through which the familiar city is transformed for the flaneur into phantasmagoria'.[62] Crucial to Benjamin's understanding of the phantasmagoria is the original meaning of the word and its relation to the living dead, here ghosts. As Cohen explains, 'The centerpiece of the phantasmagoria was a mobile magic-lantern projector that the spectacle's animator, the phantasmagorian, used to project ghosts ranging from the collective heroes and villains of the Revolution to lost private loved ones reclaimed by bereaved persons in the room'.[63] Here once again is the passage from Benjamin quoted by Cohen, which was referenced above:

> Once escaped from the hand of the producer and divested of its real particularity, [the commodity] ceases to be a product and to be ruled over by human beings. It has acquired a 'ghostly objectivity' and leads a life of its own [...]. Things have attained autonomy, and they take on human features. [...] Marx speaks of the fetish character of the commodity. This fetish character of the commodity world has its origin in the peculiar social character of the labor that produces commodities [...]. It is only the particular social relation between people that here assumes, in the eyes of these people, the *phantasmagorical* form of a relation between things'.[64]

The fetish-like commodity is haunted by the ghostly presence of the human who made it, just as the human is reified into a ghostly thing, an object. As Sanyal points out, 'The human body is presented as an inert and petrified thing, inanimate objects are invested with human characteristics'.[65] Thus in 'Une martyre', the woman as object among objects, a commodity among commodities, gives rise to the poem's phantasmagorical scene, as she becomes one of those pale visions, the spectre whose 'forme immortelle' returns to haunt her lover. As thing, as commodity fetish, she displays the psychic underside of the fetish, the threat of loss in her decapitation, which represents a generalized loss, as well as death. In the two-part structure of 'Une martyre', after the woman has appeared as commodity object and when the poem then turns to the woman as the addressee of the poet's words, her image as ghost emerges, making visible in her haunting form the loss of the human in commodity culture, and thus the living death of humans in the modern age.

Another link of Benjamin's bourgeois interior with Baudelaire's living dead resides in the cases and containers that proliferate in Baudelaire's poems. Benjamin describes these manifold containers in the bourgeois dwelling and their meaning:

> The interior is not just the universe but also the étui of the private individual. To dwell means to leave traces. In the interior, these are accentuated. Coverlets and antimacassars, cases and containers are devised in abundance; in these, the traces of the most ordinary objects of use are imprinted. In just the same way, the traces of the inhabitant are imprinted in the interior.[66]

Baudelaire's poems are the containers of many such containers, and of containers within containers, such as the 'flacon' that resides in the armoire located in the deserted house. In 'Une martyre', the bourgeois interior is the casing and coffin that surrounds the woman's body, particularly in the equation of her head, like the ranunculus flower, with the dying flowers in their glass coffins.

When Baudelaire reveals the ghostly underside of things and the interior of the poetic container, this bourgeois interior does not 'sustain [the private individual] in his illusions' as Benjamin describes it, but rather reveals loss, represented by the woman's severed head.[67] Indeed, one of those objects, the pillow, which could have cushioned her head as she dreamed (just as the bourgeois interior might sustain the dreams of the individual, according to Benjamin), instead avidly drinks her blood, as if Baudelaire were revealing the draining of the human by the consumer objects that surround human bodies and define them:

> Un cadavre sans tête épanche, comme un fleuve,
>   Sur l'oreiller désaltéré,
> Un sang rouge et vivant, dont la toile s'abreuve
>   Avec l'avidité d'un pré. (*OC*, I, 112)

[A cadaver without the head pours out, like a river, | On the sated pillow, | A blood red and living, from which the cloth drinks | With the avidity of a field.]

Thus, as in other images we have seen of containers that cannot hold their contents, such as Lazarus breaking out of his shroud, dead love emerging from its coffin/flask, as well as the shiny surfaces that disappear to reveal what lies below, this poem not only presents the illusion of the shiny, unbroken surface of the body/commodity, but also breaks open that surface, to reveal the living dead ghost, the fragmented self, and loss, which emerges ghostlike from its tomb. In this way, the room in this poem expresses the relation between bourgeois culture and the dead woman (her commodification) as the ghosting of the human.

Woman, Death, and the City: 'À une passante' and 'Le Cygne'

> It is the unique provision of Baudelaire's poetry that the image of woman and the image of death intermingle in a third: that of Paris.
>
> — WALTER BENJAMIN[68]

The poem, 'À une passante', weaves living death throughout in rich and complicated ways. It first stages the experience of the individual in the city crowd, whose contact with other humans is a brief, anonymous crossing in the street. As Benjamin famously observes, the backdrop of deafening sound represents the presence of the large population. What is odd, however, is that the noisy street of the first line strangely metamorphoses into the woman encountered by the poet in the temporality of our reading of the poem. The first line describes the street, a feminine noun in French, as deafening. This feminine form of 'la rue' in the first line appears to continue the description of the street in the second line, which begins with the feminine form of the word 'longue' — a long street. However, the list of adjectives after 'longue' pushes us off this reading path and leaves us stranded and guessing in our interpretation until the third line where we learn that these words describe a woman:[69]

> La rue assourdissante autour de moi hurlait.
> Longue, mince, en grand deuil, douleur majestueuse,
> Une femme passa, d'une main fastueuse
> Soulevant, balançant le feston et l'ourlet. (OC, I, 92)
>
> [The deafening street around me roared. | Long, slim, in full mourning, majestic grief, | A woman passed by, with a sumptuous hand | Lifting, swaying the scalloped edges and the hem.]

This technique makes it seem as if the woman slowly emerges from the street itself as she becomes a kind of product of the city, and as she 'passes' poetically from street to woman. She also relates to our other fetish objects: covered with black mourning cloth, the surface of her body harbours a reference to death.[70]

The body part that she shows, a leg, is like that of a hard, lifeless statue: 'Agile et noble, avec sa jambe de statue' [Agile and noble, with the leg of a statue]. This quality of hardness petrifies her even in her agility as it combines the conflicting qualities of movement (agility and life) and petrification (the statue and death). Thus, she is moving and living as she walks, 'passante', but also deathly in her frozen motionless state, a 'passante', as the word *passer* can also mean to die, to pass from this life into death — Ross Chambers goes so far as to call her a 'spectre en plein jour' [spectre in broad daylight].[71] The poem leaves her eternally passing between these two meanings.[72]

She fascinates the poet who gazes at her eyes, which threaten death:

> Moi, je buvais, crispé comme un extravagant,
> Dans son œil, ciel livide où germe l'ouragan,
> La douceur qui fascine et le plaisir qui tue. (*OC*, 1, 92)
>
> [I, I was drinking, tensed up like an eccentric, | In her eye, livid sky where grew a hurricane, | Gentleness that fascinates and pleasure that kills.]

Eyes are fascinating to see; however, they imperil in yet another example of their symbolism as pleasurable experience, yet which threaten death: 'le plaisir qui tue' (in 'Une martyre' the human eyes are dead). Here, eyes contain a dangerous hurricane, which, just after the mention of the sound of the roar of the city street in the first line of the poem, leads to the suggestion of a similar deafening sound of the storm, and which furthers the woman's blending with the city street, with the 'rue assourdissant' and her hurricane eyes (linking this also to another Paris poem, 'Le Cygne', which we discuss below, in which the city sounds create 'un sombre ouragan' [a sombre hurricane] in the silent air).

Also, the woman is related to brilliance, here not so much her shiny surface as the figural flash of lightning that her encounter produces and that illuminates for an instant:

> Un éclair... puis la nuit! — Fugitive beauté
> Dont le regard ma fait soudainement renaître,
> Ne te verrai-je plus que dans l'éternité? (*OC*, 1, 93)[73]
>
> [A lightning flash... then night! — Fugitive beauty | Whose gaze made me come alive again, | Shall I not see you again until eternity?]

Indeed here, the paradoxical nature of Baudelaire's much commented aesthetic theory of the eternal and fugitive character of modern art is embodied in this fetish/woman who provides both pleasure and death, light and night, street and woman, Benjamin's first and last sight of the 'eternal farewell'.[74] Ironically, the woman who wears black mourning clothes and who offers a deathly love has just brought the poet back to life by means of the very eyes that threaten death, and we must note that a variant of this line is 'm'a fait *souvenir* et renaître' [made me *remember* and come back to life] (*OC*, 1, 1023, n., my emphasis). Thus, the city woman offers life and death, life and memory, living death.

In this poem, as in 'Les Bijoux' and 'Une martyre', the final stanza distances the entrancing yet threatening woman, as she perhaps never can be attained:

> Ailleurs, bien loin d'ici! trop tard! *jamais* peut-être!
> Car j'ignore où tu fuis, tu ne sais où je vais,
> Ô toi que j'eusse aimée, ô toi qui le savais! (*OC*, 1, 93)
>
> [Elsewhere, very far from here! Too late! *Never* perhaps! | For I don't know where you flee, you don't know where I go, | O you whom I would have loved, O you who knew it to be so!]

The temporal and spatial terms and tenses in this stanza are dizzying — far away, unknown place, too late, present, future, past, the pluperfect subjunctive — and they create a limbic mix of time and space that neatly parallels the simultaneous death, rebirth, and love that the passing woman offers. Thus, in her interweaving of opposites in this poem, particularly of death and rebirth, woman represents the limbic, living death of the experience of love and modernity in the city.[75]

Through Andromache, whose name is the first word of the poem 'Le Cygne', Baudelaire gives us a foundational image for this text that represents a woman who, having lost those most precious to her, exists in the present in a kind of living-death. We see her mourning before the tomb of Hector, living in the past of death and destruction rather than in the present. Lowry Nelson says of her state, 'Her cult of the past is, as it were, an instinctive recognition that she is now among the living dead'.[76] This limbic state in life and death, present and past, permeates the poem in a number of different ways that involve the mixed time of a present past, artifice that replaces the real, monuments that contain the past, and ruins in a modern city.

The temporal structure of the beginning of this poem is as complicated as that of the end of 'À une passante'. In the *present* of the poem, the poet recalls a walk that he took in the *recent past* ('je traversais le nouveau Carrousel') [I was crossing the new Carrousel] in the *new* Haussmannian Paris. His walk in the empty, renovated place du Carrousel triggers in him an image of the *distant past* of history and myth, in which Andromache, in her *new* home of exile, remembers and mourns Hector and her *past* in the *old* city of Troy. Thus her story fertilizes the memory of the poet in his *present* life in Paris, and Andomache's ancient mourning *for the past* calls to the poet's mind his more *distant past* and the now destroyed Doyenné neighbourhood that used to occupy the place du Carrousel, which would thus be associated with *her former* destroyed home, the city of Troy.[77] As in the final stanza of 'À une passante', here moments overlap in time and place in the poet's imagination, creating a limbic temporal space in the present moment and milieu.

The physical place of Andromache's exile and the space of modern Paris are also comparable and are themselves double. Andromache's current home is a new but false Troy that has been created to replace the 'dead' city. Having lost her home with no possibility of return, she lives in this new, fake *lieu de mémoire* [place of memory] with a small and sad, artificial Simoïs — literally a 'lying' Simoïs — a false copy of the original river now lost to her. Thus, the dead past of Andromache is attached to the present in a physical place, invested and contained in the false new Troy and stream:

> Andromaque, je pense à vous! Ce petit fleuve,
> Pauvre et triste miroir où jadis resplendit
> L'immense majesté de vos douleurs de veuve,
> Ce Simoïs menteur qui par vos pleurs grandit,
>
> A fécondé soudain ma mémoire fertile,
> Comme je traversais le nouveau Carrousel. (OC, I, 85)

[Andromache, I think of you! That small river, | Poor and sad mirror where formerly shone | The immense majesty of your widow's grief, | That lying Simoïs which by your tears grew larger, | Suddenly nourished my fertile memory, | As I crossed the new Carrousel.]

The river is real and present, it exists in the living presence of Andromache's life; but because it is only a resembling form and not the original, it is also 'dead' in a certain sense, and it aptly embodies the dead past. Furthermore, Hector's tomb in the new Troy is not a real tomb for his body is not there; it is a cenotaph, a 'tombeau vide' [empty tomb]. Thus, as Andromache spills her tears into the artificial, 'living dead' Simoïs, she also mourns before an 'artificial' tomb whose corpse is absent. In discussing this scene in the *Aeneid*, Riggs Alden Smith calls this new place where Andromache dwells a ghost town.[78] Artifice, the absence or 'death' of the original, aptly embodies the dead past in a material simulacrum in the present.[79] As Terdiman notes, 'Contemporaneity is then vertiginously rewritten as a relic of the past, as a simulacrum'.[80]

This simulacrum of the Simoïs is the stimulant for the poet's memory and for the poem's allegory when the image of its waters, filled with Andromache's tears, fertilized (in the past tense) his thoughts as he walked near the 'new' Louvre and the river Seine. Indeed, in a sense, Andromache productively 'haunts' the poet and his thoughts in the same way as woman in general in Baudelaire's well-known statement in the dedication of *Les Paradis artificiels*: 'La femme est fatalement suggestive; elle vit d'une autre vie que la sienne propre; elle vit spirituellement dans les imaginations qu'elle *hante* et qu'elle *féconde*' [Woman is fatally suggestive; she lives a life other than her own; she lives spiritually in the imagination that she *haunts* and that she *fecundates*] (*OC*, I, 399, my emphasis).

Thus, Andromache's false, new stream, the empty tomb, and the *lieu de mémoire* resurrect memory in the poet, and this because of the similar story of ruin followed by disappearance that lies in the past of this newly renovated place du Carrousel. A metaphorical association forms between the new Troy's false river and the 'new' environment of the Parisian Seine (which flows under the 'new' Pont du Carrousel, built in the 1830s), and that flows near the renovated place du Carrousel and the 'new' Louvre. The word *ce* used for the new Paris, 'ce Louvre', unites with the same word used for the past, false river of Andromache, 'ce petit fleuve', uniting it with the current place of the poet. This identification of the two merges the past of Andromache at the banks of the new, fake river with the present of the poet in this new Paris near the Seine.[81] The old area of the Carrousel, the Doyenné, was razed around 1852, an early moment in the vast demolition of old, mainly poor sections of Paris. So the poet walking in the place du Carrousel sees 'ce Louvre', the new Louvre and its now empty surroundings. Vanished are the buildings and odd neighbourhood formerly set near the Louvre walls.[82] Dolf Oehler notes that many observers associated this new Paris with death, a city 'qui n'était plus vivante qu'en apparence, voire une sorte d'engeance de la mort' [that was no longer alive except in appearance, in fact a kind of brood of the dead] and quite simply, 'Paris est mort' [Paris is dead]. He goes on to say that, after the June Days uprising and its aftermath in 1848, Paris was often described as a 'nécropole' [necropolis].[83]

Much has been written about the Doyenné as it appears in 'Le Cygne', however critics have generally not emphasized that this old, destroyed neighbourhood remembered by the poet was actually already partially demolished, already half 'dead' at the time when Baudelaire frequented it, before the 'new' Carrousel.[84] Napoleon Bonaparte had begun renovation and construction work on new sections of the Louvre while he was in power, and some of the demolition of the Doyenné was carried out then.[85] Drawings of the area dating from around 1850, before the neighbourhood's final demise, show a collection of strange buildings. Their walls should have been connected to other buildings, but those buildings have been destroyed and leave a kind of ghostly presence in the outline they made on the walls that still stand. And there were apparently bird merchants that sold, among other animals, swans.[86]

The old neighbourhood that Baudelaire remembers is this partially destroyed one, whose demolition and reconstruction had been interrupted. He recalls the messy remains of the old construction site, mixed in with the hodgepodge of vendors' stalls and shops, some of which sell bric-a-brac (often used items for resale, which are thus also partially decayed in the sense that they are no longer new):

> Je ne vois qu'en esprit tout ce camp de baraques,
> Ces tas de chapiteaux ébauchés et de fûts,
> Les herbes, les gros blocs verdis par l'eau des flaques,
> Et, brillant aux carreaux, le bric-à-brac confus. (OC, 1, 86)
>
> [I see only in my mind that whole camp of shacks, | Those piles of rough-hewn capitals and columns, | The weeds, the large blocks turned green from the puddle water, | And, shining in the panes of glass, the jumble of bric-a-brac.]

The neglected building materials are mildewed, deteriorating blocks of stone.[87] The important word 'ébauchés' [partly hewn] brings us back to the 'ébauche' of the phantom form of 'Une charogne' that the artist must sketch from memory, as well as to the ghostly presence ('le fantôme') that the painter of modern life must portray.[88] These incomplete forms of the columns and cornices, along with used items for sale, contribute to the strange limbic state of the neighbourhood of the past. Stranger still, those cornices and columns, which most likely were to be its future building material, are already decayed, mossy, and overgrown: even the future seems tainted by decomposition; Ross Chambers describes 'ghosts visiting from the future'.[89] These deteriorating buildings and surrounding detritus, which in the present moment the poet is remembering, have in this present moment disappeared, 'died', but it is important to note that even in the past, they were already in a state of decrepitude, of living death.[90] This is again similar to the poet who preserves his 'amours décomposés' in 'Le Flacon'. The already dead is what returns in memory and poetry.[91]

Thus, the poet remembers several living-dead pasts. He recalls the ancient literary story of Andromache, who herself mourns her dead past, and conjures for the reader the other widows in Baudelaire's poems, such as those in 'Les Veuves'. The poet in the present mourns the Doyenné that had disappeared (which was already half-dead in the past) and its inhabitants.[92] This poem thus does not erect the past as a kind of plenitude that one can remember and that existed fully in life, but instead shows a past that is like the present, both of which are marked by living death.[93] The poem emphasizes omnipresent incompleteness and death in temporality. The alienation of the poet and the exile of Andromache work together to allegorize a present moment inhabited by a living-dead past.

Memory in 'Le Cygne' is valued, but it is not pleasurable, as it is elsewhere in a poem such as 'La Chevelure'. In 'Le Cygne', memory invades without invitation, triggered involuntarily by a being or scene in the present that is associated with the past (an already dead past) that is no more and that thus creates melancholy — as many have noted, a kind of negative example, of what Proust would later call 'mémoire involontaire'. It takes over present thoughts, showing what Terdiman calls a 'vulnerability to recollection'.[94] The insistence of these memories is expressed by repetition when the poet's memory is jarred and he says four times throughout the poem, 'Je pense' [I think]; then in another instance those thoughts have a more concrete form in vision, 'Je ne vois qu'en esprit' [I see only in my mind]; and finally he transforms the memory into a simple, hallucinatory 'Je vois ce malheureux' [I see this unhappy creature] (OC, I, 86), as the dead past of the swan becomes his present.[95] This invasive, physical nature of the past is brought home by the image of the poet's memories that are 'heavier than rocks', and he laments that these memory 'rocks' are more durable and heavier than the stone blocks with which real buildings are constructed, those decayed or fragmented 'blocs' scattered at the construction site in the past and that have disappeared in the poem's present:

> Le vieux Paris n'est plus (la forme d'une ville
> Change plus vite, hélas! que le cœur d'un mortel);
> [...]
> Paris change! mais rien dans ma mélancolie
> N'a bougé! palais neufs, échafaudages, blocs,
> Vieux faubourgs, tout pour moi devient allégorie,
> Et mes chers souvenirs sont plus lourds que des rocs. (OC, I, 85–86)

> [The old Paris is no more (the form of a city | Changes more quickly, alas! than the heart of a mortal); | [...] | Paris changes! but nothing in my melancholy | Has budged! New palaces, scaffoldings, blocks, | Old faubourgs, all for me becomes allegory, | And my dear memories are heavier than rocks.]

The weight of this dead past crushes with memories that cannot be erased and that press down and imprison, as the word *opprimer* [to oppress] has as a meaning to weigh down with a burden: 'Aussi devant ce Louvre une image m'opprime' [Thus before this Louvre an image oppresses me] (OC, I, 86).[96] This image of memories weightier than rocks and the use of the present tense in 'Je vois' make the dead past more material, heavier, and more 'present' than the current moment, as Leaky notes.[97] And as the poet says, nothing in his heart has changed: the dead past continues.[98]

Memory also presses down on Andromache, bent over by the weight of love and grief, mired in her thoughts of the past, 'Auprès d'un tombeau vide en extase courbée' [Before an empty tomb in ecstasy bowed]. The word 'extase', in its etymological sense of being outside oneself, highlights that the present moment for her is outside the present and in the past.[99] The poet describes a woman who had descended from the heights of love and grandeur with Hector in Troy to the degraded status of a traded animal, 'vil bétail' [vile beast] (thus her relation to the swan, also presumably for sale, and perhaps also as a suggestion for the personal history of the black woman in the poem).[100] The first three lines below, as they descend on the page, follow her plunge from the arms of Hector to her oppression at the hands (literally *under* the hand) of Pyrrhus, after which she becomes that statue-like figure bent over the cenotaph of Hector.[101] The fourth line takes us more rapidly down that same path from Hector to Helenus:

> Andromaque, des bras d'un grand époux tombée,
> Vil bétail, sous la main du superbe Pyrrhus,
> Auprès d'un tombeau vide en extase courbée;
> Veuve d'Hector, hélas! et femme d'Hélénus! (*OC*, I, 86)

[Andromache, from the arms of a great husband, fallen, | Vile beast, into the hands of proud Pyrrhus, | Before an empty tomb in ecstasy bowed; | Widow of Hector, alas! and wife of Helenus!]

Her fate is represented by that hand of Pyrrhus that subjects her, and seems to push physically, to weigh her down as she bows over the tomb. The image of almost material weight in this description of Andromache joins with the weight of the poet's memories, heavier than building blocks, to create a concrete and material dead past, which is itself in the poem a repetition of oppression, that presses down in the present moment.[102]

With Pyrrhus, Andromache is a *femme tombée* [fallen woman], both in the sense that she fell from her exalted position in Hector's arms, as well as in the sense that she is a woman given to Pyrrhus as his concubine. Through the joining of the image of the weight of memory with her fallen state, Andromache taps into the symbol of woman as object (related to the commodity in the modern aspect of the poem), here to be passed from man to man.[103]

Indeed, the commodity itself does appear briefly in this poem in those 'baraques', shop stalls, such as in those at fairs. Victorien Sardou described these 'shacks' of the old Doyenné quarter: 'Ces baraques [...] étaient louées à des marchands de couleurs, de gravures, de tableaux et de curiosités de toute sorte' [These shacks were rented to merchants who sold paints, engravings, paintings, and curiosities of all sorts].[104] The commodity marketplace thus makes its appearance in these stalls, and specifically in a relation to art (the engravings and paintings). It also literally appears in the 'bric-à-brac confus' [the jumble of bric-a-brac] of the small shops, where most notably we find in the display window the glitter of merchandise 'brillant aux carreaux' [shining in the panes of glass] (a shine significant in light of Benjamin's work, which we saw above, 'a profane glimmer makes the commodity phosphorescent'). Thus, this past of the bazaar-like Paris is mourned, but again it is one that was already 'fallen', half-destroyed, as well as infiltrated by the marketplace, here a kind of old-fashioned market, which was already being replaced by larger stores, as we saw even in Balzac. Here, because this old Paris was already decaying, the shiny appearance of the bric-a-brac accompanies decrepitude, this half-dead neighbourhood. The new Louvre then wiped out the physical traces of this already phantomic past, which lives only as ghostly memory in the poet's mind through its absence from the Louvre courtyard and the place du Carrousel themselves. Baudelaire shows the phantom of the dead past that dwells within the cleaned out, new, but empty, dead space of everyday life beside this new Louvre. This blank space inspires the poem, as we imagine it written on a blank page of paper.[105]

In fact, in looking at the description of Andromache, we see that there, too, a 'shine' is related to the venerated place: the new river is a 'pauvre et triste miroir où jadis resplendit | L'immense majesté de vos douleurs de veuve' [Poor and sad mirror where formerly shined | The immense majesty of your widow's grief] (*OC*, I, 85). Like the shiny commodity, the river is a glimmering surface. Furthermore, the physical objects that represent the living dead (the false city of Troy, the empty tomb, and the fake river) could be seen as fetish objects revered by Andromache. If the commodity contains the ghost of the human in the absence of the human who made it, here the tomb is venerated as a memento of the lost loved one, and it, too, is empty of the human. Andromache bows before the tomb that she knows is false and void, yet even so she continues to bow down there.[106] The presence of the fetish memorializes loss, just as this poem is, according to Burton, 'a carefully constructed poetic grave'.[107]

As mentioned above, Andromache has in fact herself been seen by Lowry Nelson as an example of the living dead. In looking at the poetic influences of Virgil on Baudelaire, Nelson writes that Andromache, who has lost so much, envies those who have died because, as Nelson says, her life is over, but she must live on in 'repetition or stasis'. In Virgil, when Aeneas comes upon Andromache 'invoking [...] the shade of Hector', and when she sees Aeneas in his Trojan garb, she at first assumes that the living Aeneas is a ghostly shade and that Hector may be with him.[108] However, as Nelson notes, 'In her living death, the distinction is not really important; she had consummated her essence in the great life she had with Hector in Troy; her life now is stasis, meaningful only in communion with the past and with the dead'.[109]

In the act of remembering Hector by the empty tomb, she seems almost to succeed in summoning him forth as the living dead. Baudelaire, however, does not represent Andromache as she invokes Hector, but rather the poet invokes Andromache by means of the famous apostrophe in the first line of the poem: 'Andromaque, je pense à vous!'. As mentioned above, Johnson has written suggestively on the way in which apostrophe itself is an invocation of the dead in Baudelaire and in general. Apostrophe is an attempt at 'rhetorical animation' as Johnson calls it:

> Apostrophe in the sense in which I will be using it involves the direct address of an absent, dead, or inanimate being by a first-person speaker [...]. The absent, dead, or inanimate entity addressed is thereby made present, animate, and anthropomorphic.[110]

Baudelaire, in his rhetorical strategy of invocation, himself calls forth the absent Andromache, as well as his own literary antecedent, Virgil, through her. In this way, the past invoked is also the literary historical past which Baudelaire reanimates in his work through his use of apostrophe.[111] Through poetic address, the poem and language itself become the place where the living dead can dwell. Johnson notes that apostrophe is actually a kind of 'fake' direct address, because the addressee is absent or even non-sentient and cannot respond. Certainly, this fake or sham address fits well with the false Troy and Simoïs, and the empty tomb.[112]

The water of Andromache's false Simoïs appears in the context of the swan and the black woman and is an important aspect of their place of exile. If Andromache's waters are false, the swan *lacks* water as it makes its way through the dust and dry pavement of a rainless Paris, beside a dry gutter.[113] In contrast, the black woman ploughs through the Parisian mud and damp fog, through a Paris that is too watery. Their opposite desires show that what is significant in human desire and lack is not what has been lost — for some it is water, for some a drier climate — but rather the universality of human lack, a kind of emptiness or death in the present moment. Oehler describes this as a melancholy that 'is always a way of actualizing, one might almost say sublimating, longing'.[114]

After the introduction of the black woman in the eleventh stanza, the poem begins to pile up images of other exiles, one after the other, building, block upon block, a structure of abject beings. Like the swan who lacks water, the poet thinks of 'maigres orphelins séchant comme des fleurs' [skinny orphans drying like flowers] (OC, I, 87); then, like the black woman who has too much water, the poet thinks of those who drink tears and the milk of sorrow, and of the 'matelots oubliés dans une île' [sailors forgotten on an island] (OC, I, 87); if they are imprisoned on this island, surrounded by insurmountable waters, the black woman misses her tropical home, perhaps itself an island (one thinks of Baudelaire's trip to Mauritius and also of Jeanne Duval's possible place of origin).[115] And there are the tears of Andromache, the 'waters' that fertilize the poet's mind.[116]

The list of the exiled then becomes vaguer and leaves the poem with an open-ended catalogue of possibilities as the poet thinks of the general types of exiles similar to the captive swan and black woman, and to the vanquished Andromache: 'Aux captifs, aux vaincus!... à bien d'autres encor!' [To the captives, to the vanquished!... To so many others!] (OC, I, 87).[117] His memories and the images they generate, which like 'rocs' stronger than the decaying and disappeared building blocks of the Doyenné, pile up to construct a strange imaginary 'structure', a community of exiles, an 'identité-identification collective', separated in time, place, and nature;[118] a community that joins up with the other wandering Parisian living-dead in Baudelaire's works — the 'fantôme débile' of 'Les Petites Vieilles' and the eternal 'spectres' of 'Les Sept Vieillards', which were to have been called 'Fantômes parisiens'.[119] These exiles create an odd new ghostly 'neighbourhood', like the Doyenné that had disappeared, in their shared living experience of absence and death. It is as if Baudelaire were compassionately wrenching from time and place a collection of people to create an imaginary city made of the symbolic living dead, another false Troy. This city in a sense expands to be the world itself through this dispersion of suffering through geographical space (Paris, the tropics, and the stranded sailors), humans and animals, old and young, from past to present. As Edward Ahearn notes, the poem shows the 'individual speaker encountering current and past French history embodied in the city, then the opening to a larger, including non-European, scope [...] an estranged sense of collectivity'.[120]

Endless Living Death

> That things are 'status quo' *is* the catastrophe.
> — WALTER BENJAMIN[121]

If Baudelaire creates an endlessly expanding community of the living dead in 'Le Cygne', another poem in the 'Tableaux parisiens' greatly expands the concept of living death itself into an endless and general state.[122] The first part of 'Le Squelette laboureur' [The Skeleton Plowman] begins with a description of anatomical prints that the poet comes across while browsing through the book stalls of the Paris quays. These books contain anatomical drawings of skeletons and *écorchés* (human bodies stripped of skin). The poet singles out one strange representation of these cadavers; they till the earth. Then in the second part of the poem, the poet explores the meaning of this image of eternal living death as he asks one appropriately long-drawn-out question of the skeletons and *écorchés*, again using a kind of apostrophe to elicit a response from the dead:

> Voulez-vous (d'un destin trop dur
> Épouvantable et clair emblème!)
> Montrer que dans la fosse même
> Le sommeil promis n'est pas sûr;
>
> Qu'envers nous le Néant est traître;
> Que tout, même la Mort, nous ment,
> Et que sempiternellement,
> Hélas! il nous faudra peut-être
>
> Dans quelque pays inconnu
> Écorcher la terre revêche
> Et pousser une lourde bêche
> Sous notre pied sanglant et nu? (*OC*, I, 94)

[Do you wish (of a destiny far too harsh | Frightful and clear emblem!) | To show that even in the grave itself | Promised sleep is not certain; | That for us Nothingness is traitorous; | That everything, even Death, lies to us, | And that sempiternally | Alas! we must perhaps | In some unknown land | Scratch the obstinate earth | And dig with a heavy spade | Under our foot bloodied and bare?]

Here Baudelaire imagines that death does not, in fact, end things, and that we will have to continue our life of hard labour 'sempiternally', a word whose length in French (seventeen letters) aptly evokes eternity, as Labarthe notes.[123] We may all thus become the living dead without end (which is perhaps worse than death).[124]

The books of anatomical prints themselves are described as cadaverous and as mummies that one finds:

> Dans les planches d'anatomie
> Qui traînent sur ces quais poudreux
> Où maint livre cadavéreux
> Dort comme une antique momie. (*OC*, I, 93)

[In the anatomy plate illustrations | That lie around the dusty quays | Where many a cadaverous book | Sleeps like an antique mummy.]

In one sense, this is because these books contain those anatomical images of the living dead *écorchés* and skeletons who labour in the fields. This mummy-book could thus be thought of as the covering or wrapping that contains the dead, which one can unwrap/open to view the contents. Indeed, the *rime embrassée* is a verse structure that embodies the idea of wrapping, containing two rhyming lines of poetry within two outer lines that rhyme, another one of those Baudelaire containers within which one finds death preserved.

This skeleton who works the earth also sets up an identification of the skeleton with the poet who works his poem. In order to develop the meaning of this symbol, we find in a poem from *Les Épaves*, 'La Rançon', a similar situation in which man must ceaselessly till fields in order to produce 'la moindre rose' [the smallest rose] and 'des fleurs' [flowers]:

> L'homme a, pour payer sa rançon,
> Deux champs au tuf profond et riche,
> Qu'il faut qu'il remue et défriche
> Avec le fer de la raison;
>
> Pour obtenir la moindre rose,
> Pour extorquer quelques épis,
> Des pleurs salés de son front gris
> Sans cesse il faut qu'il les arrose. (*OC*, I, 173)

[Man possesses, in order to pay his ransom, | Two fields of rocky soil, deep and rich, | That he must turn and clear | With the iron of reason; | In order to grow the smallest rose, | In order to extort a few wheat ears, | With salty tears from his grey brow | Ceaselessly must he water them.]

One of these two flower and grain fields to be tended is 'l'Art'. For the poet of *Les Fleurs du mal*, the act of labouring fields to create flowers, clearly stands for creating art, and if we transfer this metaphor of tilling to writing poetry, we find a number of additional similar supports for this equation of poet with skeleton as we return to 'Le Squelette laboureur'. Baudelaire uses the word *écorcher* twice in this poem, once as a name for those 'écorchés', the skinned people who labour the fields (in 'La Rançon' this is the poet), and then for what the poet/skeleton must do: 'Écorcher la terre revêche' [Scratch at the hostile soil]. If one thinks of the process of writing with a pen at the time, one can imagine the act as a kind of scratching at the page, a *griffonnage* [scribble] from the word *griffer*, which is a kind of clawing or scratching, similar to *écorcher*. One says 'chicken scratches' in American English for bad handwriting, *écrire comme un chat* in French, both expressions that conjure scratching. Furthermore, the poet asks the skeleton if it must till the soil 'sous son *pied*' [under its *foot*] with 'tout l'effort de vos *vertèbres*' [every effort of your *vertebrae*]: in this poem, the *vers*, verses, are made under one's 'pied' [foot], the *vers* of eight metered, poetic *feet*, eight *pieds*.[125] Thus, we have Baudelaire, the poet, who has tilled the soil, scratched the paper, for these poems, one of which is 'planted' in *Les Fleurs du mal*, and has given them and this living death to us from beyond the grave as we open his own cadaverous, mummy-like book.

Allegory and the Living Dead

> Baroque allegory sees the corpse only from the outside;
> Baudelaire evokes it from within.
> — WALTER BENJAMIN
>
> [...] tout pour moi devient allégorie.
> — CHARLES BAUDELAIRE[126]

If the poet in Baudelaire's works is at times represented as suspended in a state of living death, Baudelaire also relates one of the important elements of his works, allegory, to living death. I do not wish to rehearse the incredibly complicated debates about allegory that have taken place in Baudelaire studies and simply refer the reader to Susan Blood's exemplary clarification of the arguments and issues involved (based in part on work by Ross Chambers) in her introduction to *Baudelaire and the Aesthetics of Bad Faith*.[127] Rather, I start here with Baudelaire's own discussion of allegory, of 'allegorical intelligence', in *Les Paradis artificiels*. In this work, he makes one general comment about allegory itself as an important form in poetry: 'nous noterons en passant que l'allégorie, ce genre si *spirituel* [...] est vraiment l'une des formes primitives et les plus naturelles de la poésie' [we note in passing that allegory, this genre that is so *intellectual*, is truly one of the most primitive and natural forms of poetry] (*OC*, I, 430). After this, he goes on to discuss how the 'ivresse' [intoxication] of hashish intensifies the understanding of allegory, which recovers its legitimate domination of our mind: 'L'intelligence de l'allégorie prend en vous des proportions à vous-même inconnues [...]. L'allégorie [...] reprend sa domination légitime dans l'intelligence illuminée par l'ivresse' [The understanding of allegory acquires in you dimensions as yet unknown to you [...]. Allegory [...] recovers its legitimate domination in the mind illuminated by intoxication] (*OC*, I, 430).[128]

One of the examples he gives of this magical state of intensified allegorical understanding is that of the Lazarus-like resuscitation of something that has died. Even arid grammar can become a 'sorcellerie évocatoire' [evocatory sorcery] when one is in a state of 'ivresse', and here I take the word 'evocatory' in its sense of evoking, calling forth something that is absent and making it present by means of language, as in apostrophe.[129] For Baudelaire, in this sorcery something that exists in arid skeletal form in language is magically resuscitated and given flesh:

> La grammaire, l'aride grammaire elle-même, devient quelque chose comme une sorcellerie évocatoire; les mots ressuscitent revêtus de chair et d'os, le substantif, dans sa majesté substantielle, l'adjectif, vêtement transparent qui l'habille et le colore comme un glacis, et le verbe, ange du mouvement, qui donne le branle à la phrase. (*OC*, I, 431)

> [Grammar, arid grammar itself, becomes something like an evocatory sorcery; words resuscitate, clothed again in flesh and blood, the noun, in its substantial majesty, the adjective, transparent clothing that dresses the noun and colours it like a glaze, and the verb, angel of movement, that sets the sentence in motion.]

Here something that lies dormant beneath the dead surface of words arises and returns to life, '*re*vêtus de chair et d'os' [*re*-clothed in flesh and blood]. It is this idea of a return to life of words as they reawaken, like Lazarus in 'Le Flacon', that connects with the generation of rich meanings and with the allegorical image of the living dead in Baudelaire's works. This resuscitation connects also with Baudelaire's description of Guys's method of drawing in 'Le Peintre de la vie moderne', as we saw above: 'une contention de mémoire *résurrectionniste*, évocatrice, une mémoire qui dit à chaque chose: "Lazare, lève-toi!"' (*OC*, II, 699, my emphasis).[130] In this way we can understand Benjamin's linking of allegory and ruin, since a ruin, a kind of 'dead' creation, is the concrete presence and intrusion of the past in the present moment: 'Allegory holds fast to the ruins'.[131]

Indeed, the resurrection of the dead displays the temporal nature of allegory, which Paul de Man famously explicated. For de Man, allegory:

> Necessarily contains a constitutive temporal element; it remains necessary, if there is to be allegory, that the allegorical sign refer to another sign that precedes it. [...] Whereas the symbol postulates the possibility of an identity or identification, allegory designates primarily a distance in relation to its own origin.[132]

In 'Le Cygne', when the poet says 'tout pour moi devient allégorie', it is at the moment when he is in the Paris that is changing, 'Paris change', but he still 'sees' the image of the swan, 'une image m'opprime'. The past has disappeared, it is absent from the present, at a temporal distance. However, it is that disappearance that then conjures up the 'dead' buildings and beings of the past in the present. The difference between life and death, of course, must be a temporal one and thus the problem posed by the living dead necessarily relates to temporality, to a state of being that normally has a before and an after, but which is put into question in living death.[133]

The image of the living dead differs from that of a ghost or spirit that haunts because of its material, physical nature, like the rocks that weigh down the poet: Lazarus smells, his dead body lives and moves. This physicality expresses the intrusive nature of the past that exists not simply as an image in the mind but rather has a real, concrete effect on the present moment. De Man notes this insistence of the past in the present when he describes how memory occupies the present moment for Baudelaire: 'any temporal awareness is so closely tied for him to the present moment that memory comes to apply more naturally to the present than it does to the past' (p. 156). For de Man, the present thus itself becomes split, becomes temporal, which for us is represented by the paradoxical, split image of living death: 'The same temporal ambivalence prompts Baudelaire to couple any evocation of the present with terms such as 'representation', 'mémoire', or even 'temps', all opening perspectives of distance and difference within the apparent uniqueness of the instant' (p. 157).

De Man goes on to link allegory with negativity, seen in our context as the negativity of death that returns rather than the return of an ideal past: 'Allegory and irony are thus linked in their common discovery of a truly temporal predicament [...]. Both are determined by an authentic experience of temporality, which, seen from the point of view of the self engaged in the world, is a negative one' (pp. 222, 226). One might think of 'La Vie antérieure' as an illustration of this concept: in that poem, what appears to be an evocation in the present of a beautiful but finished past turns into its opposite when, at the end of the poem, we learn that this past contained not happiness but rather a 'secret douloureux qui me faisait languir' [a secret suffering that made me languish] (*OC*, I, 18).

Thus, when the living dead return in this allegorical form, it is not plenitude that is emphasized but rather division and loss, as de Man says, 'renouncing the nostalgia and the desire to coincide, it establishes its language in the void of this temporal difference' (p. 207). Benjamin before De Man also relates the allegorical form in Baudelaire to the negativity of the renunciation of totality: 'As Baudelaire, after 1850, took up the doctrine of *l'art pour l'art*, he explicitly carried through a renunciation which he had undertaken in sovereign spirit at the very instant he made allegory into the armature of his poetry: he gave up using art as [a] category of the totality of existence'.[134]

The final aspect of allegory that is significant in the idea of the living dead is that of a kind of inner difference that breaks out from the present, as in Baudelaire's dead grammar that revives. Chambers in fact links the fetish with allegory, in that fetish objects 'are or have become *allegorized*; ... if they "speak" to us, it is to bespeak "otherness"'.[135] In the allegory of the swan, the story of a bird shows itself to be like something that it is not and that is temporally removed from it, such as Andromache: the everyday space of the place du Carrousel breaks open to make present the swan's story and that of Andromache.[136] In Baudelaire's poetry, bodies, objects, and buildings become something else, as Benjamin says, 'things are raised to allegory'.[137] Thus, the present space and moment are really the tombs of past moments that can reappear, ghostlike, when jarred by any number of different kinds of connections — similarity, metonymical relations, smells — between the present and the past.

Notes to Chapter 2

1. Charles Baudelaire, letter to Félix Nadar, 16 May 1859.
2. Baudelaire refers to another scene of the resurrection of the dead in 'Les Phares', when he describes Michelangelo's 'Last Judgement' with its phantoms and fleshy dead: 'fantômes puissants qui dans les crépuscules | Déchirent leur suaire en étirant leurs doigts' [powerful phantoms who at dusk | Tear their shroud while stretching out their fingers] (*OC*, I, 13 & 853, n.).
3. Georges Poulet notes that the theme of living death is very frequent in the work of Baudelaire: *Qui était Baudelaire?* (Geneva: Skira, 1969), p. 138.
4. Charles Baudelaire, 'Le Peintre de la vie moderne' (*OC*, II, 684).
5. J. A. Hiddleston notes that the first two lines are prose-like, thus one could see another instance of the collapse of opposites when the distinction between poetry and prose is effaced: *Baudelaire and 'Le Spleen de Paris'* (Oxford: Clarendon Press, 1987), p. 62. Alain Faudemay says of this enjambment that it expresses 'le contact entre deux matières et le passage de l'une à l'autre' [the contact between two different types of matter and the passage from one to the other]: 'Sur la porosité baudelairienne: la mémoire au futur dans "Le Flacon"', *Colloquium Helveticum*, 27 (1998), 163–79 (p. 167). Peter Broome writes that, because of the enjambment, 'the verse, touched by the presence of real poetic perfume, becomes porous and allows a seeping transfusion to take

place': *Baudelaire's Poetic Patterns: The Secret Language of 'Les Fleurs du mal'* (Amsterdam & Atlanta, GA: Rodopi, 1999), p. 99. See also Dominique Rincé's analysis of the word and syllable *vers* in Baudelaire's poetry: 'Vers, vermines, vermisseaux et autres bestioles contaminantes dans l'œuvre poétique de Charles Baudelaire', *Nottingham French Studies*, 58.2 (2019), 146–55.

6. This invasion of the body by the *vers* [verse] can be performed, in other poems on the living dead, by a different type of *vers*: the worms that eat the dead body and remorse that eats at the heart; the word *remords* [remorse] from *mordre* [to bite]. In 'Remords posthume', for example: 'Et le ver rongera ta peau comme un remords' [and the worm will gnaw your skin like remorse]. John E. Jackson speaks appropriately here of 're-mort': *La Mort Baudelaire: essai sur 'Les Fleurs du Mal'* (Neuchâtel: La Baconnière, 1982), p. 113.
7. It is notably in 'La Chevelure' that we see memory brought back by a scent.
8. Broome, *Baudelaire's Poetic Patterns*, p. 77.
9. Richard D. E. Burton describes memory as being below the level of consciousness in *Baudelaire in 1859: A Study in the Sources of Poetic Creativity* (Cambridge & New York: Cambridge University Press, 1988), p. 175.
10. Another meaning for 'larva' and for the French *larve* is ghost.
11. Burton, *Baudelaire in 1859*, p. 141 and elsewhere. *Les Limbes* was the title of an early, limited collection of poems, which would later become *Les Fleurs du mal*. Burton mentions the truly astounding list of themes associated with death compiled by Jean-Paul Weber, who interprets it as an infantile theme that founds all of Baudelaire's poetry: Jean-Paul Weber, *Genèse de l'œuvre poétique* (Paris: Gallimard, 1960), pp. 185–223.
12. Robert Greer Cohn gives a psychoanalytic reading of the letter 'v' in 'Baudelaire's "Frisson Nouveau"', *The Romanic Review*, 84.1 (January 1993), 19–26 (p. 22).
13. Faudemay refers the 'mort vivant' here to fantastic literature, 'Sur la porosité baudelairienne', p. 168.
14. Patrick Labarthe notes that the 'resurrection' in this poem takes place 'sur le mode d'une survie toute *négative*' [in the mode of an afterlife that is completely *negative*]: *Baudelaire et la tradition de l'allégorie*, Histoire des idées et critique littéraire, 380 (Geneva: Droz, 1999), p. 189.
15. Alphonse de Lamartine, *Œuvres d'Alphonse de Lamartine*, 2 vols (Paris: Jules Boquet, 1826), I, 88. Poulet also sees this as a state of the decomposition of the past, but relates it to a prelapsarian paradise: 'This distance is the past; not the lost and dreamed-of past lying back beyond original sin, but the past which has elapsed since the original sin, the tainted past. It stretches back into time like the field of an existence irremediably sullied over its full extent. Nothing is more strictly worked out in Baudelaire than this system of a dual past, a remote and radiant past followed by another, a dark irreparable past [...]. The past to which this remorse refers is not the happy past directly evoked by nostalgic thoughts. What is remembered here is, on the contrary, the ineradicable succession of lapses by which, in the course of a lifetime, a man has brought about his own downfall and forfeited the patrimony that was rightfully his': *Who Was Baudelaire?*, pp. 131–32.
16. Ross Chambers explores a similar paradoxical structure, in his case of simultaneous progress and digression: *Loiterature* (Lincoln: University of Nebraska Press, 1999), p. 21.
17. These images occur in 'Spleen, J'ai plus de souvenirs', 'Spleen, Je suis comme le roi', 'Le Squelette laboureur', and 'Brumes et pluies'.
18. Richard D. E. Burton has a wonderful description of this limbic state in 'Baudelaire and the Agony of the Second Republic, "Spleen" (LXXV) ("Pluviôse irrité…")', *MLR*, 81.3 (July 1986), 600–11 (pp. 607–08). In a section of *Baudelaire in 1859*, he lists a number of texts that touch on the theme of living death, including a project for a novel or novella entitled 'L'Automate', in which a man comes back to life (pp. 138–48). And we remember that Sartre claimed that Baudelaire himself 'a examiné sa vie du point de vue de la mort' [examined his life from the point of view of death]: *Baudelaire* (Paris: Gallimard, 1947), p. 186.
19. Jackson, *La Mort Baudelaire*, p. 22.
20. Dolf Oehler, 'L'Explosion baudelairienne', *Europe: Revue Littéraire Mensuelle*, 70 (August-September 1992), 62–68 (p. 65). Broome as well notes that 'the image of the self as tomb, and its ambiguous living death, are a dark motif: *Baudelaire's Poetic Patterns*, p. 348.

21. Caroline Fischer finds in another way that 'la femme est enfermée dans l'œuvre comme le parfum dans le flacon' [the woman is enclosed in the poem just at the perfume in the flask]: 'Baudelaire et la tradition de la poésie amoureuse', in *La Main hâtive des révolutions: esthétique et désenchantement en Europe de Leopardi à Heiner Müller*, ed. by Jean Bessière and Stéphane Michaud (Paris: Presses Sorbonne Nouvelle, 2001), pp. 35–54 (p. 46). More generally, Richard Stamelman states that Baudelaire's 'poems are poetic corpses enshrouded by the endless folds of allegorical writing': 'The Shroud of Allegory: Death, Mourning and Melancholy in Baudelaire's Work', *Texas Studies in Literature and Language*, 25.3 (Fall 1983), 390–409 (p. 403).
22. This is a reference to the famous last line of the first poem in *Les Fleurs du mal*, addressed to ' — Hypocrite lecteur, — mon semblable, — mon frère!' [Hypocritical reader — my like — my brother!]. Barbara Wright observes that these verses of 'Le Flacon', instead of contaminating, 'will intoxicate the memory of future generations with its evocation of the bitter-sweet recollections of his love for his mistress': 'Baudelaire's Poetic Journey in *Les Fleurs du mal*', in *The Cambridge Companion to Baudelaire*, ed. by Rosemary Lloyd (Cambridge: Cambridge University Press, 2006), pp. 31–50 (p. 38).
23. Parts of the following analysis appeared in condensed form in my article 'Toxic Doxa in Baudelaire: "À celle qui est trop gaie" and "Une charogne"', *Symposium*, 66.4 (Winter 2012), 194–205.
24. In French *ventre plein* means a full stomach, however the word *plein* is used also for pregnancy in animals, thus obliquely suggesting gestation in this context.
25. Jean-Claude Mathieu sees this as a rhythm alternating 'entre vie et mort' [between life and death] in 'Une charogne', in *Les Fleurs du mal: actes du colloque de la Sorbonne, des 10 et 11 janvier, 2003*, ed. by André Guyaux and Bertrand Marchal (Paris: Sorbonne, 2003), pp. 161–80 (p. 165).
26. One might also link flies to the writing of alphabet letters in the expression 'écrire en pattes de mouche' [writing like fly footprints] for tiny, illegible handwriting.
27. Olivier Pot notes this same link between sounds, the strange music produced by the flies is the sound of decomposition, which becomes the sound of the poem: ' "Une charogne" de Baudelaire: autopsies d'une rencontre', in *Mémoire et oubli dans le lyrisme européen*, ed. by Dagmar Wieser, Patrick Labarthe, and Jean-Paul Avice (Paris: Champion, 2008), pp. 113–48 (p. 115).
28. John E. Jackson links this new life to the cyclical theme in Baudelaire's works: 'Vers un nouveau berceau? Le rêve de palingénésie chez Baudelaire', in *L'Année Baudelaire 2: figures de la mort, figures de l'éternité*, ed. by John E. Jackson and Claude Pichois (Paris: Klincksieck, 1996), pp. 45–61 (p. 59).
29. Gérard Gasarian writes: 'En s'effaçant au profit d'un rêve, les formes en décomposition décrivent très bien la *synthèse mnémonique* par quoi le modèle s'efface lui aussi pour n'être plus à la mémoire qu'un fantôme. La décomposition du corps par la nature est une métaphore de la mémorisation du modèle par l'artiste. De même que les formes corporelles se dissolvent au soleil, de même les formes visuelles se défont au regard de la mémoire. Mais la décomposition, dans les deux cas, est aussi bien la recomposition, "ébauche lente à venir" qui renvoie au travail de la nature comme à celui de l'artiste' [By fading out in the service of a dream, forms that are in the process of decomposing describe quite well the *mnemonic synthesis* by which the model also fades to become for memory nothing more than a phantom. The decomposition of the body by nature is a metaphor for the artist's attempt to remember the model. Just as bodily forms dissolve in the sun, so visual forms are undone in what memory sees. However, decomposition, in both cases, is also re-composition, 'a sketch slow to come forth', that relates to the work of nature just as to the work of the artist]: *De loin tendrement: étude sur Baudelaire* (Paris: H. Champion, 1996), p. 154.
30. William Olmsted notes in a similar way that 'what has been immortalized is not the addressee as she is or at her best; paradoxically, her decomposed body becomes poetically "aere perennis" ': 'Immortal Rot: A Reading of "Une charogne"', in *Understanding 'Les Fleurs du mal': Critical Readings*, ed. by William J. Thompson (Nashville, TN: Vanderbilt University Press, 1997), pp. 60–71 (p. 64). He goes on to say that in Baudelaire's representation of her death, 'what the speaker desires for his mistress is nothing less than a living death' (p. 65).
31. Chambers, *Loiterature*, pp. 223–24.
32. Resurrection and phantoms are tied together also in 'Les Phares', as we saw above. Kevin

Newmark links this ambiguous presence of the phantom to the simultaneous preserving and effacing task of memory and the displacement of representation: 'Off the Charts: Walter Benjamin's Depiction of Baudelaire', in *Baudelaire and the Poetics of Modernity*, ed. by Patricia Ward and James Patty (Nashville, TN: Vanderbilt University Press, 2001), pp. 72–84 (p. 80).

33. As Ross Chambers also notes, 'it is important to point out that all of the poet's "ghostly" allegorical figures are real-life personages — very often women — encountered in the street': 'Daylight Spectre: Baudelaire's "The Seven Old Men"', *Yale French Studies*, 125–26 (2014), 45–65 (p. 46).
34. The phantom image of 'la très belle' [the very beautiful] in 'Que diras tu ce soir' and in 'L'Aube spirituelle'; the spectre of 'Un fantôme'; the 'fantôme débile' [feeble phantom] of 'Les Petites Vieilles'; the phantom of Venus in 'Un voyage à Cythère'; the 'Femmes damnées, Delphine et Hippolyte' are 'ombres folles' [mad shades].
35. 'Cher poison préparé par les anges! Liqueur | Qui me ronge, ô la vie et la mort de mon cœur!' [Dear poison prepared by the angels! Liqueur | That eats away at me, O the life and the death of my heart!] (*OC*, I, 48).
36. One might see this disturbing underside as related to what Burton describes as Baudelaire's 'abiding horror of genital sexuality': Richard D. E. Burton, 'Poet, Painter, Lover: A Reading of "Les Bijoux"', in *Understanding 'Les Fleurs du Mal'*, ed. by Thompson, pp. 214–23 (p. 219).
37. Living death as represented by women in the poems has also been noted by Burton, *Baudelaire in 1859*, p. 139, and Poulet, *Who Was Baudelaire?*, p. 139.
38. Here Laura Mulvey's insights are useful, in the idea of the woman's body that harbours the threat of loss beneath its shiny surface. For her, the beautiful exterior of the female Hollywood star functions as follows, 'An elaborate and highly artificial, dressed-up, made-up appearance envelops the movie star in "surface" [...]. This fragile carapace shares the phantasmatic space of the fetish itself, masking the site of the wound, covering lack with beauty [...]. The fetish object also commemorates. It is a sign [...] and is also a mark of mourning for the lost object': *Fetishism and Curiosity* (Bloomington: Indiana University Press; London: British Film Institute, 1996), pp. 13, 5. Dagmar Wieser writes on fetishism in 'Une martyre' from a Freudian perspective: 'Témoignage de Baudelaire: du fétichisme dans "Une martyre"', *Versants*, 25 (1994), 97–115.
39. Sanyal, *The Violence of Modernity*, p. 22.
40. The epigraph, 'Dessin d'un maître inconnu', provides a third instance of artwork, and implies another relation of visual art to this poem through the suggestion of its influence on this text.
41. Gasarian has described this living death in another way, 'Nous assistons ici à une mort en acte, à un cadavre sans tête mais non pas sans vie puisqu'il épanche toujours, en mourant, un sang qualifié de "vivant"' [We are witness here to a death in action, to a cadaver without a head but not without life, as it pours out, while dying, a blood qualified as 'living']: *De loin tendrement*, p. 208.
42. Barbara Johnson, 'Apostrophe, Animation, and Abortion,' *Diacritics*, 16.1 Spring (1986), 28–47 (p. 31).
43. Connected with the theme of androgyny: a plaster cast of the Louvre hermaphrodite statue was in Baudelaire's father's collection as noted by Sima Godfrey in '"Ce père nourricier": Revisiting Baudelaire's Family Romance', *NCFS*, 38.1–2 (Fall-Winter 2009–10), 39–51 (p. 46).
44. Dominique D. Fisher admirably summarizes much of this work in 'The Silent Erotic/Rhetoric of Baudelaire's Mirrors', in *Articulations of Difference: Gender Studies and Writing in French*, ed. by Dominique D. Fisher and Lawrence R. Schehr (Stanford, CA: Stanford University Press, 1997), pp. 34–51 (pp. 36–38). Gasarian discusses the poet's androgynous nature extensively in *De loin tendrement*. And Burton discusses the desire of 'man-woman for woman-man' in which 'all kinds of "slippages" from one to the other are possible', in 'Poet, Painter, Lover', p. 220. Leo Bersani, coming from a different perspective, notes similarly that 'the very nature of poetic inspiration is enough to transform the poet from a man into a woman': *Baudelaire and Freud* (Berkeley: University of California Press, 1977), p. 12.
45. F. W. Leakey, *Baudelaire: Collected Essays, 1953–1988*, ed. by Eva Jacobs, Cambridge Studies in French (Cambridge: Cambridge University Press, 1990), p. 44. Leakey also states here that 'certainly one might be forgiven, on an initial reading of the middle stanzas of "Une martyre", for assuming that the amorous tonality here evoked was homosexual rather than heterosexual'.

46. *OC*, I, 1059. Pierre Laforgue also links this poem with lesbianism: 'Écrire le fantasme, ou masculin et féminin dans "Une martyre"', in *Baudelaire, une alchimie de la douleur: études sur 'Les Fleurs du mal'*, ed. by Patrick Labarthe (Saint-Pierre-du-Mont: Eurédit, 2003), pp. 163–74 (p. 171).
47. Fisher, 'The Silent Erotic/Rhetoric of Baudelaire's Mirrors', p. 35.
48. Terry Castle, *The Apparitional Lesbian: Female Homosexuality and Modern Culture*, Gender and Culture (New York: Columbia University Press, 1993).
49. Diana Fuss, 'Introduction', in *Inside/Out: Lesbian Theories, Gay Theories*, ed. by Diana Fuss (London: Routledge, 1991), pp. 3–4.
50. Théodore de Banville describes how Baudelaire wrote this poem when he went to the apartment of a woman who has been identified as either 'la reine Pomaré' (Élise Sergent) or Rosine Stoltz, both of whom were rumoured to have been lesbians: Claude Pichois, *OC*, I, 1059–60.
51. Bersani, *Baudelaire and Freud*, p. 66.
52. Furthermore, the rigid hair, the 'tresses roides', that frame this frightful head, as well as the martyr's reptile-like body, call to mind the snakes of the Medusa head in Freud's analysis: 'Medusa's Head', *Standard Edition of the Complete Psychological Works of Sigmund Freud*, ed. and trans. by James Strachey, 24 vols (London: Hogarth Press, 1953–74), XVIII, 273–74.
53. One might see 'Les Aveugles' also as making a connection between the darting eye (the verb *darder* appears in both poems) and the living dead: the blind men seem half alive, half awake, 'mannequins' and 'somnambules', and walk about 'Dardant on ne sait où leurs globes ténébreux' [Darting one knows not where their tenebrous eyes].
54. The paralysis is noted by Freud: 'Medusa's Head', pp. 273–74.
55. Sanyal describes this as an 'interplay of identification and resistance staged in the poem': *The Violence of Modernity*, p 110.
56. Benjamin, *The Arcades Project*, p. 19. My reading owes much to Sanyal's interpretation of 'Une martyre' as a text that 'both mirrors and critiques the female body's reified circulation as a commodity'; Sanyal also notes that this poem 'hovers at the margins of many passages in Walter Benjamin': *The Violence of Modernity*, p. 106.
57. Sanyal, *The Violence of Modernity*, p. 106
58. Benjamin, *The Arcades Project*, p. 20.
59. Walter Benjamin, *The Writer of Modern Life: Essays on Charles Baudelaire*, ed. by Michael W. Jennings (Cambridge, MA; Harvard University Press, 2006), p. 131; *The Arcades Project*, p. 18.
60. Benjamin, *The Arcades Project*, p. 345.
61. Ibid., p. 346.
62. Ibid., p. 21.
63. Cohen, 'Benjamin's Phantasmagoria', p. 207. Further references to this article appear in the text.
64. Benjamin, *The Arcades Project*, pp. 181–82.
65. Sanyal, *The Violence of Modernity*, p. 107.
66. Benjamin, *The Arcades Project*, p. 9. In juxtaposition to the subjectivity imprinted on objects here, one thinks of the woman who attempts to imprint the poet on her heart in 'Le Beau Navire'.
67. Ibid., p. 8.
68. Ibid., p. 10.
69. William J. Thompson sees the resemblance between the woman and the street: 'Order and Chaos in "À une passante"', in *Understanding 'Les Fleurs du mal'*, ed. by Thompson, pp. 145–59 (p. 149). Antoine Compagnon also finds that the woman is 'à la fois femme et rue': *Baudelaire devant l'innombrable: mémoire de la critique* (Paris: Presses de l'Université de Paris-Sorbonne, 2003), p. 131. And Elissa Marder observes that 'the figures for the street and for the woman converge in the adjectives through which she is introduced: "longue, mince"': *Dead Time: Temporal Disorders in the Wake of Modernity (Baudelaire and Flaubert)* (Stanford, CA: Stanford University Press, 2001), p. 83.
70. Ross Chambers notes this emerging: 'The woman is not identical with the street; rather, it is as if she is produced by it or out of it': 'The Storm in the Eye of the Poem: Baudelaire's "À une passante"', in *Textual Analysis: Some Readers Reading*, ed. by Mary Ann Caws (New York: Modern Language Association of America, 1986), pp. 156–66 (p. 160).

71. Ross Chambers, *An Atmospherics of the City: Baudelaire and the Poetics of Noise*, Verbal Arts: Studies in Poetics (New York: Fordham University Press, 2015), p. 104. Marder calls her 'a walking tombstone': *Dead Time*, p. 84. Catherine Witt also notes that 'the encounter with the woman is premised on her loss; the death she is mourning is her own': 'Passages Through Baudelaire: From Poetry to Thought and Back', in *Thinking Poetry*, ed. by Joseph Acquisto (New York: Palgrave Macmillan, 2013), pp. 25–42 (p. 31).
72. Ross Chambers enlarges this passing to a historical context, 'history as a devastating *passing-by* that gets our attention only to leave us stunned and devastated': 'Heightening the Lowly (Baudelaire: "Je n'ai pas oublié..." and "À une passante")', *NCFS*, 37.1–2 (Fall-Winter 2008–09), 42–51 (p. 48).
73. Françoise Meltzer interestingly calls the *passante* 'an afterimage; a scopic phantom whose vivid emergence from the crowd remains in the mind after the ocular stimulus has occurred': *Seeing Double: Baudelaire's Modernity* (Chicago: University of Chicago Press, 2011), p. 88.
74. Benjamin, *The Writer of Modern Life*, p. 185. Alistair Rolls briefly analyzes the fetish in 'À une passante' in *Paris and the Fetish* (Amsterdam: Rodopi, 2014), pp. 24–28.
75. Susan Blood calls this the 'everyday uncanny': 'The Sonnet as Snapshot: Seizing the Instant in Baudelaire's "À une passante"', *NCFS*, 36.3–4 (Spring-Summer 2008), 255–69 (p. 261).
76. Lowry Nelson, 'Baudelaire and Virgil: A Reading of "Le Cygne"', *Comparative Literature*, 13.4 (Autumn 1961), 332–45 (p. 335).
77. Gérard Gasarian notes this difference between the present thought of poetry and his past experience of walking across the new place du Carrousel, in which the poet narrator remembered another past experience of the old Carrousel: '"Le Cygne" of Baudelaire', in *Understanding 'Les Fleurs du Mal*, ed. by Thompson, pp. 122–32 (pp. 125–26).
78. Riggs Alden Smith, *The Primacy of Vision in Virgil's 'Aeneid'* (Austin: University of Texas Press, 2005), p. 75
79. In a sense, Andromache parallels the poet represented in 'Le Flacon' and 'Une charogne', as he preserves his dead love in the poem as container of 'un vieil amour ranci' [an old, rancid love] and 'amours décomposés' [decomposed loves], just at the cenotaph contains and preserves the dead past for Andromache.
80. Terdiman, *Present Past*, p. 144.
81. Patrick Labarthe notes that when the poet of the current day calls to Andromache, he makes the past coalesce with the present, which gives the past the intensity of the present: 'La Douleur du cygne', in *Baudelaire, une alchimie de la douleur*, ed. by Labarthe, pp. 143–61 (pp. 143–44). Nicolae Babuts says similarly, 'Consequently, the poem's story, the story of its composition, is a gesture of erasing the distance between the past and the present': *Baudelaire: At the Limits and Beyond* (Newark: University of Delaware Press; London: Associated University Presses, 1997), p. 92. Burton describes repetition of the past as a series of cities evoked in 'Le Cygne', as it 'portrays History not as an ascending curve but as a relentless downward spiral with cities following one upon the other in endless sequence, each imitating its predecessor in a debased parodic manner': *Baudelaire in 1859*, p. 152. Daniel A. Finch-Race describes the confrontation of the poet with the past in the present Paris as spectral, 'Baudelaire's unease about the mutating metropolis is channeled through the discomfiting prosody of the moments in which he is confronted with the disorienting spectres of a traditional past in the new incarnation of Paris': 'Placelessness in Baudelaire's "Les Sept Vieillards" and "Les Petites Vieilles"', *MLR*, 110.4 (October 2015), 1011–26 (p. 1013).
82. This parallels the description of the Galeries de Bois in Balzac, which were destroyed at the time of the text's writing.
83. Dolf Oehler, *Le Spleen contre l'oubli, juin 1848: Baudelaire, Flaubert, Heine, Herzen* (Paris: Payot, 1996), p. 101.
84. Several critics do mention this fact. Ross Chambers notes that renovations had already begun when the swan escaped. However, rather than using his terminology of a 'new construction' site, I would state instead that the construction site is already old: *The Writing of Melancholy: Modes of Opposition in Early French Modernism*, trans. by Mary Seidman Trouille (Chicago: University of Chicago Press, 1987), p. 166. Richard D. E. Burton mentions that 'demolition of parts of

the area was taking place as early as the 1830s': *The Context of Baudelaire's 'Le Cygne'* (Durham: University of Durham, 1980), p. 35. Franca Zanelli Quarantini gives a political reading of this old version of the Carrousel: '"Andromaque" au Carrousel: une lecture de "Le Cygne"', *Revue Italienne d'Études Françaises*, 2 (2012), 1–12. Patrick Bray mentions the 'dilapidated state' of this area: 'Prose Constructions: Nerval, Baudelaire, and the Louvre', *L'Esprit Créateur*, 54.2 (2014), 115–26 (p. 116).

85. Balzac describes this neighbourhood, where Bette lives around the year 1837, in *La Cousine Bette*. See my 'Balzac, Gender and Sexuality: *La Cousine Bette*', in *The Cambridge Companion to Balzac*, ed. by Heathcote and Watts, pp. 111–26.
86. Alfred Delvau, *Les Dessous de Paris* (Paris: Poulet-Malassis et de Broise, 1860) pp. 258–59: 'Elle était charmante autrefois, cette place du Carrousel [...] on y rencontrait, presque à chaque pas, des animaux de toute sorte [...]. On y voyait, par exemple, des nuées de ces affreux oiseaux bavards, insolents et orduriers, qu'on appelle des perroquets [...]. On y voyait aussi des cabiais, des lapins, des tortues, des serpents [...], des cygnes plus ou moins de Norvège' [It was formerly charming, this place du Carrousel [...] one found there, almost with each step, animals of all sorts [...]. One saw, for example, flocks of those chatty, insolent, and foul-mouthed birds called parrots [...]. One saw also capibaras, rabbits, tortoises, snakes [...], swans more or less from Norway]. A slightly different version of this quotation appears in Burton (quoted from Citron): *The Context of Baudelaire's 'Le Cygne,'* p. 33.
87. Théophile Gautier describes these blocks, 'Au-delà s'étendent, jusqu'à la rue des Orties, des terrains vagues parsemés de blocs de pierre destinés à l'achèvement du Louvre, entre lesquels poussent la folle avoine, la bardane et les chardons' [Beyond stretch out, all the way to the rue des Orties, vacant lots scattered with stone blocks destined for the completion of the Louvre, between which grow wild oats, burdock, and thistle]: 'Marilhat', *La Revue des deux mondes*, 23 (1 July 1848), 56–75 (p. 56).
88. Burton associates the artist's sketch with this poem's own genesis, 'Nonetheless, it is interesting to note that the idea of the sketch or of "work in progress" is suggested in the poem itself by the "tas de chapiteaux ébauchés et de fûts", the "gros blocs verdis" and the "échafaudages"': *The Context of Baudelaire's 'Le Cygne'*, p. 90.
89. Ross Chambers, 'Baudelaire's Paris', in *The Cambridge Companion to Baudelaire*, ed. by Lloyd, pp. 101–16 (p. 108).
90. Balzac's description of this *quartier* and other streets near it (see Chapter 1, as well as my 'Balzac, Gender and Sexuality') offers other similarities with the general tenor of Baudelaire's Doyenné and Paris, as well as specific instances of the living dead. Balzac writes that the inhabitants of the decaying neighbourhood are 'probablement des fantômes' [probably ghosts], and that the area itself is a 'demi-quartier mort' [dead partial neighbourhood]. The ghost in this description by Balzac is similar to that in a different Baudelaire Paris poem, 'Les Sept Vieillards', where Paris is the place 'Où le spectre en plein jour raccroche le passant!' [Where the spectre in broad daylight grabs onto the passerby!]. Balzac furthermore calls the houses in the Doyenné 'living tombs' in *La Cousine Bette*, calling to mind the empty tomb of Andromache's present: "Enterrées déjà par l'exhaussement de la place, ces maisons sont enveloppées de l'ombre éternelle que projettent les hautes galeries du Louvre, noircies de ce côté par le souffle du nord. Les ténèbres, le silence, l'air glacial, la profondeur caverneuse du sol concourent à faire de ces maisons des espèces de cryptes, des tombeaux vivants' [Buried already by the building up of the square, these houses are enveloped by the eternal shadow thrown by the high galleries of the Louvre, blackened on this side by the north wind. Shadow, silence, glacial air, the cavernous depths of the ground all vie to make these houses into crypts, living tombs] (*CH*, VII, 100). Perhaps Baudelaire evokes this Balzac text. Graham Robb shows the remarkable extent of Baudelaire's admiration for Balzac as well as his extensive knowledge of Balzac's work in *Baudelaire, lecteur de Balzac* (Paris: Corti, 1988). In any case, the rhetoric of death used to describe this neighbourhood may actually be a kind of commonplace, as it appears in a number of other descriptions of the Doyenné by the bohemian artists that frequented it around that time, and whom Baudelaire knew. For another description of the dead neighbourhood there is Arsène Houssaye's 'Vingt ans': 'Théo, te souviens-tu de ces vertes saisons | Qui s'effeuillaient si vite en ces vieilles maisons | Dont le

front s'abritait sous une aile du Louvre? | [...] | Songes venus du ciel, flottante visions, | Sortez de vos tombeaux, vieilles illusions!' [Théo, do you remember in those green seasons | That shed their leaves so quickly in those old houses | Whose fronts were sheltered under a wing of the Louvre? | [...] | Dreams that came from heaven, floating visions, | Leave your tombs, old illusions!]: *Poésies complètes* (Paris: Charpentier, 1850), p. 41. Also Gérard de Nerval writes on the disappeared ruins of a Doyenné church: *Petits châteaux de bohême: prose et poésie* (Paris: E. Didier, 1853), p. 40. The Doyenné and these authors are also mentioned in Pierre Citron, *La Poésie de Paris dans la littérature française de Rousseau à Baudelaire* (Paris: Minuit, 1961). And Élénore M. Zimmermann discusses this passage and the loss of the Doyenné: 'Notes sur la forêt du "Cygne"', *Bulletin Baudelairien*, 26.2 (1991), 51–56 (p. 55).

91. This aligns with Benjamin's analysis of the role of Paris in Baudelaire's poetry, 'His idea of the decrepitude of the big city is the basis for the permanence of the poems he has written about Paris': *The Writer of Modern Life*, p. 112. A number of critics have noted various aspects of the return of the past: Gasarian states that the poem represents, rather than 'a linear progress from antiquity to modernity', a modernity that includes 'the enduring *presence* of the past', which he views as a confrontation of allegories ('"Le Cygne" of Baudelaire', p. 131); Chambers describes this past, which, like the present, is already a kind of repetition, 'the fragmented present in "Le Cygne", opens not onto the prelapsarian past, but recalls only a history of other present moments, also and always already marked by residuality and fragmentation': *Loiterature*, p. 241. Chambers discusses this also in *The Writing of Melancholy*: 'melancholy turns memory into a remembrance of loss and links the present to a feeling of repetition and inauthenticity' (p. 159).

92. Chambers analyzes the difficulty of finding a starting point for this poem because it is 'suspended in a kind of intermediary space that separates it from any absolute point of origin, as well as from any definitive ending': *The Writing of Melancholy*, p. 157. This would provide a parallel understanding of the already-dead past of the place du Carrousel as origin of the poem.

93. In another context, Terdiman notes that the representations in this poem 'make an absence present': *Present Past*, p. 108. And Nathanial Wing relates this sense of double death to allegory, 'the loss that is allegorized here is that which is always already absent': '"On Reading Baudelaire's Allegories", in *Pre-text, Text, Context: Essays on Nineteenth-century French Literature*, ed. by Robert L. Mitchell (Columbus: Ohio State University Press, 1980), pp. 135–44 (p. 141).

94. Terdiman, *Present Past*, p. 142.

95. F. W. Leakey describes this as the 'substitution of the old for the new': *Baudelaire: 'Les Fleurs du mal'* (Cambridge: Cambridge University Press, 1992), p. 82. And Stamelman notes that in Baudelaire 'the experience of loss takes on a life of its own, coming to replace, even to eclipse, the absent object. The words, the sorrow, the unappeased desire may seem more real, more present, and more immediate than that being whose death has occasioned them': 'The Shroud of Allegory', p. 392. Sima Godfrey also notes the idea of seeing, rather than recalling, in the sense of 'seeing again': 'From Memory Lane to Memory Boulevard: *Paris change!*', in *City Images: Perspectives from Literature, Philosophy, and Film*, ed. by Mary Ann Caws (New York: Gordon & Breach, 1991), pp. 157–71 (p. 162). Her excellent reading of the poem brings out the personal past of Baudelaire's relation to his mother in his Paris Carrousel.

96. Several critics have emphasized this idea of the weight of memory. As Lowry Nelson notes, something 'presses down' or 'weighs upon': 'Baudelaire and Virgil', p. 341. For Chambers, memory is the source of 'an oppressive experience of heaviness and melancholy': *The Writing of Melancholy*, p. 164.

97. F. W. Leakey writes, 'The past, sadly, is more real than the present': 'The Originality of Baudelaire's "Le Cygne": Genesis as Structure and Theme', in *Order and Adventure in Post-romantic French Poetry: Essays Presented to C. A. Hackett*, ed. by Ernest M. Beaumont (New York: Barnes & Noble, 1973), pp. 38–55 (p. 44). Ross Chambers says of another poem, that the sameness of space 'supports memory's *rapprochement* of now and then by supplying an enabling continuity, a dimensionality of here and there that renders what is inaccessible in time as more readily accessible in space; still inaccessible, "but nevertheless" strangely, uncannily, present': 'On Inventing Unknownness: The Poetry of Disenchanted Reenchantment (Leopardi, Baudelaire, Rimbaud, Justice)', *French Forum*, 33.1–2 (Winter/Spring 2008), 15–36 (p. 26).

98. Other interesting observations of this reversal or collapse of past and present related to life and death include that of Barbara Vinken in her reading of Baudelaire against Hugo in their reinterpretations of Virgil. She writes that Hugo saw 'the living in the dead', whereas Baudelaire saw 'the dead in the living': 'Forget Vergil? The Truth of Modernity', *Literary Imagination*, 8.3 (2006), 417–36 (p. 429). Patrick Labarthe describes the first words of the poem, which 'opèrent la coalescence de strates temporelles pourtant distinctes de plus de deux millénaires, d'une manière qui rend au passé l'intensité d'un présent' [accomplish the coalescence of temporal strata, which are separated by two thousand years, in a way that gives to the past the intensity of a present]: 'La Douleur du cygne', p. 144.
99. The idea of a living dead future arises as well. Babuts describes how Andromache foresees her widowhood in the *Illiad* when she tells Hector that his leaving will turn her into an exiled widow. As Babuts notes, 'What was a foretold future becomes a haunting present; the promised widowhood ends in eternal identity': *Baudelaire: At the Limits*, p. 99.
100. The two stanzas that describe the swan and the black woman surround the stanza that describes Andromache being passed from one man to the other, as if to associate not only exile but reification, objectification, in these three beings.
101. Victor Brombert calls this an 'immobilisation plastique' [a material immobilization]: ' "Le Cygne" de Baudelaire: douleur, souvenir, travail', *Études baudelairiennes, III: Le Poète et son temps: thèmes et exégèses*, ed. by James S. Patty and Claude Pichois (Neuchâtel: La Baconnière, 1973), pp. 254–61 (p. 257).
102. Poulet finds that 'the prodigiously heightened consciousness of time results in a sense not only of indefinite extension but of oppressive heaviness. Time is a crippling load to bear': *Who was Baudelaire?*, p. 135.
103. As mentioned above, this might also be suggested by the possible history of slavery associated with the black woman, thus also suggesting commodification. Critics have noted that this widowed mother perhaps also suggests Baudelaire's mother, who mourned the loss of Baudelaire's father (thus Hector) when Baudelaire was young and, as we saw above, when he enjoyed the exclusive company of his mother. Indeed, as Burton notes, Baudelaire places the poem 'Je n'ai pas oublié' in the 'Tableaux parisiens', thus linking the act of not forgetting the idyllic time with his mother to the Paris poems, and also linking this grieving widow, who does not forget, to his mother (Burton, *The Context of Baudelaire's 'Le Cygne'*, p. 59). Barbara Vinken adds to the reification of woman the following observation: 'Andromache, the mourning woman, mourns the fate of women: that they have to give life in the face of complete indifference to their will', and Andromache stands for 'the human condition': 'Mourning Woman: Andromache', *Pequod: A Journal of Contemporary Literature and Literary Criticism*, 35 (1993), 47–65 (pp. 47–48).
104. Victorien Sardou, in Georges Cain, *Coins de Paris*, préface de Victorien Sardou, nouvelle édition (Paris: Flammarion, 1910), p. xxvii.
105. Joséphine Alida Jacquier observes that the new, empty Carrousel is a 'blank space' that spurs memory for the poet: 'From Paris to Rome: Virgil's Andromache Between Politics and Poetics in Charles Baudelaire's "Le Cygne"', in *Augustan Poetry and the Roman Republic*, ed. by Joseph Farrell and Damien P. Nelis (Oxford: Oxford University Press, 2013), pp. 161–79 (p. 174).
106. Just as the fetishist says, 'I know, but even so'. Octave Mannoni, *Clefs pour l'imaginaire, ou l'autre scène* (Paris: Seuil, 1969), pp. 9–33.
107. Actually, a grave for Baudelaire's father according to Richard D. E. Burton: 'The Dead Father: A Note on "Le Cygne" and the *Iliad*', *French Studies Bulletin*, 11.38 (Spring 1991), 7–9 (p. 9).
108. Nelson, 'Baudelaire and Virgil', pp. 333–34. Burton also takes up the concept of living death, adding that Andromaque is 'stranded, still conscious, in a limbo-world between life and death', and he mentions as well Georges Poulet's 'thème du mort vivant': *The Context of Baudelaire's 'Le Cygne'*, p. 62. As Richard E. Grimm describes, 'And the final, strange, anguished question, *Hector ubi est?*, gains greatly in pathos if we consider that after the incredulous *vivisne?* Andromache seems immediately ready to assume the opposite — that Aeneas is indeed a real shade, representing a more vivid projection of her world than any she has thus far known — and she steps readily into that domain of death to ask Aeneas where her dead Hector is, as though Aeneas could immediately point him out': 'Aeneas and Andromache in Aeneid III', *The American Journal of Philology*, 88.2 (April 1967), 151–62 (p. 155).

109. Nelson, 'Baudelaire and Virgil', pp. 334–35. Gasarian notes similarly that 'être mélancolique comme le cygne ou Andromaque, c'est ne pas pouvoir vivre ici et maintenant sans être aussitôt transporté jadis et ailleurs; c'est être poursuivi jusque dans le présent par l'image du souvenir' [To be melancholic like the swan or Andromache is to be unable to live in the here and now without immediately being transported to the past and to another place; it is to be pursued into the present by the image of the memory': *De loin tendrement*, p. 118.
110. Johnson, 'Apostrophe, Animation, and Abortion', pp. 29–30.
111. Gasarian writes also of a kind of resuscitation of Hugo, Euripides, Racine, and Homer in *De loin tendrement* (p. 98). One might say that Andromaque, as she mourns Hector, 'conjures' him, as the poet conjures her, the swan conjures its lake, and the black woman conjures her coconut trees, trees that Leakey describes as 'ghosts': 'The Originality of Baudelaire's "Le Cygne"', p. 47.
112. The poet goes on to say that he still 'sees' the swan reaching its neck to the sky, speaking to or 'apostrophizing' God, in reproach for the cruel blue clearness that brings no rain. Many have read the 'cygne', whose feathers drag in the Parisian dust, as the *signe* or metaphor for the poet; here his 'plume' (feather/feather pen) can write only of and through exile within exile. Jean Starobinski recalls that Virgil is known as the 'cygne de Mantoue': *La Mélancolie au miroir: trois lectures de Baudelaire* (Paris: Julliard, 1989), p. 58. Françoise Lionnet has also shown that Mauritius, one of the islands on which Baudelaire was 'exiled' on the trip forced on him by his mother and step-father, an island viewed as one of the origins of his exotic imagery, such as that of the black woman and coconut trees in 'Le Cygne', was known as the 'Island of the Swan', and the name of the main newspaper was a derivative of the word 'swan' in Portuguese: 'Reframing Baudelaire: Literary History, Biography, Postcolonial Theory, and Vernacular Languages', *Diacritics*, 28.3 (Autumn 1998), 63–85.
113. Starobinski makes the point that Andromache is a literary character, and thus is 'fake': *La Mélancolie au miroir*, p. 58.
114. Dolf Oehler, 'Baudelaire's Politics', in *The Cambridge Companion to Baudelaire*, ed. by Lloyd, pp. 14–30 (p. 19).
115. Starobinski expresses this in a different way, saying that there is either too much or too little water: *La Melancolie au miroir*, p. 75. Lionnet calls Baudelaire, exiled in Mauritius, one of these stranded sailors: 'Reframing Baudelaire', p. 81. Pierre Laforgue sees the liquidity as coming from the Latin 'bathe' and it unites the entire poem of Baudelaire in '"Falsi Simoentis ad undam" — autour de l'épigraphe du "Cygne": Baudelaire, Virgile, Racine et Hugo', *NCFS*, 24.1–2 (Fall-Winter 1995–96), 97–110 (p. 99).
116. Nelson, 'Baudelaire and Virgil', p. 337.
117. See more in Lionnet's 'Reframing Baudelaire' about the relation of the black woman to the swan and the poet.
118. Brombert, '"Le Cygne" de Baudelaire,' p. 260; Chambers, *The Writing of Melancholy*, p. 158. Edward Kaplan links these blocks with Baudelaire's construction of this very poem: 'Baudelaire's Portrait of the Poet as Widow: Three "Poèmes en prose" and "Le Cygne"', *Symposium*, 34 (Fall 1980), 233–48 (p. 245).
119. Victor Brombert describes Baudelaire's city as 'a world of phantoms' and a city 'filled with wandering ghosts': 'Baudelaire: City Images and the "Dream of Stone"', *Yale French Studies*, 32 (1964), 99–105 (p. 99).
120. Edward Ahearn, 'Marx's Relevance for Second Empire Literature: Baudelaire's "Le Cygne"', *NCFS*, 14.3–4 (Spring-Summer 1986), 269–77 (pp. 272, 274).
121. Benjamin, *The Arcades Project*, p. 473.
122. Chambers describes 'Le Cygne''s 'endless forward movement': *The Writing of Melancholy*, p. 157.
123. Labarthe, *Baudelaire et la tradition de l'allégorie*, p. 198.
124. This would link up with the eternal wandering of 'Les Sept Vieillards'. 'Ces sept monstres hideux avaient l'air éternel!' [These seven hideous monsters had the air of eternity!]: see Chambers, *An Atmospherics of the City*, p. 97. The idea of endless life is similarly treated in 'Le Rêve d'un curieux'. The epigraph by Benjamin at the head of this section fits the catastrophe of living death, which is that it simply continues. See also Michael Tilby's essay on the possible visual origins of the poem and how it gives us 'a meaning both absent and present': 'Poetry,

Image, and Post-Napoleonic Politics: Baudelaire's "Le Squelette laboureur"', *Studi Francesi*, 56.3 (September-December 2012), 422–36 (p. 436).
125. Or, according to the *Littré*, four 'pieds'.
126. Benjamin, *The Arcades Project*, p. 329. Charles Baudelaire, 'Le Cygne' (*OC*, I, 86).
127. Susan Blood, *Baudelaire and the Aesthetics of Bad Faith* (Stanford, CA: Stanford University Press, 1997).
128. Elements in this description by Baudelaire remind one of the descriptions of objects in the antique shop of Balzac's *La Peau de chagrin*.
129. See Johnson on apostrophe ('Apostrophe, Animation, and Abortion') and above on 'Le Cygne'.
130. This magic evocation is also related to art in Baudelaire's discussion in 'Théophile Gautier [I]': 'Manier savamment une langue, c'est pratiquer une espèce de sorcellerie évocatoire. C'est alors que la couleur parle, comme une voix profonde et vibrante; que les monuments se dressent et font saillie sur l'espace profond' [To manipulate a language skilfully is to practice a kind of evocatory sorcery. It is then that a colour speaks, like a profound and vibrant voice; that monuments rise up and stand out on the background of profound space] (*OC*, II, 118). Magic evocation is also used for writing itself in *Fusées*: 'De la langue et de l'écriture, prises comme opérations magiques, sorcellerie évocatoire' [Of language and writing, taken as magical operations, evocatory sorcery] (*OC*, I, 658).
131. Benjamin, *The Arcades Project*, p. 329. Benjamin writes as well that 'allegories are, in the realm of thoughts, what ruins are in the realm of things': *The Origin of German Tragic Drama*, trans. by John Osborne (London & New York: Verso, 1998), p. 178.
132. Paul de Man, *Blindness and Insight: Essays in the Rhetoric of Contemporary Criticism* (Minneapolis: University of Minnesota Press, 1983), p. 207. Further references to this work appear in the text.
133. Kevin Newmark further explicates this temporal nature of allegory in 'Le Cygne' in 'Who Needs Poetry? Baudelaire, Benjamin, and the Modernity of "Le Cygne"', *Comparative Literature*, 63.3 (Summer 2011), 269–90.
134. Benjamin, *The Arcades Project*, p. 324.
135. Chambers, *An Atmospherics of the City*, p. 2.
136. As Stamelman notes, 'Allegorical discourse [...] is always incomplete and imperfect because it evokes some meaning, some image, some figure lying beyond the horizon of its signification, some "otherness" that it can designate but not join': 'The Shroud of Allegory', p. 393.
137. Benjamin, *The Arcades Project*, p. 205.

CHAPTER 3

Zola: Heredity and Social Living Death

> ce mal du pays dont on ne peut guérir,
> Dont tous les jours on meurt, sans en jamais mourir.
> [this homesickness of which one cannot be cured,
> From which every day one dies, without ever dying.]
> — CASIMIR DELAVIGNE[1]

As the leading voice for the naturalist movement's scientific representation of reality, Zola surprisingly makes the rather fantastic theme of living death an integral part of his *œuvre*. In his works, living death is the product of the modern world, whereas in Balzac it is the product of the emerging modern world as it takes over the old. Living death in Zola symbolizes the death of humanity in a society dominated by money and commodities. It also acts as a figural representation of the new knowledge gained about heredity and the extent to which we are our dead and living ancestors. The first book of the *Rougon-Macquart* series, *La Fortune des Rougon*, takes us into this new world at the moment when its modernity oddly appears to become a repetition of the past — the living dead past — both in its politics and in the lives of its characters. From there we move on to later novels in the series and to one that predates it, *Thérèse Raquin*.

The Inheritance of Death in *La Fortune des Rougon* and *La Bête humaine*

Living death dominates *La Fortune des Rougon* (1871), to which Zola gave the subtitle 'Les Origines'. One of its main characters, Adélaïde Fouque, known as 'Dide', is the 'origine': as the first member of the Rougon-Macquart family in this series of twenty novels, she is also the first member of Zola's living-dead community of characters. Dide is the trunk of the family tree, an *arbre généalogique* which Zola drew in various forms dating from at least 1868.[2] This symbol of Dide's family and its spreading branches unites the books of the series, as each novel tells the tale of different family members that branch out from her. In this first novel, *La Fortune des Rougon*, her son, Docteur Pascal, who often stands in for Zola's voice, uses the tree metaphor that makes of Dide the 'souche', meaning both the first member of a particular part of a family, but also the stump or root section of a tree or vine, that spreads out over time in his scientific vision of the present and future members of her family and, on Zola's part, of the *Rougon-Macquart* series itself, as Pascal reflects:

> Et il songeait à ces poussées d'une famille, d'une souche qui jette des branches diverses, et dont la sève âcre charrie les mêmes germes dans les tiges les plus lointaines, différemment tordues, selon les milieux d'ombre et de soleil. Il crut entrevoir un instant, comme au milieu d'un éclair, l'avenir des Rougon-Macquart, une meute d'appétits lâchés et assouvis, dans un flamboiement d'or et de sang.³

> [And he mused about these growths of a family, of a trunk that sends out diverse branches, and whose bitter sap carries the same germs out to the most distant shoots, differently twisted, according to their milieus of shade and sun. He thought he glimpsed for a moment, as in a lightning flash, the future of the Rougon-Macquart, a pack of appetites let loose and sated, in a blaze of gold and blood.]

In addition, three symbolic trees in *La Fortune des Rougon* connect three important naturalist elements of this initial novel: first, heredity, with the base of the family tree, Dide herself, as the origin of Zola's representation of the process of heredity, in particular the flaw or *tare* she passes on; second, the tree of liberty that grows in the centre of Plassans, and which is poisoned at one point in the novel, symbolizes the toxic cultural and political environment, which also shapes humans; third, the word 'tordues' in Pascal's description above of the family tree's branches is the same word used to describe the 'twisted' and monstrous 'bras tordus' [twisted arms] of pear trees in the Saint-Mittre cemetery at the beginning of the novel. These cemetery trees also symbolize the physical, naturalist milieu that contributes to the shaping of human destiny, as the rotting corpses in the ground of the cemetery create the misshapen trees that grow above them. Thus, the milieu's influence combines with the hereditary aspect of Dide's flawed (and eventually living-dead) state to create her 'misshapen' offspring.⁴ Most important, each of these three trees, as symbols of naturalist ideas about the formation of human beings, are tightly connected to living death: the living dead matriarch as trunk, the living trees fed by the dead in the cemetery, and the poisoned tree of liberty that dies a slow death. Indeed, the tree symbol's relation to the living death of Dide becomes clear at the end of the novel. In *Le Docteur Pascal* (1893) she is called a skeletal tree, locked in an institution, unable to move much, dead but for her eyes: 'squelette jauni, desséché là, telle qu'un arbre séculaire dont il ne reste que l'écorce, elle se tenait pourtant droite contre le dossier du fauteuil, n'ayant plus que les yeux de vivants, dans son mince et long visage' [yellowed skeleton, dried up there, like a century-old tree that has nothing left but its bark, she however sat straight against the back of the armchair, with nothing but her eyes alive in her thin, long face] (*RM*, v, 973).⁵

La Fortune des Rougon, this novel of origins that narrates the life the family tree's first mother, is remarkable in the extent to which it develops many of the themes of later novels. Packed with different characters and plotlines, its complex development seems disconnected, moving back and forth in time and among several different power struggles.⁶ However, this complication permits Zola to establish the foundation for later novels; in particular, an important structural part of this foundation is the metaphor of living death. This first novel will guide us through our reading of this trope, before we turn to its elements in several other novels and contexts.

Dide's role is that of giver of life, who brings forth the Rougon-Macquart family, so it is odd that she should be associated in so many ways with death. Even her introduction in the novel surrounds her with death and its aftermath:

> Le nom de cette famille s'éteignait quelques années avant la révolution. Une fille seule resta, Adélaïde, née en 1768, et qui se trouva orpheline à l'âge de dix-huit ans. Cette enfant, dont le père mourut fou, était une grande créature, mince, pale, aux regards effarés [...]. Mais, en grandissant, elle devint plus bizarre encore; elle commit certaines actions que les plus fortes têtes du faubourg ne purent raisonnablement expliquer, et, dès lors, le bruit courut qu'elle avait le cerveau fêlé comme son père. (RM, I, 41)[7]

> [The family name died out several years before the revolution. Only one girl remained, Adélaïde, born in 1768 and who became an orphan at eighteen years of age. This child, whose father died insane, was a tall creature, thin, pale, with a frightened look [...]. But, as she grew, she became even more bizarre; she took certain actions that the best minds in town could not reasonably explain, and, ever since then, rumour had it that she was crazy like her father.]

This first description of her introduces both death (of the Fouque name and of her father) and hereditary madness. She carries the tainted blood of her father, presented here as having died insane and whose *tare* [defect] she will pass on to her offspring in various forms.

After this introduction, the text then rather obsessively repeats the image of Dide as a living person who is dead, particularly later in her life. She has decomposed to such an extent that she is ready for the coffin, her clothes cling to her like a shroud, and rather paradoxically, 'Elle était trop morte déjà' [She was too dead already], as if there were degrees of being dead (pp. 135–36). Although she is 'dead', she comes back to life occasionally, almost literally here, where her nervous crises are described in the quotation that begins this study: 'Parfois encore, dans cette morte, dans cette vieille femme blême qui paraissait n'avoir plus une goutte de sang, des crises nerveuses passaient, comme des courants électriques, qui la galvanisaient et lui rendaient pour une heure une vie atroce d'intensité' [Again at times, through this dead woman, through this pallid old woman, who seemed not to have even a single drop of blood left, flowed nervous attacks, like electric currents, that galvanized her and returned her for an hour to a life atrocious in its intensity] (p. 135). One might see these periodic 'resurrections' as a metaphor for her physical and mental traits that recur and 'relive' periodically in her offspring.

The cause of her living death was the death of her lover, Macquart. Yet her passion for him is relived, brought back to life for her, when she and it resuscitate in those hysterical crises. Zola describes her when she is elderly as someone who, in the past, loved with the brutality of a wolf, and whose need for love after Macquart's death devoured her. She is consumed, burned up, by this unsatisfied passion, which flares up periodically in her fits that are a 'retour à ces anciennes ardeurs' [a return of her former ardours] (p. 135). Like Freud's notion of the return of the repressed, her suppressed desire for Macquart, her dead love, comes back to haunt her and to take over her body. It is sometimes difficult for the reader to know if she is alive or dead — she is actually still alive in the following scene:

> Il vit tante Dide, roide, morte, sur le lit. [...] Les nerfs avaient comme mangé le sang; le sourd travail de cette chair ardente, s'épuisant, se dévorant elle-même dans une tardive chasteté, s'achevait, faisait de la malheureuse un cadavre que des secousses électriques seules galvanisaient encore. (RM, I, 297)[8]
>
> [He saw Aunt Dide, stiff, dead, on the bed. [...] Her nerves seemed to have consumed her blood; the hidden work of this ardent flesh, burning out, devouring itself in a belated chastity, was ending, was making of the unhappy woman a cadaver that only the electric jolts still galvanized.]

Dide has tried, however, to prevent this return of her dead desire and the past, the memories of the life she had led with Macquart: she has symbolically and physically closed off the door that she herself made in the wall between Macquart's shack and her Fouque property. It was through this door that she went to Macquart, and her piercing of this wall by the door symbolized her crossing from accepted behaviour to behaviour condemned by society, which Zola presents through the eyes of her neighbourhood: 'Un matin, les voisins furent très surpris en voyant cette muraille percée d'une porte' [One morning, the neighbours were very surprised to see this wall pierced by a door] (p. 44). As Colette Becker notes, society prefers to keep walls and doors closed to transgression, the walls that separate Plassans from the outside world (the city gates are shut each night), as well as the other symbolic walls that divide social classes, such as the roads that define the boundaries of the working-class, bourgeois, and aristocratic neighbourhoods in Plassans.[9] Her opening of the wall opens the door to the erasure of limits.

This wall between the former Fouque and the Macquart properties, impenetrable in the present of the novel because the door is locked, keeps her inside and her former world outside. Beyond this door her love lies buried, as she has psychologically buried desire within herself (a bit like the Derridean crypt that renders ambiguous outer and inner, here outside property and inside passion): 'Elle ignorait, elle voulait ignorer ce qu'il y avait maintenant de l'autre côté de cette muraille, dans cet ancien enclos des Fouque, où elle avait enterré son amour, son cœur et sa chair' [She didn't know, she didn't want to know, what was now on the other side of this wall, in the former Fouque enclosure, where she had buried her love, her heart, and her flesh] (p. 177). Just as Macquart's death brings about her state of living death, it was his death that had sealed the door 'l'avait murée' [walled her in] (p. 188). She fears that her grandson, Silvère, when he asks questions about the girl beyond the wall (Miette, his first love), will stir the ashes of this past, 'cendres' meaning ashes left from her burning passion and also suggesting the remains of the dead (p. 177).

And sure enough, in order to meet with Miette, Silvère literally does reopen that door to the past, crosses the same line that Dide had crossed, thus letting light through the opening and throwing, for Dide, an abyss of light onto her past, light as knowledge and memory (p. 188). Yet it is not just a memory, but also a more literal kind of vision of the dead past that becomes present to her, that returns to life. In the same way as Baudelaire writes 'Je vois' to express the strength of the past in the present, Dide re-sees: 'Elle se revit au milieu des clartés du matin, accourant, passant le seuil avec tout l'emportement de ses amours nerveuses. Et Macquart était là qui l'attendait [...]. Vision brusque qui la tirait cruellement du sommeil de sa vieillesse' [She saw herself again in the brightness of the morning, running, passing the threshold with all the passion of her nervous love. And Macquart was there waiting for her [...]. Sudden vision that cruelly pulled her out of her elderly woman's sleep] (p. 188). The dead Macquart in her hallucination waits for her, has emerged as from 'une tombe ouverte' [an open tomb] (p. 188).[10]

When she finally sees what is really there, it is the physical destruction, the death of her past, the razing of her family home and symbolically her youth, a bit like the place du Carrousel for Baudelaire in 'Le Cygne', however here she can no longer deliberately recall an image of the past:

> Le vieux logis, le vaste jardin potager, avec ses carrés verts de légumes, avaient disparu. Pas une pierre, pas un arbre d'autrefois [...]. Maintenant, lorsque, les paupières closes, elle voudrait évoquer les choses du passé, toujours ce chaume lui apparaîtrait, pareil à un linceul de bure jaunâtre jeté sur la terre où sa jeunesse était ensevelie. (*RM*, I, 189)

> [The old dwelling, the vast vegetable garden, with its green patches of vegetables, had disappeared. Not a stone, not a tree from the past [...]. Now when, with her eyes closed, she wanted to evoke the things from the past, it was always that stubble field that would appear, like a shroud of yellowish-brown wool thrown over the earth where her youth was buried.]

Finally, Dide feels that the death of her heart caused by the death of Macquart is repeated a second time now that she sees the razed earth: 'En face de cet horizon banal et indifférent, elle crut que son cœur mourait une second fois' [Faced with this banal and indifferent horizon, she thought that her heart was dying a second time] (p. 189). Death itself is repeated, and this is one of the forms that living death takes in this text.

The novel does not, however, begin with this first mother Dide and her living death. Rather the first few, decidedly odd paragraphs of *La Fortune des Rougon* describe a physical milieu, which in itself is not surprising in a naturalist novel. However this physical place, next to which Dide lives, is that cemetery in which grow the deformed trees discussed above, which no longer exists in the present of the novel — a 'dead' cemetery, in a sense, whose story is the first that Zola tells, thus putting death at the forefront of the story.[11] The 'aire Saint-Mittre', a vacant lot in the present moment of the novel, was formerly the Saint-Mittre cemetery, which, when it had filled to overflowing, was closed for a number of years and left idle when a new burial ground was opened on the other side of town. After a while, the town tore down the old cemetery walls, dug up the bones in the tombs, piled them in a corner, and the area became that vacant public lot. However, when children began to play boules with the skulls, the town decided to move the bones to a mass grave in the new cemetery. It took a week to finish the task, as the wagon travelled back and forth from one side of the town to the other, leaving bones along the route in its wake. Even though most of them were removed from the old cemetery, skulls still occasionally surfaced in the corner where they had been stored. There is clearly much that is significant for living death in these opening paragraphs.

As we saw above, in the early history of the cemetery the twisted pear trees become monstrous because of the tainted soil in which they grew, soil fertilized by the dead. Later, after the removal of the pear trees and the partial removal of the bones, some wheelwrights rent space in the lot and turn it into a wood yard, partially filled with neat piles of lumber. Children continue to play there, and gypsies set up camp in its space, but even so, death still lurks there in Zola's description. At night, the stack of wooden planks 'immobiles, comme raidis de sommeil et de froid, rappelait les morts du vieux cimetière' [immobile, as if stiffened by sleep and by cold, recalled the dead of the old cemetery] (p. 10).[12]

Most important, the former cemetery is the preferred meeting place of Silvère and his sweetheart, Miette, in that very corner where the bones were piled and continue to surface. The neglected and weathered tombstone of an adolescent named Marie (Miette's real name) is their place of rendezvous and the couple chat while sitting on it (p. 13). Even though the pear trees have been cut down and most of the remains moved, the couple meet on the soil where the trees grew. As trees are symbols of the family that grows from Dide and her deceased, insane father, the twisted trees that used to grow in the cemetery stand for the effect on Silvère both of Dide's heredity and of the physical milieu of the cemetery soil saturated with the dead that now foster Silvère and Miette's love.

Indeed, this milieu has a profound influence on the two innocent lovers. The dead in the cemetery seem actually to be living there underground and acting on the couple, pushing them to love each other (p. 206). In a particularly uncanny sentence, dead finger-like plants reach up out of the burial ground to grasp the couple's feet in order to retain them so that they will be together: 'Ces herbes, qui leur liaient les pieds par les nuits de feu, et qui les faisaient vaciller, c'étaient des doigts minces, effilés par la tombe, sortis de terre pour les retenir, pour les jeter aux bras l'un de l'autre' [These weeds, that tied their feet on ardent nights, and that made them stagger, were slim fingers, thinned out by the tomb, emerging from the earth to retain them, to throw them into each other's arms] (p. 207). A fecundating odour emanates from the plants that grow from the dead and seem to fertilize their love just as the dead in the cemetery fertilize these plants and want the couple to be together: 'Les morts, les vieux morts, voulaient les noces de Miette et de Silvère' [The dead, the old dead, desired the marriage of Miette and Silvère] (p. 207). As Naomi Schor notes, 'The invisible crowd of the dead is one of the most active in Zola'; here they seem to be acting, living and dead at the same time.[13]

The interconnection of love and death is, of course, a recurrent theme in Zola's works: one thinks of Jacques Lantier's linking of desire and murder, and Etienne and Catherine's lovemaking just before she dies in the Voreux coal mine in *Germinal*. For Zola in this first novel, the exquisite place to love is the cemetery: 'C'est là où il est exquis d'aimer' [It is there where it is exquisite to love] (p. 9). Love, which continues life, sets its roots in death, here again a kind of metaphor for heredity, in the sense that reproduction repeats the hereditary traits of ancestors in children: the dead are reproduced in their offspring.[14] When the cemetery cannot induce the couple to continue the bloodline, it wants instead to drink Silvère's blood, and it succeeds when he dies on Marie's tomb. The dead push for love and the reproduction of ancestors, or for death.

More than the mere linking of love and death, however, is the idea that love is connected to the pattern of eternal return, here the repeated return of dead lovers and the actual lives they lived.[15] We have seen one aspect of this when Dide hallucinates, as she thinks she sees Macquart, when it is actually Silvère who goes to meet with Miette: the existence of the young couple leads to the imagined return of the dead. Silvère and Miette also love each other in the same general space of the Fouque/Macquart/Saint-Mittre terrains, as did Macquart and Dide, thus they do repeat their tryst. The dead of the cemetery also want to love again, which they would do vicariously through Miette and Silvère: 'c'étaient les morts qui leur soufflaient leurs passions disparues au visage, les morts qui leur contaient leur nuit de noces, les morts qui se retournaient dans la terre, pris du furieux désir d'aimer, de recommencer l'amour' [It was the dead who breathed out vanished passions into their faces, the dead who told them about their wedding night, the dead who turned over in the earth, taken over by the furious desire to love, to begin love again] (p. 206). In relation to the cemetery, Schor notes that Silvère and Miette give body once more to the sprits of the deceased. The dead can return in new lovers.[16]

The eternal return is also evoked in Miette's notion that Marie's tomb is there for her (p. 208). In a sense, it *is* her tombstone, because, just before Silvère dies there, he gruesomely suggests that a part of the deceased Miette actually remains on the tomb's writing where she touched it in the past, and thus she is, at least in part, there (p. 312). Miette also claims her early death will be like Marie's, which does in fact happen when Miette dies young at the age of thirteen: 'Elle voulait absolument qu'elle fût morte à son âge, à treize ans' [She insisted absolutely that the girl had died at her own age, at thirteen years old] (p. 208). Thus, the dead Marie seems to return in Miette.

When Dide sees Miette with Silvère, who has crossed the threshold of the door that led to Dide's love, it is not just that the two young people repeat Macquart and Dide's love story from the past, Silvère actually becomes Macquart for her.[17] First, earlier in the novel, Silvère seems to look like Macquart, as the narrator speculates that Dide possibly sees the similarity (p. 136), suggesting hereditary resemblance with his grandfather. More important, in the scene at the door in the wall, Dide realizes that her love affair with Macquart will go on forever:

> Jusqu'au bout, elle devait se retrouver, elle et Macquart, aux bras l'un de l'autre, dans la claire matinée. Une seconde fois, la porte était complice. Par où l'amour avait passé, l'amour passait de nouveau. C'était l'éternel recommencement, avec ses joies présentes et ses larmes futures. (*RM*, I, 189)

> [Until the very end, she would have to find herself once again, she and Macquart, in each other's arms, in the bright morning. A second time, the door was complicit. Where love had passed through, love passed through again. It was the eternal rebeginning, with its present joys and its future tears.]

Furthermore, ancestor merges with descendant in Dide's hysterical crisis later that night. She speaks of a 'douanier' (and we assume it is the one who killed Macquart), and when she comes out of the crisis, she confuses Silvère with someone else (again presumably Macquart) and predicts that the innocent ones will also be killed (presumably Silvère and Miette). When she sees Silvère, she seems to be talking to Macquart: 'Ils sont là [...]. Vois-tu, il vont te prendre, il te tueront encore' [They are there [...]. Don't you see, they will take you, they will kill you again] (pp. 190–91). In a sense, she envisions that Macquart is going to die a second time through Silvère. In this way Zola gives us the merging of two characters from the same family, and he provides an uncanny prediction, here of the future of Silvère, who does repeat the death of Macquart when he is shot by a representative of the law, a gendarme (p. 306). In this way the dead of the past and the dead past return in a character and an event.[18]

Finally, a scene in *Le Docteur Pascal* brings back this return of the dead Macquart in a third instance: the death of Charles, Dide's great-great grandson, in an asylum. Dide, whom we saw nearly paralyzed in her living death at the end of her life, is present during Charles's death. As he expires, she returns like a spectre from her coma-like existence: 'Et de nouveau, l'oubliée vivait, sortait de son néant, droite et dévastée, comme un spectre de l'épouvante de la douleur' [And again, the forgotten woman lived, came out of her void, upright and devastated, like a spectre of terror and suffering] (*RM*, v, 1105).[19] Dide cries out three times 'Le gendarme! le gendarme! le gendarme!' after Zola has made the three terrible, repeated shocks explicit:

> Le premier, en pleine vie ardente, lorsqu'un gendarme avait abattu d'un coup de feu, comme un chien, son amant, le contrebandier Macquart; le second, à bien des années de distance, lorsqu'un gendarme encore, d'un coup de pistolet, avait cassé la tête de son petit-fils Silvère, l'insurgé, la victime des haines et des luttes sanglantes de la famille. Du sang, toujours, l'avait éclaboussée. Et un troisième choc moral l'achevait, du sang l'éclaboussait, ce sang appauvri de sa race qu'elle venait de voir couler si longuement, qui était par terre. (*RM*, v, 1105)

> [The first, in full ardent life, when a gendarme had taken down with a gunshot, like a dog, her lover, the smuggler Macquart; the second, many years later, when a gendarme again, with a gunshot, had obliterated the head of her grandson, Silvère, the insurgent, the victim of the hatreds and the bloody struggles of the family. Blood, always, had splattered her. And a third moral shock was finishing her: blood splattered her, that weak blood of her race that she had just seen flow for so long, which was on the ground.]

Although Charles dies of a blood disorder (which would seem to be haemophilia) and not by shooting, the three deaths are tied together in the image of their shared blood that was spilled, here literally when Charles bleeds to death, blood that represents the hereditary repetition of the family members and the bloody death they reenact and relive.

The new generation thus mechanically repeats the previous one; the dead return in the living, and these living dead beings are the symbol of heredity. As we saw above, if Schor sees this as each generation repeating the actions of the previous generation, it seems here for Dide, however, that in this case one family member returns physically in another, and in the case of Silvère, it is a dead ancestor, his grandfather who returns in him.[20]

In *La Fortune des Rougon* it is also the theme of the eternal return of dead political regimes that Zola emphasizes in the socio-political milieu of his characters. The romantic idyll of Silvère and Miette becomes an allegory of the fate of the republic in the text; and the familial, fraternal battles among Pierre, Antoine, Aristide (and to a different extent, Silvère), take on the connotation of the battles for and against *liberté, égalité, et fraternité*. Zola makes clear that the path that leads from monarchy, to First Republic, to First French Empire returns again beginning in 1848: power in Plassans passes from monarchists to republicans to supporters of the Empire. As David Charles notes, this cycle is allegorized by the mayor's chair.[21] It is first used by Garçonnet, a legitimist, then taken over by Antoine Macquart for the Republican uprising against Louis-Napoléon, only to be taken from him by his half-brother, Pierre Rougon, for the Empire.

Before the return of the Empire, those seated in the mayor's chair, the monarchists, rule over Plassans even though they are not represented as viable leaders, but rather as degraded and decaying vestiges of a past that has not completely disappeared. Zola describes the nobles of Plassans who favour the monarchy as the living dead: 'Ce sont les morts s'ennuyant dans la vie. Aussi leur quartier a-t-il le calme lourd d'un cimetière' [They are the dead bored in life. Thus, their district had the heavy calm of a cemetery] (p. 39). When the new Empire is declared, what is most important for the notion of the living dead is that the Rougons and Louis Napoléon have succeeded in killing the republic once again. The republic that returns when Macquart takes over the mayor's office is thus short-lived when Louis Napoléon succeeds in taking power. The first republic was 'killed' by Napoléon Bonaparte, it returned to life in the Second Republic, and now is killed again by Louis Napoléon, as Rougon says of the general killing in Plassans (which applies as well to the political context), they are *re*buried: 'Ils sont rentrés sous terre' [They have gone back under the ground] (p. 288).

In general, the powerful of Plassans accept the Second Empire, giving up on the monarchy, because they fear the republic and are glad it has been killed: 'La grande impure, la République, venait d'être assassinée' [The great impure one, the Republic, had just been assassinated] (p. 75). And it is the dead body of the republic that becomes the foundation of the Rougon fortune, just as the dead of the cemetery provide the fertile ground for the twisted richness of the pear trees:

> Ces événements fondèrent la fortune des Rougon. Mêlés aux diverses phases de cette crise, ils grandirent sur les ruines de la liberté. Ce fut la République que volèrent ces bandits à l'affût; après qu'on l'eut égorgée, ils aidèrent à la détrousse. (*RM*, I, 76)

> [These events founded the fortune of the Rougons. Involved in the diverse phases of this crisis, they thrived on the ruins of liberty. It was the Republic that these bandits, lying in wait, stole; after they slit its throat, they assisted in its plunder.]

As Naomi Schor noted, the cemetery evolves from a holy place, 'le cimetière Saint-Mittre', to a secular plot, l'aire Saint-Mittre, from *ancien régime* to modern society.[22] This transformation is certainly important for Zola's representation of Second Empire society, however we have seen that the dead in the Saint-Mittre cemetery, even though the area changed when most of the dead were removed and it was 'modernized', continue their influence on the living even in the cemetery's transformed, modern state, when they symbolically call out to Miette and Silvère. Transformation remains grounded in, and influenced by, death in the cemetery; and symbolically, the present remains grounded in and directed by the past.

It is also significant that the word *semer* [to sow] is used to describe the way the bones fall off the cart during their trip from the cemetery to a nameless, common grave. It is as if the influential and active dead were now being 'sown' through Plassans. Having nourished the soil in the cemetery, they are now being 'planted', diffused throughout the social space: 'Le pis était que ce tombereau devait traverser Plassans dans toute sa longueur, et que le mauvais pavé des rues lui faisait semer, à chaque cahot, des fragments d'os' [The worst was that the cart had to traverse Plassans for its whole length, and that the bad paving of the streets caused it to sow, with each bump, fragments of bone] (p. 6). As we shall see, *La Fortune des Rougon*, and the *Rougon-Macquart* novels in general, represent the evolution not just of the political but also of the social order, evolving from the old power held by the monarchists in Plassans to a new order, one whose ground is layered with diffused death, the symbol of a death that spreads through society and remains ever present as the social space takes on new and modern forms.

One of the major themes involving the modern that Zola inherits from Balzac is the objectification of human beings. As we saw above, for Balzac it is the role that money takes on as it becomes the common basic value and replaces morality. Money contributes to the intensification of the objectification of humans, who can be bought and sold in increasingly diverse ways, and it progressively turns them into things that are buyable or expendable for others' personal gain. Similarly, in *La Fortune des Rougon*, the city of Plassans decides to dig up the bones of the departed so the city can profit from the public land of the cemetery (p. 6). It is thus profit that makes objects of these anonymous dead, an objectification symbolized earlier when the bones in the pile are used by the town urchins for those games of boules mentioned above and are hung on the cords of doorbells in the town. And it is profit that the town eventually gains when the wheelwrights rent its space. In this text of origins, Zola links the reification of humans, here this objectification of the dead, with the desire for profit.

Another aspect of reification figured in the cemetery is its transformation to a working space, a symbol of change to an industrial and commercial society. The peacefulness of the old cemetery is replaced by the noise of the sawyers as they cut wooden planks. They and their industry represent the dehumanization and mechanization of the industrial world that will appear in *Germinal* (1885), as the men seem to be machine-like puppets: 'Pendant des heures, ces hommes se plient, pareils à des pantins articulés, avec une régularité et une sécheresse de machine' [For hours, these men would bend, like jointed puppets, with the regularity and insensitivity of a machine] (p. 8). The symbol of the mechanical human ties the theme of becoming a thing-like puppet to the loss of humanity in modernity.

Nevertheless, no matter how changed this former cemetery space might be, the stacks of industrial wooden planks that are piled there themselves create mysterious paths and a space, an aisle, where the dead show their continued presence in, and influence on, this industrial space itself: 'Dans cette allée [...], règnent encore la végétation puissante et le silence frissonnant de l'ancien cimetière. On y sent courir ces souffles chauds et vagues des voluptés de la mort qui sortent des vieilles tombes' [In this aisle [...] still reigned the powerful plants and the quivering silence of the former cemetery. One could feel those hot breaths and vague delights of death that emerged from the old tombs] (pp. 8–9). The reification and mechanization of human life, here symbolized by the sawyers' workspace grounded in the soil of the 'living dead', joined with Zola's representation of the living death of heredity, introduce the aspects of the living death of modernity that we pursue in the following analyses of other works by Zola, first with *La Bête humaine* (1890).

Jacques Lantier vividly embodies the intrusion of death and dead ancestors into the bodies of the living. Sexual arousal for him leads to the desire to murder women, the *tare*, the flaw that he inherited from an unknown male family member from the distant past: 'l'ancien mâle, emportant à son cou les femelles éventrées' [the ancient male, carrying off disemboweled females on his shoulders].[23] This ancestor takes him over, a loss of control that becomes focused on Jacques's hands, as he fears this ancestor will control them and he will kill the woman he loves, Séverine (p. 1207).[24] This other does take hold of him and seems to expel Jacques from his own body, as he flees Séverine and tries to kill another woman in her place (although he doesn't succeed): 'Dans son corps qui allait, sa personnalité était absente' [In his body that walked on, his personality was absent] (p. 1209). Thus, the dead ancestor from the past makes him act and eventually kill Séverine as Jacques becomes a kind of combination of the will and drives of his dead forerunner and his own unconscious body, a different kind of living death. As Françoise Gaillard notes, the ghosts of Zola's characters 'se cach[ent] sournoisement dans les gènes' [hide slyly in their genes].[25] The dead inhabit us and make us do their bidding in this metaphor for heredity. And it is an absence of agency, will, and the ability to choose one's destiny (p. 1044).

Zola makes clear that there are in fact two different kinds of 'heredity' that can either enter into conflict or work together. The first type is physical heredity, the second cultural heredity, again what Bourdieu would call 'habitus', the embodiment of social mores in individual ideas, habits, and practices that come from one's milieu.[26] Through Jacques, Zola illustrates both the more basic physical laws of heredity as well as the social scruples and rules that develop in human society (p. 1236).[27] This corpus of social mores and laws he calls 'the milk of generations' (p. 1236), the milk that feeds our conscience: 'la conscience n'était faite que des idées transmises par une lente hérédité de justice' [conscience was made only of the ideas transmitted by a slow heredity of justice] (p. 1241). Jacques's work on the train, his social role in life, helps to control the ancestor within him. The runaway train at the end of the novel symbolizes the failure of social laws to contain hereditary drives: the train is significantly called a 'train fantôme' [ghost train], in part a symbol of the runaway energy of the drives of dead ancestors from the past that destroy human control in the present.[28]

Indeed, for Jacques, these two heredities come into conflict: the desire to kill and the prohibition against it. When he thinks of killing Roubaud so that he and Séverine can be together, the crime seems monstrous to him because of that 'milk' of civilization that nourishes our practices: 'En lui, l'homme civilisé se révoltait, la force acquise de l'éducation, le lent et indestructible échafaudage des idées transmises' [In him, the civilized man revolted, the acquired force of education, the slow and indestructible scaffolding of transmitted ideas] (p. 1236). These transmitted ideas are another way in which the human being in Zola is made of the past, of the laws and cultural practices of ancestors. It gives additional force to the strong deterministic and mechanistic bent of his works.

However, for Jacques, when the law of his physical heredity takes over, it overrides cultural rules, the 'idées transmises', to become 'le tourment de l'idée fixe' [the torment of the *idée fixe*] (p. 1227), a kind of eternal return of an obsessional idea, and here it is the idea of murder. Jacques's original hereditary obsession with killing transforms into a specific *idée fixe* in an important scene, when Séverine recounts her role in the murder of Grandmorin. She tells its story, re-presents it in words and ideas, and this represented image of the murder begins to haunt Jacques who cannot rid himself of it:

> Chaque fois que, par un effort de volonté, il croyait glisser au sommeil, la même hantise recommençait, les mêmes images défilaient, éveillant les mêmes sensations. Et ce qui se déroulait ainsi, avec une régularité mécanique, pendant que ses yeux fixes et grands ouverts s'emplissaient d'ombre, c'était le meurtre, détail à détail. Toujours il renaissait, identique, envahissant, affolant. (*RM*, IV, 1206)

> [Each time that, by an effort of his will, he thought he was drifting off to sleep, the same obsession began again, the same images filed past, awakening the same sensations. And what thus unfolded, with a mechanical regularity, while his eyes, fixed and wide open, filled with darkness, was the murder, detail by detail. Always, it rose again, identical, invading, terrifying.]

Here the idea of death, the murder, continually returns, is reborn.

In this same scene, the image of the anonymous 'hand' comes back, not yet to kill Séverine, but to force Jacques to continue to see this hallucinatory, recurring image of the stabbing of Grandmorin when the hand holds his eyes open: 'Malgré son effort, les invisibles doigts rouvrirent ses paupières; et, dans le noir, le meurtre reparut en traits sanglants' [Despite his efforts, the invisible fingers reopened his eyes; and, in the dark, the murder reappeared in bloody strokes] (p. 1206). The hereditary drive along with the social transmission of ideas, the latter represented by the story told by Séverine, merge the two heredities in what will become for Jacques the *idée fixe* of imitating this murder, which he does later when he kills Séverine with a knife in the same fashion as, in her story, Roubaud killed Grandmorin (the words *idée fixe* are actually one of the titles that Zola imagined for his novel [p. 1758]).[29] This combination of the social transmission of the idea of the murder and natural heredity push Jacques to kill the woman he loves and then mourns, thus representing the double power of combined heredities to bring another version of that past murder back into the present, to repeat the death.

This dead ancestor who returns to haunt and control Jacques becomes a general symbol for the past that haunts several other characters in the novel. Séverine and Roubaud, having murdered Grandmorin, wish to bury this past, and so they physically 'bury' the watch and the money taken from him under the floorboards of their apartment. They try not to speak of the murder again and consider it to be, significantly, a 'chose finie, enterrée' [a thing ended, buried] (p. 1136). However, they remain aware of the cadaver buried under their floor, embodied in the watch and money that become the ghostly presence of the dead man (p. 1139). Here, the image of the living dead in the cemetery in *La Fortune des Rougon* reappears, because, for Roubaud, the hole in the floor is a 'charnier, un trou d'épouvante et de mort, où des spectres l'attendaient' [a charnel house, a hole of horror and death, where spectres awaited him] (p. 1138).

Roubaud and Séverine realize that the memory in fact is not buried, and they are troubled by the symbolic cadaver that they continue to sense at every moment under their feet (p. 1139). As we shall see in *Thérèse Raquin*, the murderers here have visions of the victim: when Roubaud makes love to Séverine, she thinks she sees the dead Grandmorin's face in his and she relives the sensation of the murder as if it were she being murdered (p. 1140). And when Roubaud decides to retrieve the buried money in order to use it and Séverine appears in the doorway, he thinks that she is a ghost (p. 1159). Even though the couple tries to bury the past and the dead man, they continue to return and to haunt them both. Other characters in the novel also experience the imagined return or the continued life of the dead: Jacques thinks he sees Flore's ghost (p. 1299); after Phasie is dead, Misard thinks he sees her eyes taunt him and her lips speak to him (p. 1281).[30] The dead return to life in the obsessions of these characters.

If imagined ghosts continue to make the past present, various kinds of language in the text speak the past, which can then intrude on the present. Human bodies display their past history, the record of their formation over time from social shaping, which is a kind of body language can be 'read', such as Jacques' hands that reveal the type of job he has (p. 1026). Sometimes bodies speak and have the uncanny ability to tell the truth about the past when words lie.[31] When Séverine denies her culpability in Grandmorin's murder while speaking with Jacques, both she and Jacques 'read' each other and know that her denial is really a confession that she did help murder Grandmorin, and both of them are completely aware of this fact.

Objects as well seem to contain the past, bring it into the present, and reveal it by 'speaking'. In the first few pages, Zola uses an object, a box made of shells seen by Roubaud, as a narrative device to call forth for us and for Roubaud the past of their marriage, a bit like Proust's later madeleine: 'Et ce petit objet avait suffi, toute l'histoire de son mariage se déroulait' [And this small object sufficed, the entire history of his marriage unfolded] (p. 1000). Séverine has such a need to confess her crime aloud to Jacques that she imagines that the objects in the room themselves tell aloud the story of her first confession to Roubaud, which took place in the same room (p. 1194). And objects can even give false information about the past, a theme central to the novel as crime fiction. Grandmorin's watch travels from Roubaud after its theft to its place in the floor, to Séverine, to Jacques, back to Séverine, then finally to Cabuche, who steals it and cherishes it because he is in love with Séverine; later it is used to convict him falsely of her murder.[32]

A building space can become a kind of object that brings back the past or people encountered there, a bit like Balzac's Conciergerie and Baudelaire's Carrousel. As we saw above, la mère Victoire's room contains objects that seem to tell the story of Séverine's confession to Roubaud when she explained Grandmorin's depraved sexual relations with her. With Jacques in this same room in which she was forced to reveal her past to Roubaud, she repeats the same 'scene' with Jacques: they eat the same food for supper, they hear the same sounds coming from the apartment next door, she again has too much to drink, and she reveals Grandmorin's abuse, just as she did with Roubaud, while this time revealing as well the later circumstances of Grandmorin's murder.[33] In a sense, Jacques takes the place of the murderer Roubaud here, rather than himself being taken over by his distant ancestor.

Séverine then begins to feel the past physically, as she thinks she senses someone's breath on her neck and she believes that she sees her husband's hand taking the knife used to kill Grandmorin (pp. 1191–93). The room is a kind of chronotope where time and space converge and the past remains in the present.[34] And specifically it is death that seems to occur again, the murder of Grandmorin as Séverine recounts it: 'Le frisson du désir se perdait dans cet autre frisson de mort, revenue en elle. C'était, comme au fond de toute volupté, une agonie qui recommençait' [The shiver of desire dissolved into that other shiver of death, which returned in her. It was, as in the depths of all sensuality, death throes that recurred'] (p. 1197). Death comes back into life, comes back to life, in a sense. This is a kind of living death of humans because they remain tied to that past, limited in their life in the present moment, again a kind of living death of past experiences, as with Stéphanie in Balzac.

Zola makes the temporal dimensions of the chronotope even thicker when, through Jacques, the narrator announces the importance of a place before anything happens there. The house at the Croix-de-Maufras, where Séverine was abused, lies on the path of the train that Jacques drives, and each time he sees it, even before he knows what happened to Séverine there, it haunts him with a feeling that it will be involved in his future: 'Elle le hantait sans qu'il sût pourquoi, avec la sensation confuse qu'elle importait à son existence' [It haunted him without his understanding why, with the confused sensation that it was important to his life] (p. 1037). It of course does become part of his tragedy when he regains consciousness after the train accident and finds himself there in the house, where he recalls his unease as he would pass by. It is in this house and even in the same bed (which he recognizes from Séverine's story), where she was subjected to Grandmorin's sexual abuse, and where Jacques will kill her because of his own sexual malady. Again, he takes the place of another man, the dead Grandmorin, this time in this house and bed. The room and house become a chronotope that predicts the future when Jacques sees it from the train, become his present when he is recovering from his injuries, and eventually mix past and present in what seems to be an inevitable repetition and recurrence of death, here of violence against Séverine in the future, a collapsing of time in this space of her death.

In this scene at the Croix-de-Maufras, Zola takes another step in the condensation of the chronotope-room: the two aforementioned rooms — that of la mère Victoire (where Roubaud's violence against Séverine and her confession occur) and the bedroom at the Croix-de-Maufras (where Grandmorin's violence against Séverine and her murder occur) — are collapsed one into the other. Jacques himself links the two rooms, because two young women who live below la mère Victoire actually come to the house at the Croix-de-Maufras after the train wreck to visit their brother (a worker on the train) as Jacques and he recover there. Jacques hears the same girlish laughter that he heard in the room when Séverine revealed her past to him and he explicitly links the two spaces (p. 1277). Later, after Jacques imitates Grandmorin's murder (which Séverine had recounted to him in Paris) by murdering Séverine in this room with the same knife, the narrator joins the two crimes together as necessarily connected through Jacques's indirect discourse:

> Comme l'autre, elle venait de culbuter [...]. Obscurément, cela avait germé, avait grandi en lui; pas une heure, depuis un an, sans qu'il eût marché vers l'inévitable; même au cou de cette femme, sous ses baisers, le sourd travail s'achevait; et les deux meurtres s'étaient rejoints, l'un n'était-il pas la logique de l'autre? (*RM*, IV, 1298)
>
> [Like the other one, she was taken down [...]. Mysteriously it had germinated, had grown in him; there was not a single hour, for a whole year, when he didn't progress toward the inevitable; even in the arms of this woman, under her kisses, the silent work drew to a close; and the two murders had joined together; wasn't one the logical result of the other?]

Two moments and two rooms from the past make their return and converge in the present moment to result in Séverine's murder as if by logical necessity from the murder of Grandmorin. Once again, death must return, and here it is Jacques who must relive the experience of his dead ancestor.

After the murder, Jacques looks at Séverine's body and notes that murder makes of a human being a thing, a puppet, and he sees that Séverine is the same kind of object as was Grandmorin's corpse: 'c'était la même loque humaine, le pantin cassé, la chiffe molle, qu'un coup de couteau fait d'une créature' [it was the same human wreck, the broken puppet, the limp rag, that a stabbing made of a human being] (p. 1298). This literal objectification of the human, along with the things that seem to speak to Séverine, open onto our important Zolian semantic field of the humanization of things and the objectification of humans.[35] In the context of this novel, the blurring of animate and inanimate, human and thing, works within the dynamics of what Michel Serres has analyzed as the engine: 'Globalement parlant, tout fonctionne comme la machine à feu: le roman, ses amours et ses crimes' [Globally speaking, everything functions like a thermodynamic machine: the novel, its loves and its crimes].[36] As Laura Salisbury notes, humans function as 'engines of their genetic instincts'.[37] In our context of living death, they must cede to the power of the mechanical reproduction of the past. In this novel, and more generally in Zola (as we shall see in more detail later in the analysis of the novels on stores and Second Empire society), people *are* things, either a Grandmorin, the 'pantin cassé' after he is killed, or something to be possessed and used, as a grateful Séverine offers herself to Camy-Lamotte saying, 'Je vous appartiens' [I belong to you] (p. 1126). And, of course, machines are like humans: la Lison, Jacques' train engine, whom he loves as if she were a woman, has a soul, a personality, a life (p. 1128) — a soul that leaves her body in her breath-like steam when she dies: 'son âme s'en allait avec la force qui la faisait vivante, cette haleine immense [...]. Elle était morte' [her soul left with the force that made her alive, that immense breath [...]. She was dead] (p. 1267).

One of the themes that express this death of the human in machine-driven modernity is that of the railroad timetable, which matches the pace of human life with the workings of engines. Jacques does not need to think when driving his machine (p. 1227). Roubaud's life is ordered and dominated by his daily activity, eternally the same (p. 1057), even when he develops his gambling *idée fixe*. The *idée fixe* of Misard is described as the tick-tock of a clock (p. 1281). However, within this regulated existence, disruptions can occur, and both humans and machines can become *détraqués*, off track, out of control, which can lead to real death.[38] The word *détraquer* — one might say 'going haywire' — is used to describe a number of heterogeneous things: Flore's mind (p. 1280), Roubaud and his marriage (pp. 1289, 1216), the train schedule once war has been declared (p. 1327), the entire railroad organization, and consequently the government itself because of Grandmorin's murder (p. 1125). The mechanization of human existence represents an absence of agency, a kind of symbolic living death of humans who do not act with will or choice, and a glitch in the machine can lead to catastrophe.

The Living Death of Reification: Shopping, Money, and Illusion

'Thérèse Raquin': Commerce and the Living Death of the Outmoded in Modern Paris

From *La Bête humaine* and its speedy mechanical modernity (well analyzed by David Bell[39]), we move back in time to a novel that preceded the *Rougon-Macquart* series, *Thérèse Raquin* (1867–68), as we begin to explore the role of Paris and commerce in the symbolism of living death in modernity.[40] This early novel centres on the representation of living death in a shop, in this case a *mercerie*, a 'notions shop' that would sell things like caps and socks, as well as buttons, boxes, and knitting needles. As Zola claims in his preface to the second edition, he wants to conduct a study of the milieu as it affects a particular character, an 'étude du tempérament et des modifications profondes de l'organisme sous la pression des milieux et des circonstances' [study of temperament and of the profound modifications of the organism under the pressure of milieus and circumstances].[41] The novel begins with a description of this milieu, Mme Raquin's shop in its location of the passage du Pont Neuf (torn down in 1912), which is described by Zola as a dark, damp, and depressing space. Walking through this arcade resembles descending into a dangerous underground and funereal passage: 'on dirait une galerie souterraine vaguement éclairée par trois lampes funéraires' [one might say a subterranean gallery vaguely lit by three funeral lamps] (p. 28).[42] The Raquin shop itself is described as a 'fosse' [grave] (p. 41) where Thérèse becomes sad enough to die in the depths of the dark vault, which smells of the cemetery (pp. 213–14). Before she meets Laurent, she has already become the living dead, as she feels buried alive there: 'On m'a enterrée vive dans cette ignoble boutique' [I have been buried alive in this foul shop] (p. 62).[43] When Laurent meets her for the first time and sees how bored she must be, he thinks to himself, ironically for any reader who knows the end of the story, that a woman would have to die in that place (p. 56). Thus, the milieu of the novel, the shop, is a kind of tomb that matches the miserable lives of Thérèse and Laurent, who dream of leaving the passage du Pont-Neuf, whose dampness seemed made for their desolate life (p. 213).

The character who most fully represents living death is Camille: his corpse returns to haunt his murderers, Thérèse and Laurent, in their joint nightly hallucinations in the shop.[44] Zola skirts the borders of fantastic literature in his descriptions of Camille by describing the real presence of the cadaver through his character's perceptions, as if he were there materially in their presence. In their bed, 'Il y avait entre eux une large place. Là couchait le cadavre de Camille' [There was a large space between them. There lay Camille's cadaver] (p. 161).[45] Laurent oddly even tries to imagine killing Camille a second time:

> Laurent pendant plus de quinze jours, se demanda comment il pourrait bien faire pour tuer de nouveau Camille. Il l'avait jeté à l'eau, et voilà qu'il n'était pas assez mort, qu'il revenait toutes les nuits se coucher dans le lit de Thérèse [...] leur victime ressuscitait pour glacer leur couche. Thérèse n'était pas veuve, Laurent se trouvait être l'époux d'une femme qui avait déjà pour mari un noyé. (p. 163)

> [For more than two weeks, Laurent wondered how he would be able to kill Camille again. He had thrown him in the water, and there it was that he was not dead enough, that he came back every night to sleep in Thérèse's bed [...] their victim resuscitated in order to chill their bed. Thérèse was not a widow, Laurent found himself to be the husband of a woman who already had a drowned man for a husband.]

Camille's return represents the return of the past, of the memory of the murder that the couple cannot kill, and the drowned man comes back each night: 'Chaque nuit, le noyé les visitait' [Each night, the drowned man visited them] (p. 128). The mention of Camille's name 'fills' them with the past and makes them relive, 'vivre de nouveau', the anguish caused by the murder (p. 148). For Laurent, these memories become reality in hallucinations that are not just visual but involve other physical senses: smell and touch (p. 121).[46] As in Baudelaire, the dead past returns as an almost physical presence. And in Zola, it is again an eternal return: Laurent 'lives' in the same nightmare of encountering the living dead Camille that is repeated numerous times: 'à plus de dix reprises, il refit le chemin, il vit le noyé s'offrir à son embrassement' [more than ten times, he retraced his path, he saw the drowned man offer himself to his embrace] (p. 124).

Furthermore, Zola describes other characters as being living and dead in various ways. As for Laurent, 'sa chair semblait morte' [his flesh seemed dead] (p. 115) (and this is the case for both Thérèse and Laurent in another point in the text, p. 147). Suzanne is a 'pauvre créature toute morte et toute blanche' [poor creature completely dead and white] (p. 139), 'vivant à demi' [half alive] (p. 170). After Camille's murder, Mme Raquin becomes paralyzed, 'locked in', and she can move only her eyes, and briefly her hand. She is described as a 'cadavre vivant à moitié' [half-living cadaver] (p. 182), and like Thérèse, she has been buried alive, in this case in her own body: 'Son esprit était comme un de ces vivants qu'on ensevelit par mégarde et qui se réveillent dans la nuit de la terre, à deux ou trois mètres au-dessous du sol' [Her mind was like that of one of those living people who are buried by mistake and who awaken in the night of the earth, at two or three meters under the ground] (p. 186).[47] If Zola claimed his goal in this novel was to do the same thing that 'les chirurgiens font sur les cadavres' [surgeons perform on cadavers] (p. 19), he has done so in an oddly literal way in his probing representation of living cadavers.

In addition to this type of living death, the return and the presence of the dead past in a particular milieu, the novel aims as well, according to Zola in his preface, at studying the way in which the characters' physiology makes of them puppets who must follow bodily drives, deprived of free will (as we saw above in the *La Bête humaine*) (p. 18). The novel shows how the two contrasting physical types of human being, Laurent, who is sanguine, and Thérèse, who is nervous, interact with each other and are transformed by this contact. However, the two also resemble each other because, as Zola claims, they have no soul (p. 18). They are beings ruled by their physical nature alone, in a kind of machine-like existence, object-like, living in movements but dead as humans.

Indeed, Zola describes other characters in the novel as mindlessly obeying routine. The friends of the family who arrive every Thursday to play dominos seem to Thérèse to be mechanical corpses in a funeral vault (pp. 47–48).[48] This mechanization can take the form of the inability to control one's body, in one case hands (we are reminded of the takeover of Jacques' hands in *La Bête humaine*). Laurent, who attempts to be an artist, is now obsessed with Camille's 'ghost' and can no longer draw anything but Camille's face. He feels that his hand is no longer his, it is mechanically governed by something else (p. 182).[49]

Is there a relation between this representation of the mechanical nature of human behaviour and the moribund shop and arcade? Benjamin provides some interesting insight into possible connections. He states that the scientific study of behaviour in *Thérèse Raquin* is not actually as convincing as the scientific study of 'the death of the Paris arcades, the decay of a type of architecture' that the book provides in the descriptions of the passage du Pont Neuf. Benjamin goes on to say: 'The book's atmosphere is saturated with the poisons of this process'.[50] Indeed, the poisoned, mechanical nature of the behaviour of the characters is, in fact, linked with this decay and the decline of the type of shop that was lodged in Zola's arcade, the family shop that was being replaced by the giant department stores of *Au Bonheur des Dames*.

We can begin to explore this connection in a section of Hippolyte Taine's letter (of 'début 1868') to Zola on *Thérèse Raquin* that interestingly prefigures some of Benjamin's later ideas. Taine is one critic who found Zola's descriptions unrealistic — they became, in his words, a 'fantasmagorie, et, en pareille histoire, la fantasmagorie devient cauchemar' [a phantasmagoria, and, in such a story, the phantasmagoria becomes a nightmare] (p. 275). As we saw in previous sections, the phantasmagoria, a form of entertainment that projected ghosts (among other things), the 'living dead', onto a screen and made them move and seem real, certainly does correspond to the ghostly haunting in the imaginations of the characters in this 'scientific' novel. As for Benjamin and phantasmagoria, Margaret Cohen notes that the term gives Benjamin a way to describe 'the persistence of the irrational in modern life', just as it gives Taine a way to describe the unrealistic nature of Zola's realist, pre-naturalist text.[51]

Furthermore, Benjamin explicitly links phantasmagoria with the arcades: 'the new economically and technologically based creations that we owe to the nineteenth century enter the universe of a phantasmagoria [...]. They are manifest as phantasmagorias. Thus appear the arcades'.[52] In addition to this general link to the experience of the arcades, the word 'phantasmagoria' (again, as we saw above) is used by Benjamin in relation to commodity fetishism and to the death of the 'human' that lies beneath the shiny surface of the commodity (from Marx's definition of human social relations that take on the phantasmagorical form of a relation between things').[53] It is here in the arcade that the loss of the human connects with the mechanization of the characters and the reification of people in *Thérèse Raquin*. Just as the novel's characters are living and dead 'phantoms', and just as they are machine-like, they become things. This is particularly salient in the case of Mme Raquin when she is paralyzed and compared to a package, a thing (p. 183). She becomes the doll, the 'poupée' of the couple (p. 206). Laurent must, in fact, carry her around like a package (p. 183).

Perhaps more important in terms of the subtext of commerce, Thérèse would seem to prostitute herself. Benjamin lists the prostitute as an ambiguous figure who is both human subject and object for sale, along with other similarly opposing things, the commodity and our arcades: 'Such an image is afforded by the commodity per se: as fetish. Such an image is presented by the arcades, which are house no less than street. Such an image is the prostitute — seller and sold in one'.[54] Thérèse, trying to escape the nightmare of her life with Laurent and the ghost of Camille, 's'habillait comme une fille, [...] elle se dandinait sur le trottoir d'une façon provocante, regardant les hommes, relevant si haut le devant de sa jupe, en la prenant à poigné, qu'elle montait tout le devant de ses jambes' [dressed like a prostitute, [...] she pranced about on the pavement in a provocative fashion, looking at men, raising the front of her skirt so high, gripping it in her hand, that she showed the entire front of her legs] (pp. 220–21). She joins a group of men and prostitutes in a cafe, leaves with a man, and goes with him to a rented room. She would seem to turn herself into an object for sale.[55] Thus we have in *Thérèse Raquin* the intertwined figures of the ghostly phantasmagoria, the decaying commerce of the arcades, and the reification of humans in Mme Raquin's paralysis and in Thérèse's prostitution, which Benjamin ties to the growing domination of commodity culture.

The other link of sexuality (prostitution) with the reification of humans occurs in one of the most famous scenes in the novel that takes place in the Paris morgue.[56] Young boys go there to look at the naked bodies of drowned women, and Zola goes so far as to say, 'C'est à la morgue que les jeunes voyous ont leur première maîtresse' [It is in the morgue that young hooligans have their first mistress] (p. 105). An upper-class woman goes to see a naked working-class man (pp. 104–05). Human bodies become a spectacle, objects to be viewed as a pastime, and the dead become passive participants in living sexuality. Yet beyond that simple objectification, Zola compares these bodies and their display in the morgue to commodities on display in a more modern shop than that of the Raquins, 'l'étalage d'un magasin de nouveautés' [the display of a novelty shop] (p. 104).

The murder of Camille and the absence of human morality or soul in Thérèse and Laurent allegorize the loss of humanity in Zola's contemporary culture. This loss is expressed in the phantasmagorical representations of both people and places in *Thérèse Raquin*: they are both living and dead. The decay of the arcades links the sale of commodities in the outdated shop to living death in the ongoing reification and modernization of human existence.

'La Curée': Dispossession and Living Death

Near the end of *La Curée* (1871), the main character, Renée, becomes aware that she has been used by her society, and this 'awakening' accompanies her act of looking at herself in a mirror, where she sees that she is dead: 'Elle se vit morte' [She saw herself dead]).[57] This novel traces the path that brought her to this living death and represents the nature of her life in this state. Zola makes her voyage an allegorical one that figures the path taken by France, specifically by Paris, during the Second Empire, which he represents as manifesting the same qualities of living death. As noted above, he announces in the preface to *La Fortune des Rougon* that he is creating 'le tableau d'un règne mort' [the picture of a dead reign], thus himself symbolically 'bringing to life' a dead society (*RM*, I, 4).[58]

The opening chapter of the novel presents *in medias res* the milieu of living death in which Renée has existed for some time. Although she is not a blood member of the Rougon-Macquart family, Zola at the outset of this second novel of the series continues his practice of the naturalist method that he established in his preface to *La Fortune des Rougon*, which we saw above and which is to answer 'la double question des tempéraments et des milieux' [the double question of temperaments and milieus] to show the 'mathematical' progression of the determinism of heredity, both physical and social, and the influence of the environment on human beings (RM, I, 3). Although Renée's physical heredity plays a rather minor role in the novel, the physical and social influence of her environment is crucial to the construction of her character.[59] Near the end of the novel, Zola makes clear, through Renée's free indirect discourse, that it is the milieu of Second Empire Paris that has contaminated her with symbolic poison and has shaped her into what she has become. He uses the image of sap, which Renée, compared to a flower by the emperor, absorbs from the infected carpets of monied Paris, an infection that creates monstrous growths in her.[60] In the scene in which she recognizes that she is the living dead, she looks back on her formation by the Parisian milieu:

> Elle assistait à son long effarement, à ce tapage de l'or et de la chair qui était monté en elle [...]. C'était comme une sève mauvaise; elle lui avait lassé les membres, mis au cœur des excroissances de honteuses tendresses, fait pousser au cerveau des caprices de malade et de bête. Cette sève, la plante de ses pieds l'avait prise sur le tapis de sa calèche, sur d'autres tapis encore, sur toute cette soie et tout ce velours, où elle marchait depuis son mariage. Les pas des autres devaient avoir laissé là ces germes de poison, éclos à cette heure dans son sang, et que ses veines charriaient. (RM, I, 573)

> [She witnessed her long stupor, and that loud din of gold and flesh that had risen up through her [...]. It was like a bad sap; it had fatigued her limbs, had placed growths of shameful affections in her heart, had made sick and beastly caprices grow in her brain. That sap, the bottoms of her feet had got it from the rug of her carriage, from other rugs as well, from all that silk and all that velvet, where she had been walking since her marriage. The steps of others must have left those seeds of poison there, blossomed at this time in her blood, and that her veins carried.]

Like the trees and flowers nourished by cadavers buried in the Saint-Mittre cemetery ground in *La Fortune des Rougon*, the flower, Renée, becomes infected by the poison in the ground of her environment.[61] It is this social milieu and its transformation of her that turns her into the living dead.

Autumn is the season of the opening scene of the novel, a season that traditionally symbolizes the marginal state between summer and winter as in Balzac's *Adieu*, and here again, significantly, between life and death, as the first chapter lays the groundwork for the more symbolic marginal state of living death that develops throughout the novel.[62] Sunset is the time of day, also significant as a liminal state between day and night, symbolically life and death. The first sentence describes how the noisy, moving carriages parading around the Bois de Boulogne have suddenly stopped, which Zola links to the immobile stillness and silence of death: 'Au loin, les voix confuses du Bois se mouraient' [In the distance, the confused voices of the Bois were dying] (p. 320). Just as in *La Fortune des Rougon*, which begins with the living dead of the cemetery, this second novel begins with the scene of a more symbolic moment between life and death, where sounds are neither alive nor dead, slowly fading, in the process of dying.

As Renée later continues moving through the park in her carriage and it becomes dark, the Bois are slowly enveloped in a 'linceul' [death shroud] in which 'tout allait en se mourant' [everything went on while dying] (p. 326). Zola makes clear that this deathly physical milieu of the park invades Renée, as the text here sets up the structure of her symbolic invasion by the social forces of her living-dead society that we saw above: 'Elle était mollement envahie par l'ombre du crépuscule; tout ce que cette ombre contenait d'indécise tristesse, de discrète volupté, d'espoir inavouée, la pénétrait, la baignait dans une sorte d'air alangui et morbide' [She was gently invaded by the shadows of dusk; all that this shadow contained of faint sadness, of discrete voluptuousness, of unadmitted hope, penetrated her, bathed her in a kind of languid and morbid atmosphere] (p. 328).

The view of this living-dead nature, once the carriage has stopped in silence (so different from the Bois during the day, which is a 'nature si artistement mondaine' [nature so artfully social] and a place of movement and noise), generates in Renée an unusual reflection on her life and an odd dissatisfaction, even as she is completely sated in her life of pleasure (p. 326). Just as she reflects on her life in the mirror scene near the end of the novel, here she examines her life and also sees death: she describes to Maxime how her boring routine is 'mortel [...]. C'est à mourir' [mortal [...]. It is deadly] (p. 327). She knows that her empty days seem to be 'killing' her, and as she looks at the horizon that opens up to the empty space of large lawns and green expanses of the Bois, it seems as if this open space makes her feel the emptiness of her existence (p. 324). The oft-noted, artificial nature of the newly constructed Bois de Boulogne presents the mirror image of her own empty life, a series of lovers, shopping trips, parties, and dinners, vacant and repetitious, always the same (p. 327).[63] She wants something else that happens to no one else (p. 327). She seems to be aiming for some kind of defining element for her life that would make of her a unique individual, different from the repetitions that surround her, and that might have some authentic value. The living death of the park makes her see the living death of her existence and spurs her desire for something else.

We learn later that her youth was spent in a different environment of living death, her father's mansion, the hôtel Béraud du Châtel. This mansion belongs to the world of the past: it is called twice a 'dead house' (pp. 400, 401) and is situated in a part of the city that resembles a 'dead city' (p. 399). Renée's father is the last of a wealthy bourgeois family of long lineage, however his family name will die out with him (he has two daughters). The mansion, like the Raquin shop (and the Vieil Elbeuf of *Au Bonheur des Dames*, as we shall see below), is at the end of a line and is itself deathly, old, dark, and damp.[64]

Renée's move after her marriage, a change in location that replaces her father's deathly mansion with her gaudy Second Empire apartment, and later her ostentatious mansion, follows the path of changes made in Haussmann's Paris, where old neighbourhoods were replaced with Haussmann's signature modernity. Thus, not only is Renée's transformation caused by the 'sap' of Paris; it also itself parallels and allegorizes changes in the city. And both city and woman begin a new phase of their existence by enduring dispossession and destruction; Saccard's plans take on symbolic importance, as he 'expropriates' Renée of her assets before he can profit from the expropriations of property in Paris: 'il fallait que Renée fût dépouillée avant que l'expropriation prochaine s'ébruitât' [Renée had to be robbed before the next expropriation became public] (p. 518). As expropriations change the nature of Paris, various dispossessions, as we shall see, take away Renée's self, and she is left to subsist in that living dead state.

The first dispossession for Paris (and France) is the takeover by the emperor, a kind of 'prise de possession', to which Zola refers by describing the city where the blood of December had barely been washed away (p. 367). The infamous scene in which Saccard describes to his first wife, Angèle, the swaths to be cut through the old neighbourhoods of Paris, emphasizes the violence of the transformations that Saccard foresees and that later take place. He describes how parts of Paris will die in slow agony as it is savagely but symbolically cut by his hand (one thinks of Jacques Lantier's violent hand), which represents the workers' hands that will physically cut down buildings in the future: 'Les tronçons agoniseront dans le plâtre [...] une entaille là, une entaille plus loin, des entailles partout' [These sections will die in plaster [...] a gash there, another gash farther on, gashes everywhere] (p. 389). Saccard, mirroring the emperor, enacts his own takeover, here of Paris when he arrives the first day from the provinces and walks down its streets: 'Ce fut une vraie prise de possession' [It was a veritable taking of possession] (p. 359).

Renée's life from the start is, in fact, plagued by a series of losses and dispossessions, first when she loses her mother, and second, after that loss, when she is sent away to the convent. Zola specifies the importance of her separation from her home, a kind of dispossession of her early, staid upbringing, embodied in her principled father. The narrator states that if Renée had remained at home in her staunchly bourgeois home, she doubtless would not have become what she is (p. 421).[65] Instead, somewhat similar to the convent education of Emma Bovary, her schooling provides a freedom that mutes the influence of her family's strict past, and she learns about vice (p. 421).

Renée's third dispossession has to do with an odd scene involving a dress that she wore as a child. Dresses later in Renée's life become a symbolic representation of the outer, beautiful shell that covers her empty interior, as well as an allegory of her identity, and so this first dress becomes highly significant.[66] Made of grey wool with red squares, it has very long sleeves and a bodice that goes up to her ears, a proper bourgeois dress, thus it covers her body so that a bracelet and necklace must be worn over the cloth. She and her sister are delighted with their new dresses until Renée wears hers at the convent school, where the other girls tease her for her 'robe de Pierrot' [Pierrot dress] (p. 573). Here Zola shows how the power of social conformity robs Renée of her pleasure in her own preferences, when, in order to fit in, she pushes up the sleeves, folds under the neck of the bodice, and wears the jewelry on her bare skin, thus uncovering her body in the first of many such instances.[67]

She remembers this event near the end of the novel in the same scene in which she looks in the mirror and sees that she is dead. Here she realizes that she is not only dead, but also naked, and she reflects on her life, wondering how she got to the point of wearing her current outfit, which essentially shows her nude body. She asks herself if those alterations to her childhood dress (which revealed more of her flesh) formed the first step in her being stripped naked.[68] Nakedness, the removal of one's clothes, here represents in a different way the removal of one's will and preferences, a kind of dispossession and death of the self as one's body is made available to others (and we might add that Zola, in presenting this stripping, also lays bare the nature of Second Empire society). In free indirect discourse, Renée ties her nudity to slavery as she sees that she wears only bracelets (significantly recalling the bracelet of her childhood outfit) around her wrists and ankles like a slave (p. 575). A third, earlier scene in the middle of the novel completes the tale of bracelets, when Renée desires a bracelet worn by a courtesan, and Maxime brings it back for her to wear, thus linking Renée with other women who have sold themselves (p. 432).[69] In the mirror scene when she sees she is like a slave, she realizes that she has abandoned her body, herself, to others, 'par l'abandon de tout son corps, par la mort de son être qui agonisait' [by the abandonment of her whole body, by the death of her being in its death throes] (p. 575).[70] Thus this explains how she sees that she is now 'dead'.

The most important dispossession, however, is the early rape of Renée, a violent 'prise de possession' analogous to the takeover of Paris.[71] The man who raped her possessed her body, in a sense dispossessed her of it, and then after that her body becomes a kind of commodity, exchanged on the marriage market, where Saccard sells himself to marry her and get her money (p. 334).[72] She despises herself for the rape and this causes her to give herself up, to abandon (once again the same word, which can have several meanings here) her very self: 'ce viol brutal [...] fut pour beaucoup dans *l'abandon* de toute sa vie' [this brutal rape [...] was a large factor in her abandonment of her whole life] (p. 421, my emphasis). The rape is thus the major cause of her dispossession and her abandonment to the values of Second Empire society. We thus see that both Paris and Renée were 'up for grabs' after a hostile takeover: a coup d'état and a rape. And thus the metaphor of 'la curée': Renée and Paris are the leftovers of that violence and are possessed by Saccard, 'a hunter', in his search for wealth (p. 518). The dress worn by Renée, which is embroidered with a hunting scene, acts as a *mise-en-abyme* of Renée's 'death': after she is hunted and possessed by Saccard, her beautiful dresses cover the growing void in her being as she immerses herself in the poisoned, materialistic, and empty life of her social circle. Her poisoning by her society, the cause of her living death, is aptly figured by her consumption of a toxic plant in her hothouse, the hothouse itself a symbol of the artifice and excess of the social order.[73]

Renée's exchange in the marriage market and Saccard's selling of himself exemplify Zola's depiction of a society where money reigns (and 'rains' in Saccard's slashing scene) and all is for sale.[74] This common theme in the nineteenth century has been well documented in Zola, in Balzac as we have seen, and in the works of many other authors. A few pertinent examples from *La Curée* will suffice: Renée herself reflects that certain women in Second Empire Paris were 'cotées dans le beau monde comme des valeurs à la Bourse' [rated in high-society like investments in the Market] (p. 510). The family group in this context evolves into a company that shares benefits (p. 426); for Saccard, money is preferable to love (p. 429).

This social environment that bases the highest value in money brings with it a kind of change in consciousness for Renée in this text, in fact a slow death of consciousness and reason. First, this transformation relates broadly to what Zola calls the 'folie', both madness and folly, of both Renée and Second Empire society. 'Cette folle de Renée' [this crazy Renée] (p. 421) has been thrown into the whirlwind of high-society life, and, as a consequence, her 'pauvre tête se détraquait un peu plus tous les jours' [her poor mind became a bit more unhinged every day] (p. 334). The city of Paris is also 'folle', and *détraquée* [unhinged or faulty] (this latter word has similar significance in *La Bête humaine*): 'on sentait le détraquement cérébral, le cauchemar doré et voluptueux d'une ville folle de son or et de sa chair' [one sensed the cerebral unhinging, the golden and voluptuous nightmare of a city crazy about its gold and its flesh] (p. 435).

More important, as a part of her madness, Renée experiences the loss of the ability to comprehend what goes on around her, an inability to think and make proper sense of her surroundings, a death of understanding. This can take the form of an inability to concentrate, to think deeply, as her head, spinning, cannot stay long on one subject (p. 405). Renée also has trouble seeing, both literally and figuratively. She has poor eyesight, as many have noted (p. 319). Her myopia then figures her inability to see what is really before her eyes, to make proper sense of reality.[75] Zola presents this in a curious way when Renée meets the emperor. At first she observes unattractive qualities in him, but then they do not affect her opinion because his repellent qualities become attractive to her:

> Renée, reprise par l'émotion, distinguait mal [...]. Elle le trouva petit, les jambes trop courtes, les reins flottants; mais elle était ravie, et elle le voyait beau, avec son visage blême, sa paupière lourde et plombée qui retombait sur son œil mort. Sous ses moustaches, sa bouche s'ouvrait mollement; tandis que son nez seul restait osseux dans toute sa face dissoute. (*RM*, I, 439)

> [Renée, taken again by her emotion, could not make out what she was seeing [...]. She found him small, his legs too short, his lower back flaccid; but she was thrilled, and she saw him as handsome, with his pallid face, his heavy, leaden eyelids that closed over his dead eye. Under his moustache, his mouth opened slackly; while his nose alone remained bony in the whole of his sagging face.]

We read a list of disagreeable adjectives, but we learn that she views him as handsome: she doesn't actually see the reality that the narrator describes for us. Zola calls the appearance of the emperor in two different places in the novel an 'apparition', a word that means simply 'appearance', but also a spectre or a ghost. The ghostly nature of his apparition could be thought of as the way Renée sees a phantom handsomeness that is not really there. She lives in a phantasmagorical world of ghostly presences, where false appearance supersedes reality.[76]

This altered perception of the real appears in images of intoxication as well (a metaphor used for shopping as addiction in *Au Bonheur des Dames*, as we shall see). Renée is both drunk and crazy: 'grisée, folle' (p. 399). Saccard predicts that this same sinking into drunken madness will happen to the city: 'Mais ce sera la folie pure, le galop infernal des millions, Paris soûlé et assommé!' ['But this will be pure madness, the infernal gallop of millions, Paris drunk and dazed!] (pp. 389–90). The literal and figurative drunkenness of this life of consumption of wines, food, and clothing, kills, drowns Renée's bourgeois conscience, even though that conscience continues to haunt her periodically (p. 347). The intoxication of the streets of Paris (the environment) enters and permeates the restaurant where Renée and Maxime make love for the first time, and it calls Renée to both pleasure and to sleep, to unconsciousness: 'Une ivresse, une langueur montaient des profondeurs plus vagues du boulevard. Dans le ronflement affaibli des voitures, dans l'effacement des clartés vives, il y avait un appel caressant à la volupté et au sommeil' [An intoxication, a languor rose from the vaguer depths of the boulevard. In the diminished rumble of the vehicles, in the disappearance of the sharp brightness, there was a caressing call to pleasure and to sleep] (p. 454).

The loss of the capacity to think appears in several other contexts, the first being that of the effects of the strange, almost mesmeric strategies of Saccard. He has the ability to stun or daze his interlocutors when he speaks about his money in such a way that they cannot see clearly what he means: 'Il avait une façon d'énumérer ses richesses qui étourdissait les auditeurs et les empêchait de voir bien clair' [He had a way of enumerating his riches that stunned his listeners and kept them from seeing very clearly] (p. 436). He also distracts Renée and others from paying attention to what he is saying when he uses a poker to build up and tear down the logs that are burning in the fireplace:

> Quand il arrivait à un chiffre, à une phrase difficile à prononcer, il produisait quelque éboulement qu'il réparait ensuite laborieusement, rapprochant les bûches, ramassant et entassant les petits éclats de bois [...]. Sa voix s'assourdissait, on s'impatientait, on s'intéressait à ses savantes constructions de charbons ardents, on ne l'écoutait plus, et généralement on sortait de chez lui battu et content. (*RM*, I, 461)

> [When he arrived at a number, at a difficult sentence to say, he produced some kind of collapse that he then laboriously repaired, bringing the logs closer together, collecting and piling up the small splinters of wood [...]. His voice grew muffled, people became impatient, they became interested in his skillful construction of burning coals, they no longer listened, and generally they left his place defeated and content.]

This artificial performance of razing and constructing is a kind of *mise-en-abyme* of real construction projects.[77] In Renée's case, he begins by building a hill in the fireplace, letting it collapse, and then rebuilding it, making her forget the financial problems she wanted to discuss: 'Ce jeu commençait à brouiller les idées de la jeune femme. Elle suivait malgré elle le travail de son mari [...] [o]ubliant Worms, le mémoire, le manque d'argent' [This game began to muddle the ideas of the young woman. Despite herself, she followed the work of her husband [...] forgetting Worms, the bill, the lack of money] (p. 469). Through his artificial performance of construction and using his intense calculations (which Zola calls a veritable phantasmagoria of calculations, p. 464), he, in a sense, hypnotizes people, lulls them into a state of happy confusion that keeps them from seeing what he is really saying and doing, just as they cannot see through the 'façade dorée d'un capital absent' [golden façade of absent capital] (p. 463). Renée's inability to get past the surface artifice represents again the death of reality for her. She accepts the phantasmagoria of Saccard's empty calculations; and the fictitious world in which she now lives is an artificial, ghostly presence that has no solidity, just like the ghosts that were the optical illusions of theatrical phantasmagorias.

Renée actively seeks this mesmerized state of half-sleep during hard times, having a blazing fire built for her that makes her drowsy (p. 470). In her superheated room, her woes become a light dream and she is freed of consciousness, again that idea of the intermittent death of consciousness: the 'terrible feu [...] lui ôtait, par instants, la conscience de son être' [terrible fire [...] took away, from time to time, the consciousness of her being] (p. 186). Her memories combine with the fire to create a strange nightmare, a bad dream of waking sleep, in which Maxime becomes a 'jouissance enflammée' [flaming pleasure] (p. 186). She has lost the ability to tell reality from dream when she thinks that Sidonie, who is really there, is a manifestation of her own reveries and thoughts (p. 473). Finally, when she is later with Maxime in reality, she sees the Maxime of her burning dreams (p. 480). Zola makes clear that Renée knows she is living in a dream early in the novel, in a kind of presentiment, in a passage written in free indirect discourse: 'Et, quelque matin, elle s'éveillerait du rêve de jouissance qu'elle faisait depuis dix ans' [And one morning, she would awaken from the dream of pleasure that she had been having for ten years] (p. 334). The waking dream of her false consciousness is another kind of living death.[78]

This artificial, dreamed reality results from Renée's own imagination, and here the symbolism of her role as Echo in the *tableaux vivants* takes on great significance. In order to understand this scene, we must first look at a passage that borders on the fantastic or phantasmagoric, in which the plants of the greenhouse take on human characteristics.[79] Through interspersed comments here and there, the narrator shows that the fantastic nature of these plants resides in the imaginations of Renée and Maxime. The narrator states that what they see is a dream, a 'rêve charnel' (p. 487). They experience hallucinations (as do Séverine, Roubaud, Thérèse, and Laurent above), like waking nightmares that put them in a stupor, presumably as a result of the greenhouse atmosphere, described in the recurrent image of sap that penetrates them (p. 487).

It is in the description of this dream shared by Renée and Maxime that Zola uses the word 'echo'. The sensual and human sounds that they think they hear coming from the plants are the echo of the sounds that they themselves make: 'des murmures, des chuchotements leur venaient des massifs, voix pâmées, soupirs d'extase, cris étouffés de douleur, rires lointains, tout ce que leurs propres baisers avaient de bavard, et que l'écho leur renvoyait' [murmurs, whisperings came to them from the flowerbeds, swooning voices, sighs of ecstasy, muffled cries of pain, distant laughter, all that their own kisses had of noisiness and that the echo sent back to them] (p. 487). What they experience as coming from reality is merely their own invention of what they think is the real.

Zola's representation of a dream or illusion shared by these two people in the contaminating atmosphere of the greenhouse suggests the communal determination by the milieu, so that it is not simply the sole individual who is shaped by lived circumstances in a social space. Rather, entire segments of a population — these two people or Second Empire upper-class society — can share traits because of their formation determined by the communal milieu. The text sets up the equation of Renée in the greenhouse with the city of Paris itself through Saccard's desire to put Paris under glass and make of it a greenhouse.[80] One might think of this as similar to Pierre Bourdieu's idea of the shared characteristics of social and economic class that he analyzes in *Les Règles de l'art*.[81] In addition, particularly given Zola's emphasis on the dreamlike state of Renée, this communal effect of the shared milieu on a group relates to Benjamin's notion of the 'dreaming collective', a social formation of collective illusions structured not by physical heredity, but by history.[82] This would be part of what Benjamin viewed as the phantasmagoric nature of Paris at this time. One of the constructions that he mentions as a 'dream house of the collective', like the phantasmagorical arcades and panoramas, is a winter garden, similar to a conservatory, where Renée and Maxime live in their dream.[83] Zola thus shows how modern society itself, as social habitus, creates the living death of this phantasmagorical state.

We saw above how one of Renée's dresses, embroidered with a hunting scene, represents her identity: she is part of the leftovers, the 'curée', that Saccard snatches up in the hunt for riches. And, since her identity is inscribed on her dress, the artificial surface that covers her body, this also represents that she has no inner life, no other identity: she is, in a sense, denuded of her interior, as all that is left is her identity as surface glamour and as body available to others.[84] Another aspect of her finally being able to see that she is naked, analyzed above, is that she understands now that she is a kind of slave. A pillar used to prop up the brilliance of the emperor (*RM*, I, 475), she finally realizes at the end of the novel that she has become a possession, an object, used to display the glory of the Empire. In free indirect discourse, she understands, having awoken from her dream state, that she is the surface gold that Saccard fabricated to cover over his iron hand (which we saw above cutting through Paris): 'Elle restait une valeur dans le portefeuille de son mari; [...] il la tordait dans les flammes de sa forge, se servant d'elle, ainsi que d'un métal précieux, pour dorer le fer de ses mains' [She remained an asset in the portfolio of her husband; [...] he twisted her in the flames of his forge, using her, like a precious metal, to gild the iron of his hands] (pp. 574–75).

Maxime, as well, seems to have no interior depth: 'Mais ce qu'il avait de caractéristique, c'était surtout les yeux, deux trous bleus, clairs et souriants, des miroirs de coquettes, derrière lesquels on apercevait tout le vide du cerveau' [However, what he had that was characteristic, was above all his eyes, two blue holes, clear and smiling, coquettes' mirrors, behind which one could see all the emptiness of his brain] (p. 426). Renée herself realizes that she has become artificial and empty, and she compares herself, again in free indirect discourse, to an empty doll (p. 574).[85] However, Renée is still a living doll, an organic human whose inner humanity is dead: 'elle se vit morte'.

This reification of Renée, her loss of humanity, finds its greatest symbol in her private apartment in the mansion, where it becomes impossible to tell which is the organic being and which is the inanimate object. The idea of nudity in this description is significantly what expresses this blurring of borders, as we have seen that nudity itself represents Renée's loss of humanity. Zola drives home this loss of difference between living and inorganic by his repetition of this word 'nue' [naked]:

> Le gris rose de la chambre à coucher s'éclairait ici, devenait un blanc rose, une chair nue. [...] La jeune femme aimait à rester là, jusqu'à midi, presque nue. La tente ronde, elle aussi, était nue. Cette baignoire rose, ces tables et ces cuvettes roses, cette mousseline du plafond et des murs, sous laquelle on croyait voir couler un sang rose, prenaient des rondeurs de chair, des rondeurs d'épaules et de seins; et, selon l'heure de la journée, on eût dit la peau neigeuse d'une enfant ou la peau chaude d'une femme. C'était une grande nudité. (*RM*, I, 479, 480)

> [The greyish pink colour of the bedroom became lighter here, became a whiteish pink, nude flesh. [...] The young woman enjoyed remaining there until noon, almost nude. The round tent, also, was nude. That pink bathtub, those pink tables and basins, that chiffon on the ceiling and the walls, under which one thought one could see pink blood flowing, took on the curves of flesh, the curves of shoulders and breasts; and, depending on the hour of the day, one might have said the snowy skin of a child or the warm skin of a woman. It was a grand nudity.]

If Renée's dresses symbolize her identity, her nude skin here becomes indistinguishable from the cloth that surrounds her.[86] Organic and inorganic have combined into a living dead state.

In Renée's apartment, her dressing room resembles a 'tente de féerie' [a fairy tent] (p. 478), a *féerie* being both the marvels associated with fairies as well as, more important for us here, a type of popular theatre during the nineteenth century that used extensive mechanical props in a fantasy genre. Under this dressing room 'tent' as theatre backstage, Renée, like an actress, dons the elaborate dresses and costumes that become her identity. This image of the *féerie* links this scene describing Renée's private chambers together with two other important scenes in the novel, which not only contain images of living death, but also share some remarkable similarities. The first of these additional scenes occurs in the restaurant where Renée and Maxime make love (and in the street in front of it), and the second is the scene of the *tableaux vivants*, in which Renée plays the role of Echo.[87] Both scenes involve spectacles of different kinds, in which women's bodies, including Renée's, are offered up for viewing, and both scenes are linked to the *féerie*.

When Renée and Maxime arrive at the restaurant, she feels a thrill as she steps down from her carriage onto the Paris pavement, which, as we saw above, forms her. On the pavement with Renée, prostitutes pass by: 'Ce large trottoir que balayaient les robes des filles, [...] qu'elle sentait sous ses pieds lui chauffait les talons, lui donnait, à fleur de peau, un délicieux frisson' [The wide pavement, swept by the prostitute's dresses, [...] which she felt under her feet, warmed her heels, gave her, on the surface of her skin, a delicious quiver] (pp. 446–47). The prostitutes, a mass of humans for sale, belong to a crucial scene of Benjamin's modernity: here crowds of them walk through the artificial street lighting in 'une pluie de rayons' [a shower of rays of light] (p. 449), part of the larger crowd walking past colourfully lit advertising kiosks and shop fronts.

When Renée looks out the window of the private room at the restaurant (a room whose door locks and that is used for sexual purposes), she sees groups of prostitutes walking by. She then spies another prostitute seated at a cafe who watches the prostitutes who are passing by. Renée watches this one woman, who watches the others, and in this passage, the phrase 'la jeune femme' is used. All becomes a bit ambiguous because Renée and the prostitute are both 'jeunes femmes', and one tends to confuse Renée with this prostitute; it almost seems as though the young woman is walking with the group even though she is merely watching them:

> Celles qui marchaient se perdaient lentement au milieu de la foule, et la jeune femme, qu'elles intéressaient, les suivait du regard, allait d'un bout du boulevard à l'autre, dans les lointains tumultueux et confus de l'avenue, pleins du grouillement noir des promeneurs. (*RM*, I, 450)[88]

> [Those who walked disappeared slowly into the crowd, and the young woman, whom they interested, followed them with her gaze, went from one end of the boulevard to the other, in the tumultuous and indistinct avenue, full of the black bustling of the strollers]

These details — the influence of the street, the streetwalkers, the ambiguity between two young women and their gazes — mix and associate Renée with these prostitutes and with prostitution in general, an association already suggested above in the exchange of Renée in the marriage market and in her transformation into a living dead object of value.

Several other telling details strengthen this association. If the prostitutes are objects of the gaze, so is Renée. On the next page, Renée realizes that she is being watched by men in the omnibus as it passes by (p. 451). Furthermore, in this long scene, Zola clothes Renée and the prostitute she watches in articles of the same colour. The blue of the prostitute's dress is mentioned twice: once in the quotation above when Renée notices her before she and Maxime make love, then again after as Renée looks out the window (p. 458). As for Renée, she wears nothing in her hair but a blue ribbon (p. 443), which is mentioned a second time when she and Maxime enter the private room at the restaurant; here the narrator notes that the blue ribbon remains in its 'proper' place even though Renée's hair is a bit dishevelled from the trip (p. 448). The final mention of the blue ribbon occurs just two sentences after Renée sees the blue dress of the prostitute the second time, and because this is just after Renée and Maxime make love, it metonymically links the two female perpetrators of illicit sex. The connection becomes even clearer here because the ribbon now is significantly not in its 'proper' place when the waiter finds it mussed in the corner of the divan (p. 458).[89] Her connection to prostitution becomes clear to her as well when, after the waiter asks her if she needs 'the comb', she understands that it is the same comb used by the courtesans whose names have been scratched into the mirror (the name 'Renée' is oddly carved there, too), and she now finds herself in the same room and in a similar situation as those women. We recall as well the courtesan's bracelet that Maxime brings to her at her request. One final detail cements the association: Renée has 'un air fille' [the look of a prostitute] (p. 451).

As Renée is also a 'grande poupée' [big doll] (p. 574), a human object emptied of her humanity; so too, the prostitutes and others walking below in the crowd are 'de petites poupées mécaniques' [little mechanical dolls] (p. 450).[90] Just as the prostitutes rely on their loud dresses (p. 450), Renée depends on her infamous dresses, on surface fashion that draws the eye to her body on display. From her interest in the pictures of courtesans and actresses, through her incognito attendance at one of their parties, to her identification with prostitutes in this scene, Zola emphasizes her status as figurative commodity and again makes of her one of those who are both alive (human) and dead (an object). Significantly, as she succumbs to Maxime in this restaurant scene, Zola describes her laughing voice — the human voice often used symbolically as the way to express one's humanity, and here as she feebly resists the incestuous act — as 'mourant', as weakening with the suggestion of dying (like the noises in the park at the beginning of the novel): 'elle dit avec son rire embarrassé et mourant: "Voyons, laissez-moi... Tu me fais mal". Ce fut le seul murmure de ses lèvres' [she said with her embarrassed and dying laugh: 'Come on, leave me alone... You are hurting me'. It was the only murmur from her lips] (p. 456). The prostitute's ambiguous status as human and commodity, which like fashion (loud dresses and Renée's fashions) 'couples the living body to the inorganic world', here shows how, in Benjamin's vision of Baudelaire's Second Empire city, 'the image of woman and the image of death intermingle in a third: that of Paris'.[91]

As mentioned above, this scene that highlights the spectacle of the crowd and prostitution also presents the city as *féerie* when Zola describes the activity of the street as a 'tohu-bohu féerique' [hurly-burly *féerique*] (p. 450), complete with the lighting of a 'rayon électrique' [electric beam of light] (p. 453) and music (when Renée calls the street noise an orchestra) (p. 451).[92] The prostitutes, who move down the street past shop windows alternately light and dark, seem like ghostly apparitions as well as a group of marionettes in a *féerie*: 'Les filles surtout, avec la traîne de leur robe, tour à tour crûment éclairées et noyées dans l'ombre, prenaient un air d'apparition, de marionnettes blafardes, traversant le rayon électrique de quelque féerie' [The prostitutes above all, with the train of their dress, in turn crudely illuminated and drowned in shadow, took on the air of an apparition, of pallid puppets, crossing the electric beam of some *féerie*] (p. 453.)[93] The prostitutes and Renée, through Zola's equation of them, are the living dead, whether ghostly apparitions or mechanical puppets, who inhabit the spectacular city in this electric and phantasmagorical *féerie* of modernity.[94]

So too the *tableaux vivants*, a kind of nineteenth-century 'mannequin challenge' with music and, in this case, an accompanying story, are associated with the objectification of women and the *féerie*. As with the prostitutes in the street, the women in the *tableaux* offer up their perfections for public view (p. 545). Here, however, their bodies seem more exposed, almost naked, echoing the symbolism of nakedness as reification. As the materials of Renée's bedroom seem to animate the immaterial, here the 'living' cloth, with which the costumes of the women are made, seems to be human flesh:

> Toutes ces étoffes légères et transparentes se fondaient si bien avec les épaules et les maillots, que ces blancheurs rosées vivaient, et qu'on ne savait plus si ces dames n'avaient pas poussé la vérité plastique jusqu'à se mettre toutes nues. (*RM*, I, 544).[95]
>
> [All of these light and transparent fabrics blended so well with the shoulders and the tights, that this pinkish whiteness lived, and one no longer knew if these women had not pushed physical truth to the point of their being completely nude.]

As women become more like objects, objects (fabrics) take on life. And the spectators of the play, invaded by its sensuality, seem almost to be the crowd mixed with the prostitutes in the street, where love is offered and accepted, 'amours offertes et acceptées d'un coup d'œil' [love offered and accepted with a glance] (p. 545).

The *féerie*-like aspect of the street scene also stands out in the *tableaux vivants*, and both belong to popular theatrical genres of the time, which Colette Becker calls a spectacle for the eyes.[96] Zola uses possible allusions to the *féerie* twice in this *tableaux* scene, first in adjectival form to describe the spectacular effects of the precious metals and stones on the stage as 'les efflorescences féeriques de cette grotte' [the *féerique* efflorescence of this grotto] (p. 548). The second usage describes Venus as resembling a fairy in an apotheosis scene, a typically spectacular ending of the *féeries* (p. 553). As in the street scene, where the prostitutes walk through electric light, the electric ray illuminates the stage set here (p. 548).[97] Finally, music fills out the *féerie*-like production. This parallelism of the two scenes brings out the collective nature of the illusion lived by this society by its linking of the high society 'crowd' with the crowd on the street, both of which are closely linked to the reification of consumer society, most particularly the reification of women.[98]

Finally, if the restaurant scene represents Renée's living death through reification, the *tableaux* scene stages this living death.[99] As Echo, she is transformed from a human to an inanimate sound, with no voice of her own, both literally (the actors do not speak) and figuratively through Echo's forced repetition of the codes of others. This metamorphosis acts as a kind of allegory of her transformation by her social milieu and by reification. Her contradictory state is frozen in time in this tableau (which lasts about five minutes, p. 542) at the moment between life and death, the moment of living death that is Renée's life: 'la nymphe Echo se mourait aussi [...]; elle se trouvait peu à peu prise dans la raideur du sol, elle sentait ses membres brûlants se glacer et se durcir' [The nymph Echo was dying also [...]; she found herself gripped by the rigidity of the ground, she felt her burning limbs chill and harden] (p. 553). Driving home her deathlike being, one of the guests claims, 'Madame Saccard, on dirait une morte' [Madame Saccard looks like a dead woman] (p. 553). Still as a statue, there is nothing left alive in Renée but her eyes, and one imagines here the reverse of Pygmalion: 'elle se renversait, n'ayant plus de vivant, dans son corps figé de statue, que ses yeux de femme' [she was leaning back, having nothing left living, in her body fixed like a statue, but her woman's eyes] (p. 553). This artificial tableau aptly represents and presents Renée's transformation into a living, artificial object, the statue.[100]

Renée of course does awaken from her illusion in the mirror scene where she sees that she is naked. She grasps that the distinction she had been seeking by her incestuous crime is actually meaningless. In her social milieu, Renée's incest, which goes against the social law common to different human societies according to Lévi-Strauss, is simply not viewed as being a crime. She realizes this as Saccard, after learning of her affair with his son, walks out with Maxime arm and arm, while holding in his hand the financial document signed by Renée. Her name, her signature as her identity, has meaning only as a financial instrument, and that is the only law that exists in Zola's representation of Second Empire society.[101]

Renée's youthful formation in her father's rule-bound but dying world returns to haunt her periodically during the novel and is what enables her to see both that dying world and the new world of Saccard. The final scene of the novel shows her trying to escape Saccard's world as she returns to her playroom in her father's home and looks at the city and at her dolls which, like her, have lost their inner being. What follows is not symbolic but real death, her death. Zola here closes off the possibility of redemption in the world of the Second Empire.[102]

He does, however, show the mortal future of that society, represented by Maxime and his future wife Louise. Maxime combines the bad hereditary traits of both his parents and symbolizes his rotting society as well as his dying family line: 'les défauts des parents se complétaient et s'empiraient. Cette famille vivait trop vite; elle se mourait déjà dans cette créature frêle [...], hermaphrodite étrange venu à son heure dans une société qui pourrissaient' [the flaws of his parents completed each other and worsened. This family lived too quickly; it was dying already in this frail creature [...], strange hermaphrodite who came at the right time in a society that was rotting] (p. 425). We learn in *Le Docteur Pascal* that Maxime, not many years later, suffers from ataxia, is relegated to an armchair in a kind of living death, similar to his ancestor Dide, and dies young.[103]

Also, as we saw above, Maxime's son Charles, who is Dide re-embodied because of their uncanny resemblance, represents both literally and symbolically the degradation of this blood-line, 'l'usure de la race' (*RM*, v, 975), when Charles bleeds to death in front of Dide (an emptying out of blood curiously similar to the symbolic emptying of Renée and her doll). Humanity has died in Charles who is animal-like, nothing but a vicious little dog with no brain, no heart (p. 965). Zola describes his beauty as that of a dead person, repeating the image we saw above: he has a 'beauté de mort' (p. 975), and 'sa beauté inquiétante avait une ombre de mort' [his disturbing beauty had a touch of death] (p. 965). Charles resides at the Tulettes asylum with Dide, who is now paralyzed, and as Charles dies, Dide watches him with her own eyes that live in a dead body (p. 973). Charles looks back eerily with living eyes in a dead body: 'Toute la face de cire était morte déjà, lorsque les yeux vivaient encore' [his whole waxen face was dead already, as his eyes still lived] (p. 1104). Dide wakes at this moment of Charles's death one final time: as her mental life returns, she is described as a ghost, as we saw above, 'un spectre de l'épouvante et de la douleur' [a spectre of terror and suffering] (p. 1105), witness to the death of her offspring.

Finally, it is Maxime's wife, Louise, who perhaps symbolizes most completely Zola's representation of living death in the *Rougon-Macquart* series by embodying several of its characteristics. As noted above, she is in part her dead mother and relives that past life, 'dans cette seconde vie qu'elle revivait' [in this second life that she was reliving] (p. 434). Hence, Louise and Maxime, the next generation, are completely at home enjoying the *curée* of this living dead, Second Empire society, as seen when they enjoy the *leftovers* of their parents' dinner, where Zola uses a symbolic vocabulary of decadent gluttony, pillage, dirt, and destruction:

> Au milieu des dressoirs pillés, des bouteilles et des assiettes qui traînaient, Maxime et Louise soupaient tranquillement, à un bout de la table, côte à côte, sur une serviette qu'ils avaient étalée. Ils paraissaient à l'aise, ils riaient, dans ce désordre, ces verres sales, ces plats tachés de graisse, ces débris encore tièdes de la gloutonnerie des soupeurs en gants blancs. Ils s'étaient contentés d'épousseter les miettes autour d'eux. (*RM*, v, 565)
>
> [In the midst of the pillaged sideboards, the bottles and plates that remained, Maxime and Louise supped tranquilly, at one end of the table, side by side, on a napkin that they had spread out. They seemed at ease, they were laughing, in this disorder, these dirty glasses, these plates spotted with grease, these leftovers still warm from the gluttony of the diners in white gloves. They were content to sweep up the crumbs around them.]

As the Second Empire is dissolved later, so the family line of Maxime and Louise has no future, when Louise dies during their honeymoon.

'Au Bonheur des Dames': The Living Death of Shopping

If in *Thérèse Raquin*, the moribund milieu of the shop corresponds to the living death of the people who live there, in *Au Bonheur des Dames*, human space actively transforms those who live, work, or shop there into the living dead. As so many have noted, in this novel the blurring of borders between human beings and artificial products figures the increasingly commercial, artificial, and mechanical life of the modern world, represented by the happenings in the giant department store and the destruction in its surrounding area. Although much has been written on these topics in this Zola novel, I look at them here through the lens of their imbrication in the topos of living death.[104] The reification of modernity, with its concomitant loss of will and humanity, becomes a new type of living death: the dead commerce of the family shop evolves into the demise of human will brought about by the department store as representative of the new consumer society.[105]

Zola begins *Au Bonheur des Dames* with a now iconic description of the city space and its protagonist, Denise, as she arrives in Paris, along with her two brothers, newly embarked from the provinces, as they look for the shop of their uncle, Baudu. Significantly, they move to Paris because her father has just died (their mother is already dead, thus again we have orphans like Silvère and Miette), and this death grounds the beginning of the novel in a significant way (as does the cemetery at the outset of *La Fortune des Rougon*) and paves the way for the signifying power of death in the novel, as the young people leave behind the dead past of their family life and Denise's work in a smaller novelty shop in the provinces to embark on a new kind of dying in the city.[106]

As they reach their uncle's neighbourhood, they stop in their tracks, mesmerized by the huge new department store, Au Bonheur des Dames, and the vast space that it occupies.[107] They remain riveted to the spot, absorbed in contemplation, and do not realize that their uncle's shop is just across the street, and that he is looking at them, without knowing they are his family, and that he is exasperated by their interest in the Bonheur. Denise and her family are literally, physically, in between the old and the new, the old shop and the new, the past and the future, a liminal state fruitfully explored by Rachel Bowlby in *Carried Away: The Invention of Modern Shopping*. Passers-by, as described by Bowlby, are in a state of psychological vagueness as they walk down city streets. They are distracted from this distraction by the spectacle of the store window, which compels them to look, attracts them like a magnet.[108] In Zola, the store retains Denise, takes her over in a sense, and makes her 'oublieuse du reste', 'absorbée' [unmindful of the rest, absorbed], even forgetful of her very purpose in going to Paris.[109] She and her brothers behave 'machinalement [...] ils furent séduits' [mechanically [...] they were seduced] (*RM*, III, 391). Their experience of awe and their almost mesmeric and mechanical state introduce the ability of the new store and modern Paris to inhibit one's will and purpose, a kind of death of the will, our new form of living death in the social programming caused by marketing.

It is not until a few minutes later that they notice Baudu's obscure boutique, a store described as 'cette vieille maison agonisante' [this old, dying shop] (p. 403) — a dying space like that of the Raquin shop. Brightness and life belong to the Bonheur, and all of the negative and dark qualities of Mme Raquin's shop are bestowed on Baudu's place with its old-fashioned name, which even contains the word 'vieil' [old]: Au Vieil Elbeuf. It is low-ceilinged, prison-like, dark, dusty, with 'les ténèbres humides d'une cave' [humid shadows of a cellar] (p. 394).

This shop resembles that of the deathly Raquin shop in another way; in both cases, most of the people who live in these family shops succumb to the same fate in the novels: death. For the daughter of the Baudu family, Geneviève, both heredity and environment contribute to her poor health. She had always been weak, shaped both by her mother's physical character and also by the unwholesome environment, the dankness of the Vieil Elbeuf. When Geneviève is dying, Denise looks at her pitiful face 'où agonisait la dégénérescence dernière d'une longue famille poussée à l'ombre, dans cette cave du vieux commerce parisien' [where was dying in agony the final degeneration of a long family line pushed into the shadows, into this cellar of the old Parisian commerce] (p. 737). Throughout the novel, she dies slowly, existing in a kind of living death, and at the end, Denise sees her as a bodiless, almost ghostly creature, 'si fluette sous les couvertures, qu'on ne sentait même pas la forme et l'existence d'un corps' [so skinny under the covers that one couldn't even make out the form and existence of a body] (p. 737).[110] However, it is not only the moribund shop that causes her death: she dies indirectly because of the new Bonheur, heartbroken when her fiancé leaves her for a clerk at the big department store. The text makes the fault of the Bonheur explicit when the shopkeepers of the other small establishments in the area gather for Geneviève's funeral and partake in a kind of 'manifestation contre le Bonheur des Dames, que l'on accusait de la lente agonie de Geneviève' [demonstration against the Bonheur des Dames, which was being accused of the slow death of Geneviève] (p. 737). The reason for her death reminds one of Miette, in Geneviève's case struck down at a time of commercial and cultural, rather than political, revolution (p. 742).[111]

Zola goes beyond the simple influence of the environment, however, to represent a kind of symbiosis between the shop and its owners (one thinks of Madame Vauquer and her pension in Balzac), particularly in Madame Baudu's case, who was born in her shop and knows that its end will be her own (p. 412). Both her shop and daughter are taken by the Bonheur, described as a monster, just as she herself fades slowly away (p. 742). A kind of physical and inverse balance links her shop and the Bonheur, as it grows in power and activity, the Vieil Elbeuf diminishes (p. 588). And as the Bonheur slowly kills her shop, she too dies, looking out of her window at the department store, by means of which Mouret has 'semé le quartier de ruines, dépouillé les uns, tué les autres' [sown the neighbourhood with ruins, having despoiled some, killed others] (p. 761). Again, the word *semer* expresses the sowing of death throughout the *quartier*, which recalls the way the human bones were sown through Plassans in *La Fortune des Rougon*.

Zola thus turns a building space into an allegory of the transformation to modern capitalist commerce as the old family commerce and retailers exist in a dying state. Mouret himself places the blame on the owners of these old shops, as he claims it is their fault for persisting in a failing enterprise (p. 746). Mouret's business thrives as it gobbles up both Baudu's customers and the commercial space occupied by the other shops in the area: it feeds on their demise as it kills them off and builds on the 'graves' of their shops.[112] As Denise has a nightmare about this destruction, we find again *La Fortune des Rougon*'s metaphor of the dead fertilizing the living, here as manure: 'le petit commerce du quartier Saint-Roch s'en allait sous une pioche invisible [...] et [Denise] avait conscience que cela était bon, qu'il fallait ce fumier de misères à la santé du Paris de demain' [the small businesses of the Saint-Roch quarter disappeared under an invisible pickaxe [...] and Denise was aware that this was good, that this manure of miseries was necessary for the health of tomorrow's Paris] (p. 748). Once again, the dead serve to fertilize new life and, in a sense, become part of it.[113]

The Bonheur is built not only symbolically on the dead 'bodies' of the old shops, it is also literally built with the blood of a woman who died in its construction, Mouret's first wife, Caroline Hédouin, which has been seen as a kind of sacrificial ritual.[114] A relative of Mme Baudu, she inherited the shop from her father when he and her uncle died. She herself then died three years later after she fell while visiting the construction site, and Mme Baudu blames Mouret for her death, as well as for the Baudus' own 'assassination' (p. 408). Thus, the real blood of Caroline bonds with the cement of the foundation of the giant department store, and once again, the dead 'fertilize' the living, the Bonheur: 'le sang [de Caroline] avait scellé les pierres de la maison' [the blood [of Caroline] had sealed up the stone blocks of the store] (p. 442). Denise even imagines seeing bloody mortar in the basement (p. 408). Most important, this dead woman returns in a somewhat fantastical scene: Mouret imagines that Denise is 'channelling' his dead wife's voice when she speaks. Here we have once again the dead, his wife, 'resurrected', coming back in Denise: 'il avait cru entendre sa femme morte prononcer la phrase, une phrase à elle, qu'il reconnaissait. Et c'était comme une résurrection [he had thought he heard his dead wife say that phrase, one of her phrases that he recognized. And it was like a resurrection] (p. 724).[115]

Indeed, Denise thinks that the fear she feels when she looks at the store may be a result of Caroline's blood, which accomplishes a kind of haunting of the building. If Mme Baudu claims that Caroline 'a laissé les os dans les fondations' [had left her bones in the foundations] (p. 408), we perhaps see in those bones a reference to the bones of the Saint Mittre cemetery that shape the foundation of the *Rougon-Macquart* series. Indeed, other real human bones appear in the construction site of the Bonheur when the workers attempt to lay the foundation of the new wing of the store, bones that had in the past been brought there in the dirt from elsewhere (in a sense, they resemble the bones in the wall of Chabert's house): 'On avait eu d'abord de grandes difficultés à établir les sous-sols, car on était tombé sur [...] des terres rapportées, pleines d'ossements humains' [They had at first grave problems laying the basement levels, because they came across [...] fill-soil full of human bones] (p. 596). This commercial revolution founded on these human remains significantly succeeds and thrives.

The main thrust of this novel, however, is not the semi-fantastic living death of the old shops and the return of the dead past in bones, blood, and female ghosts, but rather their fertilization of and transformation into the phantasmagoria created by new forms of selling, what Ross calls 'Zola's phantasmagoric hymn to the marvels of modern commerce'.[116] Baudu actually uses the word 'fantasmagories' to describe and criticize Denise's description of the new developments in modern commerce in evolutionary terms: 'l'évolution logique du commerce, les nécessités des temps modernes, la grandeur de ces nouvelles créations [...] ce sont des fantasmagories' [the logical evolution of commerce, the necessities of modern times, the grandeur of these new creations [...] these are phantasmagorias] (p. 590). Baudu remains anchored in the old system of commerce and cannot understand why customers would want to shop at the Bonheur.

Many have analyzed the reification of the consumer in this novel, however my analysis here takes the particular path of bringing out the ways in which this reification is anchored in the topos of living death. The idea of the living dead and the phantasmagoria, the ghost-producing 'magic lantern' of the large department store, is the consuming experience of shopping that takes away one's humanity, 'consuming' in both its meaning of buying but also in the meaning of being consumed, being overtaken oneself. It is first and foremost the seduction offered by the phantasmagoria of the merchandise displays that lure women, like Denise in the first pages of the novel, who are taken over, 'possessed' by the experience.

In looking at the display of umbrellas (a marvellous scene analyzed by numerous scholars), Madame de Boves is immobilized as she looks up (p. 619); like Denise in the first pages of the novel, she is spellbound. Her friend, Madame Marty, then exclaims, 'C'est féerique!' [It's a fairyland!] (p. 619). The word 'féerique' again suggests the type of popular play that used extravagant stage machinery and sets to create a fantastic, unrealistic illusion on stage.[117] The stage here is the department store, where illusions are created as everyday things take on fantastic qualities. The extremely useful umbrella becomes something other than its use value: it becomes an element in an extravagant display that gives the illusion of Venetian lanterns, garlands that descend the columns of the arcade of the store, stars, and cranes that fly in a purple sky.[118] The reality of the useful umbrella dies, disappears into the phantasmagoria, where surface and spectacle alone matter, but where its ghostly use-value remains in its identifiability as umbrella. The store thus erases mundane matters and provides an artificial fairyland of dreams.[119]

The public is seduced by the awe-inspiring displays, and again, as so many have noted, those seduced are primarily women. Mouret states honestly that his aim is their exploitation (p. 408). And he describes his tactics of seduction, which seek to lure them with his display and, most important for us here, to take over their will, and here Madame Marty, seduced by Mignot, cannot help herself, she has lost her will: 'il l'attaqua plus rudement, en lui mettant sous les yeux les gants brodés: et elle fut sans force, elle en acheta une paire' [he took up the attack more aggressively, by putting before her the embroidered gloves: she had no strength, she bought a pair] (p. 622). Shopping then develops into a kind of intoxicant when alcohol becomes its metaphor (pp. 612, 637, 644), and becomes an illness, the 'névrose' [neurosis] that can develop into the malady of shoplifting in 'les voleuses par manie, une perversion du désir, une névrose nouvelle' [the thieving women who shoplift compulsively, a perversion of desire, a new neurosis] (p. 632). The phantasmagoria produces the living death of the human in the disappearance of will in automatic responses to environmental stimuli: the body continues but the ability to control one's behaviour has died (akin to the experience of Jacques in *La Bête humaine*).

As in *Thérèse Raquin*, physiology dominates, and woman's seduction by these displays, which create a new form of modern desire through their phantasmagorias, is physical: 'Ils avaient éveillé dans sa chair de nouveaux désirs' [They had awakened new desires in her flesh] (p. 461). This desire is explicitly sexual in nature, in a kind of displacement of sex onto shopping. Thus, it is a physical desire that demands to be satisfied, and in one famous scene it appears as a kind of fetishism (also seen in Raphaël's love of cloth in Balzac) as Madame de Boves and her daughter fondle the goods, with fingers trembling and face warmed from the sensual pleasure (p. 493).[120] In the following metaphor, which takes place at the end of a frenzied sale, it almost seems as though the women have indeed indulged in sexual activities, having flung off underwear in their passion: 'les dentelles et la lingerie, dépliées, froissées, jetées au hasard, faisaient songer à un peuple de femmes qui se serait déshabillé là, dans le désordre d'un coup de désir' [the lace and the lingerie, unfolded, crumpled, thrown haphazardly, made one imagine a crowd of women who had undressed there, in the disorder of a fit of desire] (p. 500).[121] Since women go to the department stores for this sexual experience, it makes sense that Bouthemont would call the stores 'brothels of commerce' (p. 681). However, this is an odd kind of reversal of prostitution in which it is the women who buy the merchandise, who pay for 'sex', in a sense.[122]

Madame Marty not only loses her willpower, her 'humanity', in this seduction, but her physical force as well, a loss that is actually pleasurable to her, perhaps symbolizing that the loss of her humanity in her loss of control is part of the pleasure. And it is here where Zola explicitly links this pleasure in succumbing to symbolic death: 'Madame Marty se disait aussi morte de fatigue; et elle n'en jouissait pas moins profondément de cette fatigue, de cette mort lente de ses forces, au milieu de l'inépuisable déballage des marchandises' [Madame Marty claimed she was dead tired; and she took no less profound pleasure in this fatigue, in this slow death of her energy, in the midst of the unending unpacking of merchandise] (p. 636). This fetishistic enjoyment that is linked to dying fits well with another kind of fetishism, the concept of the fetishism of commodities, in which the ghostly presence that haunts the commodity is the loss of the human. Here it takes the different form of the loss of the humanity of the shopper who, seduced, loses willpower and freedom of choice, addicted to her fetishistic desire for the ghostly commodity. Zola shows that these women choose to lose their human will for the illusory pleasure of the commodity fairyland, thus creating a different, more symbolic type of living death. In this combination of the erotic and the mortal, Freud's union of the life instincts with the death instincts seems here exemplified in symbolic form.

The loss of humanity is further represented in the women shoppers by their reification in the text; women become objects like the merchandise.[123] As Baudu notes, clerks treat women shoppers like 'paquets' [packages] (p. 409), a word used numerous times for the store merchandise (and for Madame Raquin). Clerks, too, become things. When Denise is new and inexperienced, she is forced to play the role of a mannequin (p. 496).[124] Later, she is forced to do the same in a client's home.

This reification becomes a kind of symbolic mutilation in several scenes, when humans are reduced to moving body parts. Seen at ground level, potential customers on the pavements outside become shoes and feet walking on their own: 'les pieds des passants [...] filaient vite au ras du trottoir, des pieds coupés aux chevilles, gros souliers, bottes élégantes, fines bottines de femme, un va-et-vient continu de pieds vivants, sans corps et sans tête' [the feet of the passersby [...] dashed along swiftly at the pavement level, feet cut off at the ankles, large clodhoppers, elegant boots, fine women's ankle boots, a continual to-and-fro of living feet, without body or head] (p. 550).[125] This partially present human being fits well with Bowlby's vision of the passerby who is 'neither here nor there', distracted, partially present and absent, ghostlike, or in the following quotation, a headless mannequin in the store window who seems to be running off to a party: 'Le grand manteaux de velours, garni de renard argenté, mettait le profil cambré d'une femme sans tête, qui courait par l'averse à quelque fête' [The large velvet coat, trimmed with silver fox, had the arched profile of a woman without a head, who was running through the downpour to some party] (p. 414).[126] Mirrors, which add to the phantasmagorical spectacle of the merchandise in the store with their artificial reflections and distortions of reality, significantly change and 'cut' the human body into parts, in another kind of dehumanization: 'partout les glaces reculaient les magasins, reflétaient des étalages avec des coins de public, des visages renversés, des moitiés d'épaules et de bras' [everywhere mirrors pushed the stores deeper, reflected the displays including bits of the crowd, upside-down faces, parts of shoulders and arms] (p. 627).[127]

The equation of human with thing becomes even more explicit when the mannequins in the store resemble their mutilated human counterparts, in this well-known passage:

> Les corsets et les tournures occupaient un comptoir [...] dont on avait fait ce jour-là un étalage spécial, une armée de mannequins sans tête et sans jambes, n'alignant que des torses, des gorges de poupée aplaties sous la soie, d'une lubricité troublante d'infirme. (*RM*, III, 780)
>
> [The corsets and bustles took up one counter [...] which was made that day into a special display, an army of headless and legless dummies that aligned only torsos, dolls' bosoms flattened under the silk, with the troubling lubricity of the disabled.][128]

Moreover, merchandise seems more alive than the manipulated humans in the store, as the clothing trembles, breathes, has a soul and a heartbeat in this equally famous passage:

> Et les étoffes vivaient, dans cette passion du trottoir; les dentelles avait un frisson, retombaient et cachaient les profondeurs du magasin, d'un air troublant de mystère; les pièces de drap elles-mêmes, épaisses et carrées, respiraient, soufflaient une haleine tentatrice; tandis que les paletots se cambraient davantage sur les mannequins qui prenaient une âme, et que le grand manteau de velours se gonflait, souple et tiède, comme sur des épaules de chair, avec les battements de la gorge et le frémissement des reins. (*RM*, III, 402)[129]
>
> [The fabrics lived, in this passion of the pavement; the laces shivered, then fell back and hid the depths of the store, with a troubling air of mystery; the swaths of cloth themselves, thick and square, breathed, exhaled a tempting breath; while the jackets bent closer around the dummies who gained a soul, and the grand velvet coat filled out, supple and tepid, as if on shoulders of flesh, with the heartbeat of the chest and the quivering of the loins.]

Customers who carry the Mouret balloons from the store become 'une réclame vivante' [a living advertisement] (p. 613). And perhaps the oddest mixture of the organic and inorganic is the daily take of a million francs that sits on Mouret's desk, 'chaude et vivante' [hot and alive] (p. 800). The department store blends organic and inorganic in its irresistible lure of the crowd into the living death of modern consumer culture, which has become our own culture, and aptly ends our detailed readings of living death in the novels.

In general in Zola's texts, living death can be an unwanted invasion of the past into the present moment, in the form of dead family members or destroyed spaces that seem to return in reality, as in the case of Dide; however there is at the same time a realistic explanation for this incursion. Living death can also take the form of the invasion of a body, taken over by a dead ancestor as Zola explores the effects of heredity, in particular for Jacques Lantier. The invasion can also be that of the modern world that takes over and slowly destroys past forms of socialization and commerce, as these past modes continue to exist in a state of living death, as in *Thérèse Raquin* and *Au Bonheur des Dames*.

Living death can also act as a kind of dispossession. Humans treated as objects are dispossessed of their humanity and survive in a state between human and object, life and death. In a different way, those who are lured into the new addiction of shopping lose their human will, becoming machine-like in their drive to acquire, again having lost their humanity. These novels show how this invasion and dispossession wrought by the modern world entails loss for those who don't succeed there or cannot master the 'rush to the spoil', as the title of Zola's *La Curée* has been translated. Saccard represents the precarious success of the winner, a man with no values other than getting ahold of more and more. Octave Mouret also appears to be primed for that path, however Denise seems to be able to channel some of this drive into good practices, one small flicker of hope in his dark representation of his world in these novels.

Notes to Chapter 3

1. Casimir Delavigne, *Marino Faliero* (newspaper clipping in the *dossier préparatoire* of *La Fortune des Rougon*; BNF/Gallica vue 775, folio 59r).
2. See Nicholas White's excellent analysis of Zola's trees and structure: 'Family Histories and Family Plots', in *The Cambridge Companion to Zola*, ed. by Brian Nelson (Cambridge: Cambridge University Press, 2007), pp. 19–38.
3. Émile Zola, *La Fortune des Rougon*, RM, I, 5–315 (p. 301). All further references are to this edition unless otherwise noted.
4. Henri Mitterand discusses Dide and this metaphor of the pear trees as the 'première image de l'Arbre généalogique': 'Une archéologie mentale: *le roman experimental* et *La Fortune des Rougon*', in *Le Discours du roman* (Paris: PuF, 1980), pp. 164–85 (p. 174). Dide's body is also 'tordu' [twisted] during one of her 'crises', like the tree branches (RM, I, 190)
5. As a number of critics have noted, other characters in Zola are paralyzed but for their eyes: here Dide, also Mme Raquin, and the main character in a novella about a man who was buried alive, *La Mort d'Olivier Bécaille*. This is remarkably similar to Balzac's description of Don Juan's father in 'L'Élixir de longue vie'. See my article 'The Marriage of Don Juan: Balzac and the Inheritance of Culture', *Dix-Neuf*, 11 (October 2008), 49–58, for an analysis of living death in this Balzac text.
6. Auguste Dezalay explores this disorder in his article 'Ordre et désordre dans les Rougon-Macquart: l'exemple de *La Fortune des Rougon*', *Travaux de Linguistique et de Littérature*, 11.2 (1973), 71–81.
7. The words 'cerveau fêlé' mean literally a 'cracked brain', which works as well in English for a person who is unsound in mind; the word *fêlé*, cracked, comes up in many contexts relating to living death, with a number of different connotations, so it is important to note the word here.
8. László Szakács notes that in this novel, 'la plupart des personnages ont la hantise d'être poursuivis par un mort' [the majority of the characters have an obsession with being pursued by a dead person], here it would be Macquart who pursues Dide; Szakács interprets the symbolism as two-sided — the spatial structure of the realist aspect of the text, which exists above ground,

and the interference of the mythical aspect of the dead underground: 'Les Vivants et les morts dans *La Fortune des Rougon*', *Acta Litteraria Scientarium Hungaricae*, 32.1–2 (1990), 91–95.
9. Colette Becker, 'Zola, un déchiffreur de l'entre-deux', *Études Françaises*, 39.2 (2003), 11–21 (p. 15).
10. Robert Ricatte sees this as a kind of eternal present for Dide, 'cette sorte d'éternel present': 'Espace et temps dans *La Fortune des Rougon*', in *Les Critiques de notre temps et Zola*, ed. by Colette Becker (Paris: Garnier, 1972), pp. 135–40 (p. 135).
11. Here again Baudelaire's living death of a past that was already dead comes to mind. For Zola, this dead place of death perhaps invokes as well Zola's preface to the work, in which the dead Second Empire, the cemetery of that Empire in a sense, is the historical ground of this 'tableau d'un règne mort' [picture of a dead reign] (*RM*, I, 4). Marie-Sophie Armstrong shows how Hugo influenced this scene in its echoes of the sewer scenes; one could also imagine an echo of the cemetery in which Jean Valjean was buried alive: 'Hugo à l'aire Saint-Mittre: Zola et la problématique de la propriété littéraire', *The French Review*, 76.2 (December 2002), 346–57.
12. It is clear why Mitterand describes this book as 'l'éternelle confrontation des vivants avec leurs morts': 'Une archéologie mentale', p. 176. The metaphor of the cemetery itself recurs in Zola's works as a kind of obsessive literary return. From an 1868 essay on his 'fertilizing' visit to Musset's tomb in Père Lachaise (as well as the later reuse of this material), through the beginning pages of the serialized publication of *La Fortune des Rougon* and its cemetery in 1870–71, through revisions made to the novel form of *La Fortune* (after the Commune and after Zola's reports on the massacred corpses scattered among the Père Lachaise tombstones, one of which bears information about the deceased that is uncannily similar to that of Silvère), we find a kind of eternal return of the cemetery in Zola's writings. See David Charles's excellent article: '*La Fortune des Rougon*, roman de la Commune', *Romantisme*, 131.1 (2006), 99–114, as well as that of Henri Mitterand, 'Zola devant la Commune', *Les Lettres françaises*, 732 (3 July 1958), 5–6.
13. Naomi Schor, *Zola's Crowds* (Baltimore, MD: Johns Hopkins University Press, 1978), p. 120.
14. Schor shows how Zola rotates love and death to put in motion what she calls the 'Life/Death/Life cycle': *Zola's Crowds*, p. 13. She notes that this cycle 'condemns each generation to repeat the actions of the preceding one. Silvère must die like Macquart, Miette, like the Marie on whose tombstone the lovers sit. The cycle appears to be a metaphor for heredity': 'Zola: From Window to Window', *Yale French Studies*, 42 (1969), 38–51 (p. 50). It is curious that the name 'Miette' is so close to the name of the cemetery, 'Mittre' — perhaps another link to Miette's destiny.
15. Philip D. Walker has an excellent section on eternal *recommencement*: 'Life Continuing and Recommencing', in *Germinal and Zola's Philosophical and Religious Thought*, Purdue University Monographs in Romance Languages, 14 (Amsterdam & Philadelphia: John Benjamins, 1984), pp. 73–86. Mitterand observes similarly that 'l'existence biologique et social est donnée, d'entrée de jeu, comme le lieu d'un cycle éternel, d'un constant échange de la mort et de la vie' [biological and social existence is given, from the beginning, as the place of an eternal cycle, of a constant exchange of death and life] and that the book presents the 'mariage de l'amour et de la mort' [marriage of love and death]: 'Une archéologie mentale', pp. 174, 176. Jean Borie describes 'un *éternel retour* de la bête humaine' [an *eternal return* of the human beast]: *Zola et les mythes ou la nausée au salut* (Paris: Seuil, 1971), p. 69.
16. Schor, *Zola's Crowds*, 13.
17. In a similar way, Dide thinks that Pierre is her first husband, Rougon, come back from the dead to punish her for Macquart: 'Elle se disait que Rougon ressuscitait pour la punir de ses désordres' [She told herself that Rougon resuscitated to punish her for her debauchery] (*RM*, I, 49).
18. It appears that gendarmes return from the dead as well, according to Dide: 'Le gendarme était mort, murmura-t-elle, et je l'ai vu, il est revenu... Ça ne meurt jamais, ces gredins!' [The gendarme was dead, she murmured, and I saw him, he has come back... They never die, those scoundrels] (*RM*, I, 300). It is notable that Miette's father was also killed by a gendarme, and that both Miette and Silvère are orphans.
19. Kate Griffiths states that each of Zola's works contains a woman spectre: 'The Haunted Mirrors in Émile Zola and Guy de Maupassant', *Bulletin of the Émile Zola Society*, 26 (October 2002), 3–13 (p. 8). She also reviews the numerous ghostly female figures in Zola and their relation to writing

and gender: 'Scribbling Ghosts', in *Possessions: Essays in French Literature, Cinema and Theory*, ed. by Julia Horn and Lynsey Russell-Watts (Oxford: Peter Lang, 2003), pp. 3–13. Schor also notes that 'the spectre of a dead woman haunts the *Rougon-Macquart*', haunts Miette, Albine, Clotilde, and Denise in *Au Bonheur des Dames: Zola's Crowds*, pp. 21–22.

20. Schor, 'Zola', p. 50. In another instance in *Le Docteur Pascal*, Charles represents the return of Dide, for he looks exactly like her, even with hints of death in the resemblance: 'Mais ce qui frappait surtout, en ce moment, c'était sa ressemblance avec Tante Dide, cette ressemblance qui avait franchi trois générations, qui sautait de ce visage desséché de centenaire, de ses traits usés, à cette délicate figure d'enfant, comme effacé déjà elle aussi, très vieille et finie par l'usure de la race. En face l'un de l'autre, l'enfant imbécile, d'une beauté de mort, était comme la fin de l'ancêtre, l'oubliée' [But what struck one above all, at this moment, was his resemblance to Tante Dide, this resemblance that skipped three generations, that jumped from this dried up face of the centenarian, from her worn traits, to this delicate face of a child, as if it were also erased, very old and finished off by the weakening of the race. Face to face, the imbecile child, with a deathlike beauty, was like the end of the ancestor, the forgotten woman] (*RM*, v, 975).

21. Charles writes, 'Se succèdent ainsi dans ce fauteuil un monarchiste, un "communiste", un bonapartiste: c'est la répétition de 1848 et l'inverse de la succession que Zola dit craindre en 1871–1872' [Thus succeed in this armchair a monarchist, a 'communist', a Bonapartist: it is the repetition of 1848 and the inverse of the succession that Zola said he feared in 1871–1872]: '*La Fortune des Rougon*, roman de la Commune', p. 112.

22. Naomi Schor, 'Mythe des origines, origine des mythes: *La Fortune des Rougon*', *Les Cahiers Naturalistes*, 52 (1978), 124–34 (p. 125).

23. Émile Zola, *La Bête humaine*, *RM*, IV, 997–1331 (p. 1235). All further references are to this edition unless otherwise noted. See Dorian Bell's useful analysis of the scientific understanding of atavism in Zola's time: 'Cavemen Among Us: Genealogies of Atavism from Zola's *La Bête humaine* to Chabrol's *Le Boucher*', *French Studies*, 62.1 (January 2008), 39–52. Sophie Ménard notes that, for Zola, the phantom in the age of positivism is biological: 'Les Fantômes nuptiaux chez Zola', *Romantisme*, 149.3 (2010), 97–110 (p. 99).

24. Kate Griffiths also observes the phantomlike aspect of Jacques's ancestor in his uncontrolled hands in her study of ghostly authorship in the novel and its adaptations: *Émile Zola and the Artistry of Adaptation* (London: Legenda, 2009), pp. 107–08, 110–11, 123.

25. Françoise Gaillard, 'La Peur des revenants', in *Littérature et médecine, ou les pouvoirs du récit*, ed. by Gérard Danou (Paris: BPI, Centre Pompidou, 2001), pp. 89–105 (p. 91).

26. Gaillard also notes these two types which she describes as 'hérédité comportementale' [behavioural heredity] and 'hérédité physiologique' [physiological heredity]: 'La Peur des revenants', p. 91. These types are a bit different from the categories established by Gilles Deleuze, who analyzes 'big heredity' (general inheritance of instincts) and 'little heredity' (the way heredity works in a particular body, what he calls 'la fêlure' [the crack]): *La Logique du sens* (Paris: Minuit, 1969), p. 376. My definition here fits, however, with Zola's description of his project: a study of the accidents of a family's heredity in a particular milieu. He expounds this in the preface to the *Rougon-Macquart* series, where the word 'race' means rather, in this context, a family line: 'les accidents nerveux et sanguins qui se déclarent dans une race, à la suite d'une première lésion organique, et qui déterminent, selon les milieux, chez chacun des individus de cette race [...] toutes les manifestations humaines, naturelles et instinctives' [accidents in the nerves and in the blood that manifest themselves in a family line, after a first organic lesion, and which determine, depending on the milieus [...] all human manifestations] (*RM*, I, 3).

27. Andrew Counter has an interesting interpretation of the *tare* that de-emphasizes the caveman aspect and integrates the sociological and psychological, revising Deleuze's formulation, 'While Lombroso speaks of 'instinct' as animal in the sense of pre-human, Zola refers to 'des offenses,' 'la rancune,' 'la première tromperie,' words which participate in a moral symbolism suggestive of creatures more sophisticated than the prominent-jawed reprobates of Lombroso's reductive pathology. Zola's primal vision is not animalistic, but theological, civil and economic, a poetics of sin, guilt and retributions': 'The Legacy of the Beast: Patrinlinearity and Rupture in Zola's *La Bête humaine*, and Freud's *Totem and Taboo*', *French Studies*, 62.1 (January 2008), 26–38 (p. 28).

I am interested in the scenes in which the animal comes into conflict with the social.
28. I study *La Bête humaine* from the angle of gender and psychoanalysis in 'Gender, Metaphor, and Machine: *La Bête humaine*', *French Literature Series*, 16 (1989), 110–22.
29. Several other characters in the novel are taken over by these *idées fixes* and periods of lost agency. Misard has only one purpose in life, to find where Phasie has hidden her money: 'depuis des années, il n'avait pas eu d'autre idée dans la tête, de jour et de nuit' [for years, he had no other idea in his head, day and night] (*RM*, IV, 1280). Roubaud 'ne se possédait plus' [no longer possessed himself] when he comes up with the idea of murder, and then after he accomplishes it, he turns to gambling as his *idée fixe*. Flore remains intent on the 'idée fixe, [...] la chose qui la hantait' [the *idée fixe*, [...] the thing that haunted her], and 'l'idée brusque s'était plantée, enfoncée en elle' [the brusque idea had planted itself, driven itself into her], which is the killing of Jacques and Séverine (*RM*, IV, 1249). Séverine can be overwhelmed by the need to speak of the past: when she has a glass of wine, the barriers seem to be lowered and she lets slip a detail of her past that gives the truth to Roubaud, and again when she has a glass of wine with Jacques, she tells the story of the murder.
30. Griffiths studies the *Rougon-Macquart* novels through the psychoanalytic frame of mirrors, ghostly women, and identity in 'Scribbling Ghosts'.
31. Samantha Peterson analyzes gender and difference in this non-linguistic communication: 'Experimenting on Difference: Women, Violence, and Narrative in Zola's Naturalism' (unpublished doctoral thesis, Boston University, 2015).
32. Mathew Yost first brought this circulation to my attention.
33. Michael Mayerfeld Bell, in his investigation of the sociology of space, describes 'the ghosts of place', the way a room can be associated with a person, who seems to inhabit it, ghostlike, because of memories of events that took place there, and these imaginary ghosts can 'have real consequences for social life'; thus, la mère Victoire's room becomes one of these ghostly places: 'The Ghosts of Place', *Theory and Society*, 26.6 (December 1997), 813–36 (pp. 815, 831).
34. Henri Mitterand discusses the genesis of the chronotope of traffic and the railway line in this novel: 'The Genesis of Novelistic Space: Zola's *La Bête humaine*', in *Naturalism in the European Novel: New Critical Perspectives*, ed. by Brian Nelson (New York & Oxford: Berg, 1992), pp. 666–79.
35. Lewis Kamm notes that, as early as 1885, Jules Lemaître claimed that Zola gives to things the life that he takes away from humans: 'People and Things in Zola's *Rougon-Macquart*: Reification Re-humanized', *Philological Quarterly*, 53.1 (1974), 100–09 (pp. 102–03).
36. Michel Serres, *Feux et signaux de brume: Zola* (Paris: Grasset, 1975), p. 131.
37. Laura Salisbury, 'Michel Serres: Science, Fiction, and the Shape of Relation', *Science Fiction Studies*, 33.1 (March 2006), 30–52 (p. 33).
38. Mitterand discusses this as a kind of ludic play on Zola's part, in which he builds a railroad, makes it function, and then brings about accidents, a 'double game' of rules and their transgression: 'The Genesis of Novelistic Space', p. 71.
39. David F. Bell, *Real Time: Accelerating Narrative from Balzac to Zola* (Urbana: University of Illinois Press, 2004).
40. The transformation from *ancien régime* to modern commercial society also finds expression in the first novel of the *Rougon-Macquart* series, *La Fortune des Rougon*, in the evolution of the type of work that the family pursues. Pierre Rougon sells the property of his mother's truck-farming business, which makes a living from the land, to use the money to 'acheter Félicité', clearly making an object of a human being, by marrying into her family and entering into her business, helping her run their olive oil store (*RM*, I, 53). Rougon becomes a middleman in commerce, and even makes minor speculative investments in olive oil. From farming and direct contact with the land, the Rougons move into shops and speculation.
41. Émile Zola, *Thérèse Raquin* (Paris: Librairie générale française, 1997), p. 22. All further page references are to this edition.
42. Agnieszka Tworek associates this description with that of the morgue, and the room's resemblance to a burial vault: 'Death Masks in *Thérèse Raquin*', *Excavatio*, 23.1–2 (2008), 195–202 (pp. 197–98).

43. As David F. Bell discusses, in Zola's time the literary critic Louis Ulbach describes characters such as Thérèse as being 'ces fantômes impossibles qui suintent la mort, sans avoir respiré la vie, qui ne sont que des cauchemars de la réalité' [those impossible phantoms that sweat death, without having breathed life, who are but nightmares of reality]. Bell emphasizes that this relates to Zola's task of exposing the real: '*Thérèse Raquin*: Scientific Realism in Zola's Laboratory', *NCFS*, 24.1–2 (Fall-Winter 1995–96), 122–32 (p. 122).
44. As Sophie Ménard notes, Camille is actually a 'revenant' from the start, as his mother has fought against his death all his life: *Émile Zola et les aveux du corps: les savoirs du roman naturaliste* (Paris: Classiques Garnier, 2014), p. 347.
45. Ménard reveals connections between ghosts and marriage in 'Les Fantômes nuptiaux chez Zola'.
46. This happens to both of them in another scene: 'tous leurs sens s'hallucinaient' [all of their senses hallucinated] (p. 161). Susan Harrow notes that the hallucinations even have an acoustic dimension: '*Thérèse Raquin*: Animal Passion and the Brutality of Reading', in *The Cambridge Companion to Zola*, ed. by Nelson, pp. 105–20 (pp. 113–14).
47. Tworek describes Mme Raquin as 'a living corpse' and ties Thérèse's deathly state to Ophelia: 'Death Masks in *Thérèse Raquin*', pp. 198, 201. Zola's short work *La Mort d'Olivier Bécaille* is a first-person narrative by a man who was buried alive. We also remember Dide who suffers a similar, symbolic fate, buried alive in her own body.
48. Jonathan Strauss remarks on mechanization and living death in their relation to necrophilia: *Human Remains: Medicine, Death, and Desire in Nineteenth-century Paris* (New York: Fordham University Press, 2012), pp. 172–73.
49. We recall in a different way Mme Raquin's hand; when she is paralyzed, she tries to trace an accusation with her fingers, but cannot control her hand long enough to express her thought: her body will not follow her commands (p. 195).
50. Benjamin, *The Arcades Project*, pp. 203–04.
51. Cohen, 'Benjamin's Phantasmagoria', p. 208.
52. Benjamin, *The Arcades Project*, p. 14.
53. As Rolf Tiedemann states, 'The concept of phantasmagoria that Benjamin repeatedly employs seems to be merely another term for what Marx called commodity fetishism': Benjamin, *The Arcades Project*, p. 938.
54. Benjamin, *The Arcades Project*, p. 10.
55. It is never stated outright by the narrator that she sells herself: we see what happens through Laurent's eyes as he spies on her. Later, when he decides to take up vice as well, he notes that it is more difficult for a man, and he envies 'le sort des filles qui peuvent se vendre' [the lot of prostitutes who can sell themselves] (p. 223). Even though her prostitution is not made explicit, she is certainly associated with prostitution here. In a slightly different context, Tworek notes that Thérèse's face, which resembles a death mask, makes her appear to be an object rather than a person: 'Death Masks in *Thérèse Raquin*', p. 96.
56. See Vanessa R. Schwartz's excellent history of the morgue as spectacle: 'The Morgue and the Musée Grévin: Understanding the Public Taste for Reality in Fin-de-Siècle Paris', in *Spectacles of Realism: Gender, Body, Genre*, ed. by Margaret Cohen and Christopher Prendergast (Minneapolis: University of Minnesota Press, 1995), pp. 268–93.
57. Émile Zola, *La Curée*, RM, I, 319–599 (p. 576). All further references are to this edition unless otherwise noted.
58. This 'tableau' also ties in with the important *tableaux vivants* scene in the novel (discussed below).
59. As for physical heredity, there is the general influence of the bourgeois blood of her father, and only a vague suggestion of a maternal influence in the mention of a secret drama related to her mother, who died when Renée was a child. Anthony Zielonka describes this maternal heredity, 'Peut-être avait-elle dans les veines un filet de sang vicié' [Perhaps she had in her veins a trickle of tainted blood]: 'Renée et le problème du mal', in *La Curée de Zola ou 'la vie à outrance': actes du colloque du 10 janvier 1987*, ed. by David Baguley (Paris: SEDES, 1987), pp. 161–70 (p. 164). Heredity for Louise, Maxime's wife, is more important. She is also the living dead, because she, somewhat like Jacques Lantier, is, in a sense, taken over by a dead person from her past: her mother. She remembers, relives her dead mother's life, as Zola writes: 'Portée dans ces flancs

malades, Louise en était sortie le sang pauvre, les membres déviés [...]. Parfois, elle croyait se souvenir confusément d'une autre existence, elle voyait se dérouler, dans une ombre vague, des scènes bizarres, des hommes et des femmes s'embrassant, tout un drame charnel où s'amusaient ses curiosités d'enfant. C'était sa mère qui parlait en elle. [...] A mesure qu'elle grandissait, rien ne l'étonnait, elle se rappelait tout, ou plutôt elle savait tout, et elle allait aux choses défendues, avec une sûreté de main, qui la faisait ressembler, dans la vie, à une personne rentrant chez elle après une longue absence' [Carried in a sick womb, Louise emerged with poor blood, twisted limbs [...]. At times, she thought she confusedly remembered another existence, in which she saw unfold, in a vague shadow, bizarre scenes of men and women embracing, an entire carnal drama in which her childish curiosities were amused. That was her mother speaking in her. [...] As she grew up, nothing astonished her, she remembered everything, or rather she knew everything, and she approached forbidden things with a sureness of hand that made her resemble, in life, a person returning home after a long absence] (RM, I, 434).

60. The metaphor of the growth of her incestuous love also draws on the soil image: 'Dans le monde affolé où ils vivaient, leur faute avait poussé comme sur un fumier gras de sucs équivoques' [In the crazed world where they lived, their transgression had grown as if on manure rich with dubious saps] (RM, I, 481). And this love is also nourished by the artificial nature of Paris, as represented in the artificial nature of her greenhouse: 'La sève qui montait aux flancs des arbres les pénétrait, eux aussi, leur donnait des désirs fous de croissance immédiate, de reproduction gigantesque' [The sap that rose up the sides of the trees penetrated them also, gave them mad desires of immediate growth, of gigantic reproduction] (p. 487).

61. The Saint-Mittre cemetery: 'C'était une mer d'un vert sombre, profonde, piquée de fleurs larges, d'un éclat singulier. On sentait en dessous, dans l'ombre des tiges pressées, le terreau humide qui bouillait et suintait la sève' [It was a deep sea of dark green, spotted with large flowers that had a singular radiance. One sensed below, in the shade of the crowded stems, the humid, fertile ground that boiled and sweated sap (RM, I, 5). The pavement of Paris, like the rugs and the cemetery, also stimulates desire in Renée, as we see in more detail below: 'Ce large trottoir [...] cette asphalte grise [...] réveillaient ses désirs endormis' [That wide pavement [...] that grey asphalt [...] reawakened her sleeping desires] (RM, I, 446). Griffiths discusses this influence in *Emile Zola and the Artistry of Adaptation*, pp. 89, 92.

62. The title of Chateaubriand's *René* and the importance of autumn in that text, the time when René would visit his home and take long walks with his incestuous sister through the 'grand bois' [great woods], resembles this autumn trip of Renée through the Bois de Boulogne with her soon-to-be incestuous 'son-brother' (Maxime says she could be his sister) (RM, I, 405); Saccard calls both of them his children (p. 414). This sets up parallels between the two works, which both describe the empty, valueless, and dead new world created after a regime change. Zola's novel might be seen to resurrect the dead past of the milieu of Chateaubriand's work. See André Benhaim, 'De René à Renée', *Les Cahiers Naturalistes*, 73 (1999), 151–66, for an analysis of many of these similarities between the two works; particularly interesting are his observations that Chateaubriand is a literary 'aïeul impossible à mettre en terre' [a literary ancestor impossible to put in the ground] (p. 151) and that he had an aesthetic 'rapport avec la tombe' [relationship with the tomb] (p. 153) exemplified in the *Mémoires d'outre tombe*. Sandy Petrey also notes the autumn scene that begins the novel, which represents time coming to an end: 'Stylistics and Society in *La Curée*', *MLN*, 89.4 (May 1974), 626–40 (p. 629).

63. Jacques Noiray observes that people in *La Curée* are either 'surface beings' or 'empty beings': 'La Symbolique de l'espace dans *La Curée*', *L'Information Littéraire*, 39.1 (1987), 16–20 (p. 20). In a different context, Philippe Berthier looks at the environment of the novel — Paris, the luxurious house — as a surface that covers emptiness: 'Hôtel Saccard: états des lieux', in *La Curée de Zola*, ed. by Baguley, pp. 107–18.

64. The hôtel Béraud and its contents are described by such words as 'glaciale', 'moroses', 'noirâtres', 'marbrés de moisissures', 'vieux meubles', 'silence', 'ombre', 'froide', 'humide' [glacial, morose, blackish, mottled with mould, old furniture, silence, shadow, cold, humid] (RM, I, 400–01). Renée, who moves between the past of her father's house and the modernity of her new abodes, exemplifies Priscilla Parkhurst Ferguson's description of Haussmannization as 'caught [...]

between the old and the new': *Paris as Revolution: Writing the Nineteenth-century City* (Berkeley: University of California Press, 1994), p. 126.
65. Renée herself notes that she would have been different had she remained in her father's home: 'Certes, elle serait devenue meilleure, si elle était restée à tricoter auprès de la tante Elisabeth' [Certainly, she would have become better, if she had stayed to knit at Aunt Elisabeth's side] (*RM*, I, 573).
66. Later in the text another dress, which has a hunting scene embroidered on it, suggests the 'curée' (in the hunt, the scramble by the hunting dogs for the remains of the kill), a metaphor for Paris and Renée (see below).
67. When Renée first meets Maxime, there is a similar scene in which he suggests alterations in her dress that end up showing more of her flesh. He begins by saying, 'Je trouve plutôt qu'il y a quelque chose de trop' [I find, rather, that there is something excessive], and then tells her she should scoop out the lace of the bodice and replace it with a necklace (significantly recalling the necklace of her childhood), which she does. At the end of the novel, she identifies Maxime as one of those who denuded her: 'Saccard avait dégrafé le corsage, et Maxime avait fait tomber la jupe' [Saccard had opened the front of her blouse, Maxime had pulled down the skirt] (*RM*, I, 575). Clara Pauw reads this as Renée's early sexualization as she learns how to seduce: '(Un)Dressing Renée: Clothing and Identity in Zola's Novel *La Curée*' (unpublished doctoral thesis, Emory University, 2011), pp. 13–14.
68. Hannah Thompson discusses how Renée progressively undresses herself in the novel up to the moment of this self-revelation: *Naturalism Redressed: Identity and Clothing in the Novels of Émile Zola* (Oxford: University of Oxford Press, 2004), p. 48. Griffiths also mentions this in *Emile Zola and the Artistry of Adaptation*, p. 85.
69. This perhaps pays homage to Flaubert's *Éducation sentimentale*, when Rosanette's bracelet reveals to Frédéric that she has sold herself to someone else. See Jennifer Yee's analysis of the bracelet: 'Mementoes and the Memory of the Reader in *L'Éducation sentimentale*', *Dix-Neuf*, 14.1 (April 2010), 1–12 (p. 4). Zola greatly admired this Flaubert novel and wrote an article on it immediately after its appearance in 1869: F. W. J. Hemmings, 'Zola and *L'Éducation sentimentale*', *Romanic Review*, 50 (1959), 35–40. One also notes similarities between the two novels when the upper-class receptions resemble those of the demi-monde and when carriages get slowed down in traffic jams.
70. In this scene, Renée also notes that someone has deepened the crease on her forehead, has 'marked' her with a wound like a whip lash; she wonders if it was Saccard, but notes that he never raised his hand against her. The reader recalls that it is Saccard's hand that symbolically slashed through sections of Paris in his conversation with his first wife. This 'mark' once again links Renée's dispossession, here as cutting, to that of Paris (*RM*, I, 572).
71. Colette Becker notes that 'Zola avait voulu assimiler le viol de la France par Louis-Napoléon Bonaparte à celui de Renée, identifier le destin de la jeune femme à celui du pays' [Zola had wanted to assimilate the rape of France by Louis-Napoléon Bonaparte to that of Renée, to equate the destiny of the young woman to that of the country]: 'L'Intrigue', in *Genèse, structures et style de La Curée*, ed. by Henri Mitterand, Colette Becker, and Jean-Pierre Leduc-Adine (Paris: SEDES, 1987), pp. 29–50 (pp. 47–48). Auguste Dezalay also links the two events in 'L'Infortune des Rougon ou le mal des origines', in *Le Mal dans l'imaginaire littéraire français (1850–1950)*, ed. by Myriam Watthee-Delmotte and Metka Zupančič (Paris: Harmattan, 1998), pp. 181–92 (p. 186).
72. Zola explicitly links Saccard's machinations with prostitution when Saccard and Laure work together: 'La fille et le spéculateur, dans la demi-ivresse du dessert, s'entendirent' [The prostitute and the speculator, in the semi-intoxication of dessert, understood each other] (*RM*, I, 465). Susan Harrow shows how this novel 'strips the gloss of aestheticization to reveal the female body as an object of masculine speculation in an economy of desire in which erotic and financial values become almost indistinguishable': 'Myopia and the Model', in *L'Écriture du féminin chez Zola et dans la fiction naturaliste /Writing the Feminine in Zola and Naturalist Fiction*, ed. by Anna Gural-Migdal (Bern: Peter Lang, 2003), pp. 251–70 (p. 252).
73. Like the poison of the hothouse and plant, the streets of Paris also seem to invade Renée and her space. When she is with Maxime in the private room of the restaurant, the shadows of the people

walking outside on the pavement are projected onto the ceiling of their room: 'sur le plafond, dans les reflets du café d'en bas, passaient les ombres rapides des promeneurs' [on the ceiling, in the reflections of the cafe below, passed the rapid shadows of the pedestrians] (*RM*, I, 448). Significantly, the wheels of the boulevard seem to be turning in her head: 'toutes ces roues, par instants, semblaient lui tourner dans la tête' [all of these wheels, at times, seemed to be turning in her head] (p. 453). As Borie puts it, 'Dans ce beau passage, nous découvrons avec surprise que la rue n'est pas, comme nous l'avions supposé, *au-dehors*' [In this wonderful passage, we discover with surprise that the street is not, as we had supposed, *outside*]: *Zola et les mythes*, p. 162.

74. As Saccard says to Angèle: 'Oh! vois, dit Saccard, avec un rire d'enfant, il pleut des pièces de vingt francs dans Paris!' ['Oh! See,' said Saccard with a childish laugh, 'it's raining twenty-franc coins in Paris!] (*RM*, I, 388).
75. Caitlin McGrath describes this problem of vision as 'agnosia', when someone is 'unable to attach symbolic meaning to what they see': '"Crippled by Sight": Detail in *Au Bonheur des Dames*', *Modernism /Modernity*, 21.3 (September 2014), 641–64 (p. 644). Harrow also notes that 'hampered by blurred vision, Renée is uncertain as to what she sees and confused as to how she will interpret the world': 'Myopia and the Model', p. 261.
76. The phantasmagoria will appear also in images in *Au Bonheur des Dames*.
77. The narrator uses the same word, *trou*, for the collapsing logs, for gutted buildings, and for the collapsing foundation of Saccard's fortune: 'Renée souffrait, le regardait faire un grand trou dans la cendre pour enterrer le bout d'une bûche' [Renée was suffering, watching him make a large hole in the ashes to bury a bit of log] (*RM*, I, 462); 'Rien n'était plus lamentable que les papiers peints de ces chambres [...] qui s'en allaient en lambeaux, indiquant, à une hauteur de cinq et six étages [....] de pauvres cabinets, des trous étroits, où toute une existence d'homme avait peut-être tenu' [Nothing was as pathetic as the wallpaper of these rooms [...] which fell away in tatters, revealing, at a height of five or six stories, shabby rooms, narrow holes-in-the-wall, all cramped, where an entire human existence had perhaps taken place] (p. 581); 'Il vivait sur la dette, [...] de nouveau trous se creusaient plus profonds, par-dessus lesquels il sautait, ne pouvant les combler' [He lived on his debt, [...] new and deeper holes opened, over which he jumped, unable to fill them] (p. 463).
78. Harrow also notes this living death in another way as Renée's abdicating the right to see: 'Myopia and the Model', p. 262.
79. This humanization is in a way similar to certain passages of *La Faute de l'abbé Mouret*.
80. Tullio Pagano makes the connection between the two greenhouses: 'Allegorizing *La Curée*', *Excavatio*, 6–7 (January 1995), 166–76 (p. 171).
81. Pierre Bourdieu, *Les Règles de l'art: genèse et structure du champ littéraire* (Paris: Seuil, 1992).
82. See Susan Buck-Morss on the 'dreaming collective' as 'socially specific constellations, inherited historically rather than biologically': 'Walter Benjamin — Revolutionary Writer (II), *New Left Review*, 129 (September-October 1981), 77–95 (p. 77). Ferguson in another way discusses the system of the real estate market as 'not unlike an elaborate fiction in which people must believe for it to work': *Paris as Revolution*, p. 131.
83. Benjamin, *The Arcades Project*, p. 405.
84. Harrow analyzes how 'the gaze of the onlookers fixes upon the layers of fabric [...] that produce Renée as pure surface': 'Myopia and the Model', p. 254. For Thompson, the states of being dressed and undressed reveal the 'confusion of the female body with its artificial adornments': *Naturalism Redressed*, pp. 66–67.
85. This image makes her strangely like one of her old dolls that she finds in her father's home: 'elle retrouva une de ses anciennes poupées; tout le son avait coulé par un trou' [she found one of her old dolls; all the sawdust stuffing had poured out from a hole] (*RM*, I, 598).
86. In speaking of architecture in the novel, Berthier observes, 'l'architecture d'intérieur est devenue, au sens propre, incarnation; le décor réellement s'est fait chair' [the interior architecture has become, literally, an incarnation; the décor has really become flesh]: 'Hôtel Saccard', pp. 112–13.
87. Arnaud Rykner notes the presence of the *féerie* in both the street and the *tableaux vivants* scenes and considers the *féerie* to be constitutive of the society on which the narrative is built. His analysis centres mainly on the role of silence in the *tableaux vivants*: 'Les Fulgurances du corps

muet: Zola, les tableaux vivants et la pantomime', in *Studies in French Literature: Naturalisme et excès visuels: pantomime, parodie, image, fête. Mélanges en l'honneur de David Baguley*, ed. by Catherine Dousteyssier-Khoze and Edward Welch (Newcastle upon Tyne: Cambridge Scholars Publishing, 2009), pp. 17–35 (pp. 19, 20). In another essay Rykner studies the relation between narration and image: the tableaux do not actually reveal anything to the public viewing them. For Rykner, works by Gérôme and other painters lie behind the visual image of the tableaux: 'The Power of Tableaux Vivants in Zola: The Underside of the Image', *Image & Narrative*, 12.3 (2011), 98–112 (p. 105).

88. Sophia Mizouni has interesting discussions relating to this scene and others in *La Curée* in terms of the visibility afforded by the new architecture of Paris, theatricality, voyeurism, mechanical behaviour, and illness: 'Nineteenth-century Paris, Capital of Illusion' (unpublished doctoral thesis, Boston University, 2016).

89. The prostitute's dress of blue with white lace mirrors that of Sylvia, one of Maxime's lovers: ' "Je vous assure que Sylvia avait une robe de satin bleu dans son rôle de Dindonnette"; et une autre voix d'enfant ajoutait: "Oui, mais la robe était garnie de dentelles blanches" ' ['I assure you that Sylvia wore a blue satin dress in her role of Dindonnette'; and another childlike voice added: 'Yes, but the dress was garnished with with lace'] (*RM*, I, 344). Sylvia is also the owner of the bracelet furnished to Renée, the person who signed 'I love Maxime' on the restaurant mirror, and one of the courtesans who might have left her hair in the restaurant comb. Like Renée, Sylvia shared her favours with father and son (*RM*, I, 345). In the first chapter, Renée also wears the jewels of another courtesan, Laure d'Aurigny, which Saccard got for her.

90. The crowd on the street is described in the same terms as the photograph album perused by Renée and Maxime. The photo album is a: '*Monde singulièrement mêlé*, image du tohu-bohu d'idées et de personnages qui traversaient la vie de Renée et de Maxime' [*Society strangely mixed*, a hurly-burly of ideas and people who crossed the paths of Renée's and Maxime's lives] (*RM*, I, 427, my emphasis). The street is a '*monde étrangement mêlé* et toujours le même [...] dans le tohu-bohu féerique de ces mille flammes dansantes' [*society strangely mixed* and always the same [...] in the hurly-burly *féerique* of the thousand dancing flames] (p. 450, my emphasis). The album itself is a kind of visual but artificial spectacle, a 'crowd' of photos of high and low society. It is also a kind of simulacrum of the prostitution police-album, 'un veritable catalogue vivant, où toutes les filles de Paris étaient numérotées' [a veritable living catalogue, where all the prostitutes of Paris were numbered] (p. 426), which in an interesting way links Maxime and Saccard, whose hands 'meet' around the same women, both Renée and the prostitutes (p. 430) to the symbolic place of the authorities who control women.

91. Benjamin, *The Arcades Project*, p. 10. Susan Buck-Morss notes that the *Arcades Project* 'was originally conceived as a 'dialectical fairy scene' (dialektische Feen)': *The Dialectics of Seeing: Walter Benjamin and the Arcades Project*, Studies in Contemporary German Social Thought (Cambridge, MA: MIT Press, 1989), p. 271.

92. Zola himself later wrote both a *féerie*, *Violaine la chevelue*, as well as an essay on this type of play, which he admits he enjoyed, 'J'avoue donc ma tendresse pour la féerie' [I thus admit my fondness for the *féerie*': *Le Naturalisme au théâtre: les théories et les exemples* (Paris: Charpentier, 1895), pp. 353–71 (p. 356). It is interesting that a fairy in his *féerie* is named 'Nérée', almost an anagram of 'Renée' (one accent shy), who is herself called a 'fairy' in the *La Curée*: 'la fée excentrique des voluptés mondaines' [the eccentric fairy of socialite pleasures] (*RM*, I, 421). Another character in the *féerie* is named 'Silvère' (one of the main characters of *La Fortune des Rougon*).

93. This description of the prostitutes as they walk by shopfronts that are alternately light and dark conjures up another kind of spectacle, a toy that was popular around this time, the zoetrope, *zootrope* in French (*Le Figaro*, 27 April 1868, pp. 1–2). A precursor of film, it is a spinning cylinder, black on the outside, with spaced cutouts on the side. Inside are specially designed images on white paper, which, when one spins the cylinder and looks from outside through the slots to the inside, create a moving picture, such as a dog catching a ball. It represents another kind of spectacle created by an optical illusion, such as the phantasmagorias.

94. The 'véritable fantasmagorie de calcul' [phantasmagoria of calculations] (*RM*, I, 464) of Saccard's financial dealings help to build this phantasmagoria of Paris.

95. As Renée is both spectator and spectacle at the window in the restaurant, here she is again spectacle on view, and in the tableau, in her role as Echo in the spectacle, she becomes the spectator as she gazes at Maxime.
96. Colette Becker, 'Illusion et réalité: la métaphore du théâtre dans *La Curée*', in *La Curée de Zola*, ed. by Baguley, pp. 119–28 (p. 120). Jacques Noiray notes that the theatrical traverses the entirety of the novel, presented as a series of 'scenes': 'Une "mise en abyme" de *La Curée*: les amours du beau Narcisse et de la nymphe Écho', *Littératures*, 16 (Spring 1987), 69–77 (pp. 70–71).
97. Zola mentions the electric ray three times in this scene (*RM*, I, 544, 548, 552).
98. See Harrow's excellent analysis of reification in 'Myopia and the Model'.
99. Noiray views the *tableau vivant* as a *mise-en-abyme*, or echo, of the entire novel: 'Une "mise en abyme" de *La Curée*', p. 69.
100. We might think here as well of the paralysis of Dide and Madame Raquin.
101. Borie remarks on something similar in *Zola et les mythes*: 'elle découvre que ce péché auquel elle croit n'a autour d'elle, qu'une existence "économique"' [she discovers that what she believed to be a sin had only, in those around her, an 'economic' existence] (p. 26). Zola represents the two men walking arm and arm several times in the novel, which conjures up the patriarchal collusion of men in this reification of women.
102. Arthur Goldhammer, in the introduction to his translation of the novel, writes that Zola, given the choice between old and new, chooses tradition, however it cannot take the form of tragedy but only of satire: Émile Zola, *The Kill*, trans. by Arthur Goldhammer (New York: Modern Library, 2005), p. xiii.
103. Émile Zola, *Le Docteur Pascal*, *RM*, V, 913–1220 (p. 1144). All further references are to this edition unless otherwise noted. We recall Madame Raquin, paralyzed as well.
104. Rosalind Williams's *Dream Worlds: Mass Consumption in Late Nineteenth-century France* (Berkeley: University of California Press, 1982) and Bowlby's *Just Looking* contain early, influential studies of modernity and woman in the novel. Kristin Ross's introduction to the translation of the novel is excellent: 'Introduction', in Émile Zola, *The Ladies' Paradise*, intro. by Kristin Ross (Berkeley: University of California Press, 1992), pp. v–xxiii. And there are many more fine studies; I cite here only those that touch on my particular topic.
105. This notion of the active power of the department store to change people fits nicely with Stephen Wilson's discussion of the store as a machine that changes people: 'Nana, Prostitution and the Textual Foundations of Zola's *Au Bonheur des Dames*', *NCFS*, 41.1–2 (2013), 91–104 (p. 94).
106. One thinks here of Lucien de Rubempré and his move from the dying provinces to a new living death in Paris.
107. Williams opens her book *Dream Worlds* with a description of the hypnotic power of the Bonheur des Dames in this scene, glossed by so many later analyses.
108. Rachel Bowlby, *Carried Away: The Invention of Modern Shopping* (New York: Columbia University Press, 2001), pp. 62–66.
109. Émile Zola, *Au Bonheur des Dames*, *RM*, III, 389–803 (pp. 390–91). All further references are to this edition unless otherwise noted.
110. As Barbara Vinken observes, what is being killed is something that is 'the already dead': 'Temples of Delight', in *Spectacles of Realism*, ed. by Cohen and Prendergast, pp. 247–67 (pp. 247–48).
111. Brian Nelson's wonderful title for an article on this novel adds an amusing touch to this consumer 'revolution': 'Zola and the Counter Revolution: *Au Bonheur des Dames*', *Australian Journal of French Studies*, 31.2 (1993), 233–40. Bowlby looks at Geneviève's death as representing a woman who is 'separated from modern forms of female sexuality': *Just Looking*, p. 76.
112. Bowlby writes of a kind of 'resurrection after death' in the 'replacement of the outworn, outdated 'dead shop windows' of the small local store by the showy vitality of the new': *Just Looking*, p. 75.
113. Vaheed Ramazani observes in the context of gender that Mouret 'extracts the new *from* the old': 'Gender, War, and the Department Store: Zola's *Au Bonheur des Dames*', *SubStance*, 36.2 (2007), 126–46 (p. 134).
114. Schor uses the Girardian notion of sacrifice in her *Zola's Crowds*, and many since have developed

her vision. About Caroline's blood in the foundation, Wilson notes appropriately for us, 'The Bonheur des Dames is a store that is born of the ineluctable memories of a bloody past; it is a structure that rises out of decomposition and death. The imagery of Mme Hédoin's blood in its foundation permeates a whole series of descriptions': 'Nana, Prostitution and the Textual Foundations of Zola's *Au Bonheur des Dames*', p. 94.

115. Janet Beizer discusses Mme Hédoin as a revenant and the idea of return in several guises: 'Au (delà du) Bonheur des Dames: Notes on the Underground', *Australian Journal of French Studies*, 38.3 (September-December 2001), 393–406 (pp. 396–97). Ramazani describes her role as womb and tomb: 'Gender, War, and the Department Store', p. 133. Naomi Schor sees a similarity here with the Gothic genre, in which the young woman identifies with the hero's dead first-wife: 'Devant le château: femmes, marchandises et modernité dans *Au Bonheur des Dames*', in *Mimesis et Semiosis: littérature et représentation*, ed. by Philippe Hamon and Jean-Pierre Leduc-Adine (Paris: Nathan, 1992), pp. 179–86 (p. 180).

116. Ross, 'Introduction', in *The Ladies' Paradise*, p. v.

117. As noted above, Zola actually wrote on the *féerie*, and the first paragraph of his essay describes how much money one can make or lose on this popular genre (*Le Naturalisme au théâtre*). He analyzes why this type of play is interesting: one doesn't have to think and can just watch and be rocked by the music (a bit like the 'headless' mannequins and addicted shoppers who have lost their heads and cease thinking in *Au Bonheur des Dames*). And, according to Zola, *féeries* composed by the best poets and artists could be a dream world, 'le rêve éveillé de toutes les grandeurs et de toutes les beautés humaines' [the waking dream of all of human grandeur and all of human beauty]. All lies in the artificial spectacle, in 'le dédain du vrai' [disdain for the real]; 'le charme est d'y mentir, d'y échapper à toutes les réalités de ce bas monde' [their charm is in lying, in escaping from all the realities of this base world]. This certainly applies to the experience of the shoppers in the Bonheur. Colette Becker reminds us that Zola described the *féeries* of his time as a 'spectacle pour les yeux' in her article on *La Curée*: 'Illusion et réalité', p. 121.

118. This analysis clearly owes much to Williams in her excellent discussion of this scene: *Dream Worlds*, pp. 69–70.

119. As Williams in *Dream Worlds* describes this phenomenon: 'the umbrellas shed their banality' and become a kind of art that shows 'a deep confusion of commercial and aesthetic values' (pp. 69, 71). The fictional artistry of the display joins with the reality of the object to compose an odd 'making real' in art. If in the phantasmagoria, fictional ghosts seem real, in department store windows, the artistic display of merchandise creates a new kind of reality, what Williams calls a 'fairyland', where 'dreams of distant places are materialized in exotic imagery and fairyland ones in electric light displays' (pp. 84, 90).

120. Deborah Parsons writes that the department store makes a place for female desire in the form of voyeurism and fetishism, and that it partakes of the contemporary psychology of the crowd and the woman in public as prostitute: *Streetwalking the Metropolis: Women, the City, and Modernity* (Oxford & New York: Oxford University Press, 2000), pp. 48–49. Peter Brooks views this fetishism generally as that of Zola's male narrator: *Body Work* (Cambridge, MA: Harvard University Press, 1993), p. 153. Thompson, on the other hand, explores the idea of lesbian fetishism and the blurring of gender boundaries and desires in her book *Naturalism Redressed*, a desire that threatens the male economies of desire and commerce in the novel.

121. Hannah Thompson analyzes this woman-centered sexuality more fully in *Naturalism Redressed*, pp. 83–85, and in her excellent article, '"Une perversion du désir, une névrose nouvelle": Female Sexuality in Zola's *Au Bonheur des Dames*', *Romance Studies*, 16.2 (Autumn 1998), 81–92.

122. Bowlby observes that when shopping became a 'feminine leisure activity', it took the form of a masculine appeal (men as store clerks) to women (shoppers): *Just looking*, p. 19. Parsons notes a similar trend, 'In a subtle role reversal, the salesmen take on the traits of the prostitute, vying for customers and trying to attract those most inclined to spend': *Streetwalking the Metropolis*, p. 49.

123. Ross discusses the reification of the women who become fodder for the store as engine, machine: 'Introduction', in *The Ladies' Paradise*, pp. xii–xiii.

124. Kamm notes this reification: in his article 'People and Things in Zola's *Rougon-Macquart*'.

125. Brian Nelson in his introduction to *The Ladies' Paradise* notes this fragmentation of women:

'Introduction', in Émile Zola, *The Ladies' Paradise*, trans. and intro. by Brian Nelson (Oxford: Oxford University Press, 2012), pp. vii–xxiii (p. xix). The feet of these 'passants' echo the 'jambe de statue' of Baudelaire's 'passante'.

126. Bowlby, *Carried Away*, p. 66.
127. Others who discuss commodification, alienation, and dehumanization are Alison Walls, 'Symbolism and Commodified Identity in Rachilde and Zola's Department Store Novels', *New Zealand Journal of French Studies*, 28.2 (November 2007), 36–48 (p. 42); Susan Harrow, 'Velocity, Vacancy and Consciousness: Female Character as Culture Critic in *La Bête humaine* and *Au Bonheur des Dames*', *Excavatio*, 23.1–2 (2008), 214–26 (pp. 222, 226); and Bowlby, *Just Looking*, pp. 20–29.
128. Eleanor Salotto discusses the store dummies and their ghostly aspect: *Gothic Returns in Collins, Dickens, Zola, and Hitchcock* (New York: Palgrave Macmillan, 2006), p. 82.
129. Thompson sees this rather as the women and clothing being indistinguishable: *Naturalism Redressed*, pp. 74–75.

CONCLUSION

Bare Life and the Living Death of Modernity

> La famille sans père dont l'image est évoquée par le biais d'une tombe.
> [The family without a father, whose image is evoked by means of a tomb.]
> — Walter Benjamin[1]

Many of the characters in the literary texts studied here share some remarkably similar characteristics: they are widows, orphans, or both. In the Balzac texts, Raphaël, Lucien, and Esther have lost at least one parent, and Chabert was an orphan raised in state care. Stéphanie watches her husband die. In the Zola texts, Dide is an orphan and a widow; Silvère and Miette lose both parents (the former's both die, the latter's mother dies and her father is imprisoned); Thérèse Raquin's mother dies and her father abandons her, leaving her to live with his sister; Jacques is given up by his parents to be raised by his godmother; Renée is motherless; Denise is an orphan. In the Baudelaire works, several poetic characters are somewhat different, but still have lost a loved one: the 'passante' is in mourning, and the widow Andromaque summons for readers the widows of the prose poem 'Les Veuves'.[2] Edward Kaplan argues that, in this prose poem, the lyric poet identifies with the widow who is accompanied by her child, and he becomes 'the poet as widow' of the title of his article.[3] Even though the poet himself is not literally a widow, the lyric voice frequently mourns and appreciates ruined love as one might mourn and appreciate a dead spouse. The poem 'Le Cygne' adds orphans to the widow and to the other dispossessed figures there. This loss of important family members shapes the lives of these individuals, or more precisely, destroys the life they knew and moves many of them into a different identity and social space. These nineteenth-century authors converge in their similar representations of loss and a living death that emerges as the world moves into these new physical and social spaces of modernity.

Agamben's concept of 'bare life' can give us a framework for examining these characters in their shared relation to loss and to the living death of their ongoing life. We begin with some examples that Agamben gives of bare life, because their specificity makes the political and social concepts more readily understandable in our context. One aspect of bare life for Agamben is similar to that of our authors' depictions of a character who has been separated from the life that he or she used to have. Karen Quinlan, for example, is a well-known case of a comatose patient who was kept alive by machines: 'Her biological life [...] has been entirely separated from the form of life that bore the name Karen Quinlan: here life becomes (or at least seems to become) pure *zoē* [...]. It is no longer life but rather death in motion'.[4] She is, then, both alive and dead, 'moving' but with no consciousness.

It is also important to note that Karen's life was maintained because of a legal decision that was made. Her continuation in this living-dead state is the result of a kind of social decree: 'life and death are not properly scientific concepts but rather political concepts'.[5] Agamben's idea of the political intrusion into the private life of the body stems from Foucault's work on discipline and power, which is no longer simply the 'sovereign' ruler or state, but rather the more diffuse 'l'administration des corps et la gestion calculatrice de la vie' [administration of bodies and the calculated managing of life] by social forces.[6] Another salient example in Agamben is that of concentration camp detainees: 'Precisely because they were lacking almost all the rights and expectations that we attribute to human existence, and yet were still biologically alive, they came to be situated in a limit zone between life and death [...] in which they were no longer anything but bare life'.[7] Excluded from the human, political sphere, they inhabited a symbolic and literal space of non-being outside the political, social world.

Thus, for Agamben, a human in the condition of bare life is a kind of living-dead person who dwells in a zone of indistinction and exception from the norm. Following Foucault's concept of 'biopower', as that which disciplines or regularizes the bodies of humans, Agamben's biopower is the political/social sphere itself. This regularization (or Foucault's idea of discipline) is what Agamben calls 'the politicization of life',[8] by means of which exceptions are identified in the political/social sphere: 'Through its division and its capture in the apparatus of the exception, life assumes the form of bare life, which is to say, that of a life that has been cut off and separated from its form'.[9] Karen Quinlan's stagnant, unconscious life of the body has been separated from its social form; concentration camp inmates have no rights and have been wrenched from their physical homes and previous forms of life. Important for us here is how humans become separated from the life they knew in the past; again, how their full life becomes that bare life.

Stephanie presents a first example of bare life: her body is physically alive, but the form of life she knew as Stephanie has been taken from her by the horrors of war, by the society and world in which she lives. She exists in a state between the animal and the human, similar to the example of the werewolf given by Agamben; she is both living and dead.[10] Chabert, too, experiences the first aspect of bare life when he loses his memory: he is a body that lives without social identity. Subsequently, when he recovers his memory, he lives a different kind of bare life, because the social and political world around him, his wife and the Restoration, continue to strip him of his social identity and rights. He accepts the state of living death when he joins the ranks of delinquents and the homeless.

Raphaël de Valentin and his father have experienced hardships because of political regime changes in France and Europe: they struggle to retrieve his father's property now disputed by the powers that be. When they lose that battle and Raphaël's father dies, and when he gambles and tosses away his last money, Raphaël has lost everything and aims to end his biological life, as the form of his previous political, social life can no longer exist. His postponed suicide, the period of time between his decision to die and his pact with the *peau*, takes him into a strange, living-dead space both symbolically and literally when he goes 'shopping' in the antique store and hallucinates the animation, the living aspect of inanimate things, which match his state between life and non-life, life and death. Significantly, he then chooses to 'sell himself' in this commercial space, to accept the pact with the *peau*.

This human 'sale' or exchange in a shop allegorizes the rapid growth in Balzac's society of a consumer- and money-driven social order. Because of this contract with the *peau*, each wish for success brings his slow physical death closer, and the pact marks his symbolic acceptance of this new world where money reigns and founds all values. The last part of his life, just before he 'kills himself' (by acting on his desire for Pauline), is spent in an animalistic, coma-like existence provided by opiates, a bare life existence: 'Grâce à la puissance matérielle exercée par l'opium sur notre âme immatérielle, cet homme d'imagination si puissamment active s'abaissa jusqu'à la hauteur de ces animaux paresseux qui croupissent au sein des forêts' [By virtue of the material power exercised by opium on our immaterial soul, this man with such a powerfully active imagination lowered himself to the level of those languid animals that stagnate in the heart of forests] (*CH*, x, 289). One might think of his submission to this new social order as a kind of suggestion that it is fruitless to attempt to escape from its power: once he has made the pact, there is no life without the *peau*; with the *peau*, there is only bare life/living death, and finally death.

Lucien Chardon experiences two changes in the form of his life. The first, typical of the *Bildungsroman*, is his abandonment of his provincial life and his immersion in the modern culture of Paris, where, in order to survive, he morally prostitutes himself and undergoes the symbolic death of his integrity as a poet and as a man, of the form of life that had been important to him. Then, when he is on the verge of killing himself after financially ruining himself and risking the ruin of his sister, he too makes a pact and 'sells himself' to Vautrin in order to begin a reincarnated life in this new political order as the noble Lucien de Rubempré. He represents this state as the dispossession of himself, a kind of death of agency, as he is a kind of slave: 'Je ne m'appartiens plus' — a living death of sorts. However, in prison, he discovers that he cannot exist as this immoral person who has betrayed his partner Vautrin, he can no longer accept this bare life, in the sense that it is a life stripped of the values he had held before and to which he was reduced in the new Paris. So he ends his life, which is at that moment a relic of the past like the ancient structure of the Conciergerie where he commits suicide, and he, like Chabert, opts out of that new social order in a different way.

Esther also experiences two changes in form of life. She first renounces prostitution and attempts to earn her living in order to be worthy of Lucien. However, her quest fails when she is recognized by Lucien's journalist friends, as she is identified as aberrant and 'excluded' from normality. She consequently attempts to kill herself, not wishing to go back to her old life, thinking Lucien would find her unworthy, and finding herself unable to live without Lucien. She, like Lucien, is rescued from death by Vautrin, and she is transformed, at least for the most part, into a faithful and cultured companion for Lucien through her convent education.

Once again, however, this cannot last in the new social order, and she must destroy this new Esther in order to save Lucien. In the interim before she kills herself, she is in part living, in part dead: she has killed the pure Esther and awaits the completion of her bargain with Nucingen before killing her reinstated prostituted body. Vautrin also changes and is transformed by his 'double mort' [double death] (*CH*, VI, 835) when Lucien dies, and the 'force' of the new social order, like Foucault's discipline and Agamben's regularization, also pushes Vautrin to submit to this social order, to the 'force'. He joins the police, giving up his criminal state of exception to become a member of society, 'né pour une vie nouvelle' [born for a new life] (*CH*, VI, 928), even if he might still seek revenge for Lucien:

> J'ai reconnu qu'il y a dans la marche des choses une force [...]. Ainsi, tout en voulant renoncer à une lutte avec la loi, je n'ai point trouvé de place au soleil pour moi. Une seule me convient, c'est de me faire le serviteur de cette puissance qui pèse sur nous, et quand cette pensée m'est venue, la force dont je vous parlais s'est manifestée clairement autour de moi. (*CH*, VI, 922, 924)
>
> [I have realized that there is in the way of the world a force [...]. Hence, all the while wanting to renounce battling with the law, I have not found a place in the sun for myself. Only one place works for me, that is to make myself the servant of this power that weighs on us, and when this idea came to me, the force that I mentioned to you showed itself clearly around me.]

In Baudelaire, Andromaque represents most clearly the character wrenched from a past life and placed in a zone of indistinction between past and present, life and death, between animal and human, most clearly as the 'vil bétail' under Pyrrhus.[11] She lives on, beside the emptiness of the false Simoïs and the empty tomb of her husband. The form of her life changed radically, from highborn wife and mother, to a woman stripped of that identity and forced to leave her home. Through all this she retains her majesty, 'l'immense majesté de vos douleurs de veuve' [the immense majesty of your widow's grief] (*OC*, I, 85), just as the similar widow in the prose poem 'Les Veuves', 'une femme grande, majestueuse' [a tall, majestic woman] (*OC*, I, 294). The orphans, the swan, the black woman, the marooned sailors have all been wrenched from their previous form of life and home. The martyr in Baudelaire's eponymous poem has been literally cut off from her form of life, her body in pieces, and the poet follows her after her death to her new resting place in her tomb and beyond, as, in a state of living death, she haunts her killer. We might also mention the poet himself, whose father died when he was young, and for whom the remarriage of his mother was an ongoing trauma.

As for Zola (who as a child lost his father), his character Tante Dide lost a husband and then a lover when she was wrenched from the form of life of the passionate love that she had for Macquart. She lives an isolated, bare life until Silvère comes to live with her, yet she still suffers from bouts of madness that leave her body rigid, in bare life, outside of normality and considered strange by her community, until she is sequestered, living an isolated, semi-paralyzed, bare life in an asylum. Silvert and Miette are wrenched from their childhood homes and that form of life, and must move to a different home and family. Miette suffers violence in her new family; Silvère lives first in the home of his uncle, Pierre Rougon, where he is mistreated and 'grandissait dans les larmes, comme un malheureux abandonné' [grew up in tears, like a miserable, abandoned being] (*RM*, I, 134). He finds a better life with Dide, however he isolates himself from those in his age group and prefers his books to 'normal' social life. These two social outcasts find companionship in each other before they die young.

When Jacques Lantier is taken over by his ancestor, what remains of him is bare life, his body periodically separated from his inner being, from its form of life. Séverine is a powerless orphan, separated from life with her parents, who is sexually abused by her guardian, after which she is handed over to a husband she does not love. She submits to life passively, like a kind of object passed from one to the other. She does not feel desire and remains in this passive state of bare life until she meets Jacques, who later literally takes her life. Thérèse Raquin was taken from her home and the form of life she knew in Algeria when her mother died; she was then transplanted into a deadening form of life in the Raquin family, both in Vernon and in Paris. Eventually, her widowed aunt, Mme Raquin, lives a kind of death-in-life when she becomes paralyzed and cannot move or speak. Renée, like Séverine, has her form of life stolen from her by her abuser and is 'sold' to a man she does not love. Denise must leave the comfortable life she knew in Valognes to work at the Bonheur des Dames, where she is mistreated by her fellow workers, must take on additional night work to feed her family, is fired, and then forced to live in a disreputable apartment while scratching out a bare living by doing piecework. Denise is a rare exception in these characters subjected to the loss of their form of life, as in the text she not only survives, but also flourishes in the end.

The *lieux de mémoire* of Pierre Nora become in some of our texts memorial spaces of living death, where personal or communal history, or something an individual has lost, has been invested in a particular place or monument, which makes that past return.[12] In *Splendeurs et misères des courtisanes*, it is the Conciergerie that reveals the dead yet glorious history of the building to Lucien, as he is preparing to die in order to redeem the purity and 'glory' he lost. His hallucination, in which the present structure transforms into the building of the past, matches his limbic state as the tainted living being in the act of dying.

The area of the Louvre in Baudelaire's 'Le Cygne' creates a rich, multi-layered storage-house of memory and association for the poet, who remembers the colourful and quirky neighbourhood from his past, which used to be there but has been wiped away, leaving an empty space in the new courtyard of 'ce Louvre' of the poet's present. His mourning for the former space calls up for him the imaginary space of Andromache, who mourns her dead husband in another empty space, in the sense that it contains the empty tomb/monument and the empty artifice of a fake Simoïs. For Andromache, this space parallels her own living death, as well as the living death that the lyric poet at times claims for himself.

Balzac represents the imperfect return of city spaces which, like the false Troy, are artificially rebuilt. In 'Adieu', the village of Studzianka itself was dismantled, transported, and more or less rebuilt on the plain next to the Berezina river. Again, this ruined 'cité,' this 'ville improvisée' matches the living dead humans, soldiers and civilians, that inhabit it. The dead city is once again resurrected when Philippe builds an artificial replica on his property, and this personal *lieu de mémoire* finally kills Stéphanie.

The Doyenné neighbourhood near the Louvre was just a short distance from the rue de Langlade, where Esther lives at the beginning of *Splendeurs et misères des courtisanes*. A neighbourhood of prostitution, of people who sell themselves as things, becomes at night a limbic space, where objects seem to be people and people seem to be objects; where the beings who walk there are from no known world, 'ne sont d'aucun monde' (*OC*, VI, 447); and where white, ghostly forms line the walls — a neighbourhood of the living dead, of humans who have lost their humanity.

In Zola's works, the tombs in the cemetery of *La Fortune des Rougon* hold not only the remains of the dead, but also the uncanny living-dead whose fingers seem to creep towards Miette and Silvère, as previously cited: 'Ces herbes, qui leur liaient les pieds par les nuits de feu, et qui les faisaient vaciller, c'étaient des doigts minces, effilés par la tombe, sortis de terre pour les retenir, pour les jeter aux bras l'un de l'autre'. In this symbol of the influence of the heredity and the environment on Zola's characters, the dead do not disappear but remain to act in the present, a bit like Baudelaire's *squelette laboureur*, who continues to till the earth even after death.

Balzac and Zola both feature antiquated city spaces and their inhabitants, which continue to exist in a living-dead state in the present. In *Illusions perdues*, the deathly immobility of Angouleme's old aristocratic quarter, with its nobles, entrenched in the outdated values and practices of the past and living inside the remains of the town's fortress, contrasts with the modern and active commercial and industrial section of the town by the river. Similarly, the neighbourhood of Renée's father resembles a 'ville morte' [dead city], and the Béraud family, which lives in a 'maison morte' [dead house], is nearing the end of the line of its family name. Contrasted with the Bérauds' living-dead neighbourhood, Renée's brand-new mansion, throbbing with the superficial life of the Paris rich, sits next to the recently built Parc Monceau.

In addition to these public, exterior spaces of living death, our authors also represent private residences that reflect the living death of their inhabitants. In the old abbey where Stéphanie and her uncle live, she ruins the furnishings, whereas nature has ravished the exterior terraces, stairs, and railings. The half-destroyed abbey echoes Stéphanie's half-destroyed state as a 'fantôme' whose body exists in the present but who is stuck in the past, repeating the word *adieu*. Chabert's ramshackle, *newly*-built temporary abode in Paris seems ready to 'tomber en ruine'; newly constructed with the old materials of demolished buildings, it boasts a shutter constructed with that old store sign that displays the words 'Magasin de nouveautés'. In front of this ambiguous home is a new wall built with bones, with the literal dead. This new and old building aptly houses the living-dead Chabert.

In Baudelaire's 'Le Flacon', the interior space preserves memories of dead love in the armoire that releases what seems to be the perfumed smell of the poet's lover, for whom his love has died. This living-dead state of love represents the heart of the poet, 'la vie et la mort de mon cœur' [the life and death of my heart]. The androgynous woman of 'Une martyre' meets her end in a luxurious interior space, yet she goes on in living death.

The sumptuous room in which the body of the martyr lies leads us to the places where those goods can be bought: various types of shops in these texts, which are linked to living death. In *La Peau de chagrin*, the antique shop is rife with objects and preserved animals and humans, some of which seem to be alive, in this phantasmagorical space where even human remains are for sale. This leads to the link of living death with growing consumerism and commodification in the nineteenth century: when, eventually, all is for sale, and when humans sell themselves, they become commodities, things, their humanity killed. In *Illusions perdues*, the Galeries de Bois are the haunt of prostitutes and of booksellers, and Michel Chrestien makes explicit in the text that an author who enters this game becomes a kind of prostitute. *Splendeurs et misères des courtisanes* goes even further when the second-hand clothing shop sells items that seem to store bodily elements of their owners who died, a death rattle of one, a face of another: they become a kind of object-person, living and dead. Commerce enters even in Baudelaire's verse: the poet of 'Le Cygne' reminisces about the shacks that sold shiny knick-knacks, which are now destroyed and remain in a kind of living death in his memory. And the 'Squelette laboureur' toils away in a 'livre cadavéreux', the book itself like a living-dead mummy, which one finds for sale on the book stalls of the Paris quays.

In Zola, who wrote later, when consumerism was exploding in the city with the new department stores and ubiquitous advertising, Thérèse's outdated shop is a place of living death, as is the Baudu shop in *Au Bonheur des Dames*. In Mouret's new department store, built on the blood of Mouret's first wife, and whose new wing was also built on an area where human bones were discovered, women succumb to the death of their will as they are seduced by the goods and give in to rampant consumerism. In all three authors, shops are linked to living death, in a kind of allegory of the triumph of money. In Zola's text, we see the birth of the zombie-like shopper who mechanically keeps 'consuming' goods. Thus, in this century of ideas of the influence of the environment on human identity, these living dead milieus represent not just the physical influence but also the social influence of the modern consumer society rapidly spreading and growing.

Notes to the Conclusion

1. Walter Benjamin, *Baudelaire*, ed. by Giorgio Agamben, Patrick Charbonneau, and Barbara Chitussi (Paris: La Fabrique, 2013), p. 47.
2. See Rosemary Lloyd's discussion of the importance of widows in Baudelaire's poetry and his relation with his mother in *Baudelaire's World* (Ithaca, NY: Cornell University Press, 2002), p. 35.
3. Edward K. Kaplan, 'Baudelaire's Portrait of the Poet as Widow: Three "Poëmes en prose" and "Le Cygne"', *Symposium*, 34.3 (Fall 1980), 233–48; the widow is the poet's 'moral and esthetic model' (p. 241).
4. Agamben, *Homo Sacer*, p. 186.
5. Ibid., p. 164.
6. Michel Foucault, *Histoire de la sexualité, tome 1: La Volonté de savoir* (Paris: Gallimard, 1976), p. 184.
7. Agamben, *Homo Sacer*, p. 159.
8. Ibid., p. 119.

9. Giorgio Agamben, *The Use of Bodies*, trans. by Adam Kotsko (Stanford, CA: Stanford University Press, 2016), pp. 263.
10. Agamben, *Homo Sacer*, p. 106.
11. Giorgio Agamben has written some interesting interpretations of Baudelaire, as well as having found some of the papers that would have formed Benjamin's book on Baudelaire. He places Baudelaire at the moment of radical change in the way the past relates to the present — the loss of tradition: 'Baudelaire was the poet who had to face the dissolution of the authority of tradition in the new industrial society'. For Agamben, Baudelaire makes the intransmissibility of the past the very subject of art. For our purposes, it is interesting to note that, for Agamben, 'contrary to what one might think at first sight, the breaking of tradition does not at all mean the loss or devaluation of the past: it is, rather, likely that only now the past can reveal itself with a weight and an influence it never had before'. Here one thinks of the weight of the past bearing down on Andromache: *The Man Without Content*, trans. by Georgia Albert (Stanford, CA: Stanford University Press, 1999), pp. 106–08.
12. *Les Lieux de mémoire*, ed. by Nora.

BIBLIOGRAPHY

AGAMBEN, GIORGIO, *Homo Sacer: Sovereign Power and Bare Life*, trans. by Daniel Heller-Roazen (Stanford, CA: Stanford University Press, 1998)
—— *The Man Without Content*, trans. by Georgia Albert (Stanford, CA: Stanford University Press, 1999)
—— *The Use of Bodies*, trans. by Adam Kotsko (Stanford, CA: Stanford University Press, 2016)
AHEARN, EDWARD, 'Marx's Relevance for Second Empire Literature: Baudelaire's "Le Cygne"', *NCFS*, 14.3–4 (Spring-Summer 1986), 269–77
APPADURAI, ARJUN, ed., *The Social Life of Things: Commodities in Cultural Perspective* (Cambridge: Cambridge University Press, 2013)
ARMSTRONG, MARIE-SOPHIE, 'Hugo à l'aire Saint-Mittre: Zola et la problématique de la propriété littéraire', *The French Review*, 76.2 (December 2002), 346–57
BABUTS, NICOLAE, *Baudelaire: At the Limits and Beyond* (Newark: University of Delaware Press; London: Associated University Presses, 1997)
BALZAC, HONORÉ DE, *La Comédie humaine*, ed. by Pierre-Georges Castex and Pierre Citron, 12 vols (Paris: Gallimard, 1976–1981)
—— *Œuvres complètes de H. de Balzac*, 24 vols (Paris: Calmann Lévy, 1869–79)
—— *La Peau de chagrin*, ed. by Guillaume Kichenin (Paris: Gallimard, 2003)
BAUDELAIRE, CHARLES, *Œuvres complètes*, ed. by Claude Pichois, 2 vols, Bibliothèque de la Pléiade (Paris: Gallimard, 1975–76)
BECKER, COLETTE, 'Illusion et réalité: la métaphore du théâtre dans *La Curée*', in *La Curée de Zola ou 'la vie à outrance': actes du colloque du 10 janvier 1987*, ed. by David Baguley (Paris: SEDES, 1987), pp. 119–28
—— 'L'Intrigue', in *Genèse, structures et style de 'La Curée'*, ed. by Henri Mitterand, Colette Becker, and Jean-Pierre Leduc-Adine (Paris: SEDES, 1987), pp. 29–50
—— 'Zola, un déchiffreur de l'entre-deux', *Études Françaises*, 39.2 (2003), 11–21
BEIZER, JANET, 'Au (delà du) Bonheur des Dames: Notes on the Underground', *Australian Journal of French Studies*, 38.3 (September-December 2001), 393–406
—— 'Encore *Adieu*: de la répétition à la mort', *L'Année Balzacienne*, 7.1 (2006), 55–66
BELL, DAVID F., 'Fantasy and Reality in *La Peau de chagrin*', in *The Cambridge Companion to Balzac*, ed. by Owen Heathcote and Andrew Watts (Cambridge: Cambridge University Press, 2017), pp. 52–66
—— *Real Time: Accelerating Narrative from Balzac to Zola* (Urbana: University of Illinois Press, 2004)
—— '*Thérèse Raquin*: Scientific Realism in Zola's Laboratory', *NCFS*, 24.1–2 (Fall-Winter 1995–96), 122–32
BELL, DORIAN, 'Cavemen Among Us: Genealogies of Atavism from Zola's *La Bête Humaine* to Chabrol's *Le Boucher*', *French Studies*, 62.1 (January 2008), 39–52
BELL, MICHAEL MAYERFELD, 'The Ghosts of Place', *Theory and Society*, 26.6 (December 1997), 813–36
BENHAIM, ANDRÉ, 'De René à Renée', *Les Cahiers Naturalistes*, 73 (1999), 151–66

BENJAMIN, WALTER, *The Arcades Project*, ed. by Rolf Tiedemann, trans. by Howard Eiland and Kevin McLaughlin (Cambridge, MA: Harvard University Press, 1999)
—— *Baudelaire*, ed. by Giorgio Agamben, Patrick Charbonneau, and Barbara Chitussi (Paris: La Fabrique, 2013)
—— *The Origin of German Tragic Drama*, trans. by John Osborne (London & New York: Verso, 1998)
—— *Selected Writings*, ed. by Michael William Jennings, Howard Eiland, and Gary Smith, trans. by Rodney Livingstone and others, 4 vols (Cambridge, MA: Belknap Press, 1996–2003)
—— *The Writer of Modern Life: Essays on Charles Baudelaire*, ed. by Michael W. Jennings (Cambridge, MA: Harvard University Press, 2006)
BERNHEIMER, CHARLES, *Figures of Ill Repute: Representing Prostitution in Nineteenth-century France* (Cambridge, MA: Harvard University Press, 1989)
BERSANI, LEO, *Baudelaire and Freud* (Berkeley: University of California Press, 1977)
BERTHIER, PHILIPPE, 'Histoire du texte', in Honoré de Balzac, *Splendeurs et misères des courtisanes*, ed. by Philippe Berthier (Paris: Garnier Flammarion, 2006), pp. 41–43
—— 'Hôtel Saccard: états des lieux', in *La Curée de Zola ou 'la vie à outrance': actes du colloque du 10 janvier 1987*, ed. by David Baguley (Paris: SEDES, 1987), pp. 107–18
BLOOD, SUSAN, *Baudelaire and the Aesthetics of Bad Faith* (Stanford, CA: Stanford University Press, 1997)
—— 'The Sonnet as Snapshot: Seizing the Instant in Baudelaire's "À une passante"', *NCFS*, 36.3–4 (Spring-Summer 2008), 255–69
BORGOMANO, MADELEINE, 'Adieu, ou l'écriture aux prises avec l'histoire', *Romantisme*, 76 (1992), 77–86
BORIE, JEAN, *Zola et les mythes ou la nausée au salut* (Paris: Seuil, 1971)
BOURDIEU, PIERRE, *Les Règles de l'art: genèse et structure du champ littéraire* (Paris: Seuil, 1992)
—— *Le Sens Pratique*, (Paris: Minuit, 1980)
BOWLBY, RACHEL, *Carried Away: The Invention of Modern Shopping* (New York: Columbia University Press, 2001)
—— *Just Looking: Consumer Culture in Dreiser, Gissing, and Zola* (New York: Methuen, 1985)
BRAY, PATRICK M., *The Novel Map: Space and Subjectivity in Nineteenth-century French Fiction* (Evanston, IL: Northwestern University Press, 2013)
—— 'Prose Constructions: Nerval, Baudelaire, and the Louvre', *L'Esprit Créateur*, 54.2 (2014), 115–26
BRESNICK, ADAM, 'The Paradox of Bildung: Balzac's *Illusions perdues*', *MLN*, 113.4 (1998), 823–50
BROMBERT, VICTOR, 'Baudelaire: City Images and the "Dream of Stone"', *Yale French Studies*, 32, (1964), 99–105
—— '"Le Cygne" de Baudelaire: douleur, souvenir, travail,' *Études baudelairiennes, III: Le Poète et son temps: thèmes et exégèses*, ed. by James S. Patty and Claude Pichois (Neuchâtel: La Baconnière, 1973), pp. 254–61
BROOKS, PETER, *Body Work: Objects of Desire in Modern Narrative* (Cambridge, MA: Harvard University Press, 1993)
—— 'Narrative Desire', *Style*, 18.3 (Summer 1984), 312–27
—— 'Narrative Transaction and Transference (Unburying *Le Colonel Chabert*)', *Novel*, 15.2 (1982), 101–10
BROOME, PETER, *Baudelaire's Poetic Patterns: The Secret Language of 'Les Fleurs du mal'* (Amsterdam & Atlanta, GA: Rodopi, 1999)
BUCK-MORSS, SUSAN, *The Dialectics of Seeing: Walter Benjamin and the Arcades Project*, Studies in Contemporary German Social Thought (Cambridge, MA: MIT Press, 1989)

―― 'Walter Benjamin ― Revolutionary Writer (II)', *New Left Review*, 129 (September-October 1981), 77–95
BURTON, RICHARD D. E., 'Baudelaire and the Agony of the Second Republic: "Spleen" (LXXV) ("Pluviôse, Irrité...")', *MLR*, 81.3 (1986), 600–11
―― *Baudelaire in 1859: A Study in the Sources of Poetic Creativity* (Cambridge & New York: Cambridge University Press, 1988)
―― *Baudelaire and the Second Republic: Writing and Revolution* (Oxford & New York: Clarendon Press, 1991)
―― *The Context of Baudelaire's 'Le Cygne'* (Durham: University of Durham, 1980)
―― 'The Dead Father: A Note on "Le Cygne" and the *Iliad*', *French Studies Bulletin*, 11.38 (1991), 7–9
―― 'Poet, Painter, Lover: A Reading of "Les Bijoux"', in *Understanding 'Les Fleurs du Mal': Critical Readings*' ed. by William J. Thompson (Nashville, TN: Vanderbilt University Press, 1997), pp. 214–23
BUTOR, MICHEL, *Le Marchand et le génie: improvisations sur Balzac I* (Paris: La Différence, 1998)
CAIN, GEORGES, *Coins de Paris*, préface de Victorien Sardou, nouvelle édition (Paris: Flammarion, 1910)
CARUTH, CATHY, 'The Claims of the Dead: History, Haunted Property, and the Law', in *Literature in the Ashes of History* (Baltimore: Johns Hopkins University Press, 2013), pp. 18–39
CASTLE, TERRY, *The Apparitional Lesbian: Female Homosexuality and Modern Culture*, Gender and Culture (New York: Columbia University Press, 1993)
CAZAURAN, NICOLE, 'Le "Tableau" du magasin d'antiquités dans *La Peau de chagrin*', in *Mélanges de langue et de littérature française offerts à Pierre Larthomas*, ed. by Jean-Pierre Seguin (Paris: École normale supérieure de jeunes filles, 1985), pp. 87–98
CHAMBERS, ROSS, *An Atmospherics of the City: Baudelaire and the Poetics of Noise*, Verbal Arts: Studies in Poetics (New York: Fordham University Press, 2015)
―― 'Baudelaire's Paris', in *The Cambridge Companion to Baudelaire*, ed. by Rosemary Lloyd (Cambridge: Cambridge University Press, 2006), pp. 101–16
―― 'Daylight Specter: Baudelaire's "The Seven Old Men"', *Yale French Studies*, 125–26 (2014), 45–65
―― 'Heightening the Lowly (Baudelaire: "Je n'ai pas oublié ..." and "À une passante")', *NCFS*, 37.1–2 (2008), 42–51
―― *Loiterature*, (Lincoln: University of Nebraska Press, 1999)
―― 'On Inventing Unknownness: The Poetry of Disenchanted Reenchantment (Leopardi, Baudelaire, Rimbaud, Justice)', *French Forum*, 33.1–2 (2008), 15–36
―― 'The Storm in the Eye of the Poem: Baudelaire's "À une passante"', in *Textual Analysis: Some Readers Reading*, ed. by Mary Ann Caws (New York: Modern Language Association of America, 1986), pp. 156–66
―― *The Writing of Melancholy: Modes of Opposition in Early French Modernism*, trans. by Mary Seidman Trouille (Chicago: The University of Chicago Press, 1987)
CHARLES, DAVID, '*La Fortune des Rougon*, roman de la Commune', *Romantisme*, 131.1 (2006), 99–114
CITRON, PIERRE, *La Poésie de Paris dans la littérature française de Rousseau à Baudelaire* (Paris: Minuit, 1961)
CNOCKAERT, VÉRONIQUE, 'L'Empire de l'ensauvagement: *Adieu* de Balzac', *Romantisme*, 145.3 (2009), 37–49
COHEN, MARGARET, 'Benjamin's Phantasmagoria: The *Arcades Project*', in *The Cambridge Companion to Walter Benjamin*, ed. by David S. Ferris (Cambridge: Cambridge University Press, 2004), pp. 199–220

COHEN-VRIGNAUD, G., 'Capitalism's Wishful Thinking', *Modern Language Quarterly*, 76.2 (2015), 181–99

COHN, ROBERT GREER, 'Baudelaire's "Frisson Nouveau"', *The Romanic Review*, 84.1 (January 1993), 19–26

COMPAGNON, ANTOINE, *Baudelaire devant l'innombrable: mémoire de la critique* (Paris: Presses de l'Université de Paris-Sorbonne, 2003)

COUNTER, ANDREW, 'The Legacy of the Beast: Patrilinearity and Rupture in Zola's *La Bête humaine* and Freud's *Totem and Taboo*', *French Studies*, 62.1 (2008), 26–38

DALY, NICHOLAS, 'That Obscure Object of Desire: Victorian Commodity Culture and Fictions of the Mummy', *Novel*, 28.1 (Fall 1994), 24–51

DELEUZE, GILLES, *La Logique du sens* (Paris: Minuit, 1969)

DELVAU, ALFRED, *Les Dessous de Paris* (Paris: Poulet-Malassis et de Broise, 1860)

DE MAN, PAUL, *Blindness and Insight: Essays in the Rhetoric of Contemporary Criticism* (Minneapolis: University of Minnesota Press, 1983)

DEZALAY, AUGUSTE, 'L'Infortune des Rougon ou le mal des origines', in *Le Mal dans l'imaginaire littéraire français (1850–1950)*, ed. by Myriam Watthee-Delmotte and Metka Zupančič (Paris: Harmattan, 1998), pp. 181–92

—— 'Ordre et désordre dans les Rougon-Macquart: l'exemple de *La Fortune des Rougon*', *Travaux de Linguistique et de Littérature*, 11.2 (1973), 71–81

FAUDEMAY, ALAIN, 'Sur la porosité baudelairienne: la mémoire au futur dans "Le Flacon"', *Colloquium Helveticum*, 27 (1998), 163–79

FELMAN, SHOSHANA, 'Women and Madness: The Critical Phallacy', *Diacritics*, 5.4 (1975), 2–10

FERGUSON, PRISCILLA PARKHURST, *Paris as Revolution: Writing the Nineteenth-century City* (Berkeley: University of California Press, 1994)

FINCH-RACE, DANIEL A., 'Placelessness in Baudelaire's "Les Sept Vieillards" and "Les Petites Vieilles"', *MLR*, 110.4 (2015), 1011–26

FISCHER, CAROLINE, 'Baudelaire et la tradition de la poésie amoureuse', in *La Main hâtive des révolutions: esthétique et désenchantement en Europe de Leopardi à Heiner Müller*, ed. by Jean Bessière and Stéphane Michaud (Paris: Presses Sorbonne Nouvelle, 2001), pp. 35–54

FISHER, DOMINIQUE D., 'The Silent Erotic: Rhetoric of Baudelaire's Mirrors', in *Articulations of Difference: Gender Studies and Writing in French*, ed. by Dominique D. Fisher and Lawrence R. Schehr (Stanford, CA: Stanford University Press, 1997), pp. 34–51

FORTESCUE, WILLIAM, *France and 1848: The End of Monarchy* (London & New York: Routledge, 2005)

FOUCAULT, MICHEL, *Histoire de la sexualité, tome 1: La Volonté de savoir* (Paris: Gallimard, 1976)

FRAPPIER-MAZUR, LUCIENNE, 'Violence et répétition dans *Adieu* de Balzac', in *Pratiques de l'écriture: mélanges de poétique et d'histoire littéraire offerts à Jean Gaudon*, ed. by Jean Gaudon and Pierre Laforgue (Paris: Klincksieck, 1996), pp. 157–66

FREUD, SIGMUND, 'Medusa's Head', in *Standard Edition of the Complete Psychological Works of Sigmund Freud*, ed. and trans. by James Strachey, 24 vols (London: Hogarth Press, 1953–74), XVIII, 273–74

FUSS, DIANA, ed., *Inside/Out: Lesbian Theories, Gay Theories* (London: Routledge, 1991)

GAILLARD, FRANÇOISE, 'L'Effet peau de chagrin', in *Le Roman de Balzac: recherches critiques, méthodes, lectures*, ed. by Roland Le Huenen and Paul Perron (Montreal: Didier, 1980), pp. 213–30

—— 'La Peur des revenants', in *Littérature et médecine, ou les pouvoirs du récit*, ed. by Gérard Danou (Paris: BPI/Centre Pompidou, 2001), pp. 89–105

GARVAL, MICHAEL, 'Balzac's *La Comédie humaine*: The Archival Rival', *NCFS*, 25.1–2 (Fall-Winter 1996–97), 30–40

GASARIAN, GÉRARD, '"Le Cygne" of Baudelaire', in *Understanding 'Les Fleurs du Mal': Critical Readings*, ed. by William J. Thompson (Nashville, TN: Vanderbilt University Press, 1997), pp. 122–32
—— *De loin tendrement: étude sur Baudelaire* (Paris: Champion, 1996)
GASCAR, PIERRE, 'Préface', in Honoré de Balzac, *Le Colonel Chabert, suivi de El Verdugo, Adieu, Le Réquisitionnaire*, ed. by Patrick Berthier (Paris: Gallimard, 1974)
GAUTIER, THÉOPHILE, 'Marilhat', *La Revue des deux mondes*, 23 (1 July 1848), 56–75
GENGEMBRE, GÉRARD, 'Temps et argent ou la politique du temps fantastique dans *La Peau de chagrin*', *Otrante*, 9 (1997), 113–17
GILL, MIRANDA, 'Psychomachia and the Limits of Masculine Agency in Balzac's *Adieu*', *MLR*, 110.4 (2015), 1027–44
GODFREY, SIMA, '"Ce père nourricier": Revisiting Baudelaire's Family Romance', *NCFS*, 38.1–2 (2009), 39–51
—— 'From Memory Lane to Memory Boulevard: *Paris change!*', in *City Images: Perspectives from Literature, Philosophy, and Film*, ed. by Mary Ann Caws (New York: Gordon & Breach, 1991), pp. 157–71
GOERGEN, MAXIME, 'Les Noms du *Colonel Chabert*: langage et pouvoir après Napoleon', *Romance Notes*, 54.3 (2014), 353–68
GOULET, ANDREA, *Optiques: The Science of the Eye and the Birth of Modern French Fiction*, Critical Authors & Issues (Philadelphia: University of Pennsylvania Press, 2006)
GRIFFITHS, KATE, *Emile Zola and the Artistry of Adaptation* (London: Legenda, 2009)
—— 'The Haunted Mirrors in Émile Zola and Guy de Maupassant', *Bulletin of the Émile Zola Society*, 26 (October 2002), 3–13
—— 'Scribbling Ghosts', in *Possessions: Essays in French Literature, Cinema and Theory*, ed. by Julia Horn and Lynsey Russell-Watts (Oxford: Peter Lang, 2003), pp. 3–13
GRIMM, RICHARD E., 'Aeneas and Andromache in *Aeneid* III', *The American Journal of Philology*, 88.2 (1967), 151–62
GUICHARDET, JEANNINE, ''Illusions perdues' : quelques itinéraires en pays parisien,' in *Balzac: 'Illusions perdues': l'œuvre capitale dans l'œuvre*, ed. by Françoise van Rossum-Guyon (Groningen: University of Groningen; 1988), pp. 89-93.
—— 'Errance et folie dans *Adieu*', in *Balzac mosaïque*, Cahiers romantiques, 12 (Clermont-Ferrand: Presses universitaires Blaise Pascal, 2007), pp. 205–15
HARROW, SUSAN, 'Myopia and the Model', in *L'Écriture du féminin chez Zola et dans la fiction naturaliste /Writing the Feminine in Zola and Naturalist Fiction*, ed. by Anna Gural-Migdal (Bern: Peter Lang, 2003), pp. 251–70
—— '*Thérèse Raquin*: Animal Passion and the Brutality of Reading', in *The Cambridge Companion to Zola*, ed. by Brian Nelson (Cambridge: Cambridge University Press, 2007), pp. 105–20
—— 'Velocity, Vacancy and Consciousness: Female Character as Culture Critic in *La Bête humaine* and *Au Bonheur des Dames*', *Excavatio*, 23.1–2 (2008), 214–26
HARVEY, DAVID, *Paris: Capital of Modernity* (New York: Routledge, 2006)
HEATHCOTE, OWEN, 'Negative Equity? The Representation of Prostitution and the Prostitution of Representation in Balzac', *Forum for Modern Language Studies*, 40.3 (2004), 279–90
HEMMINGS, F. W. J., 'Zola and *L'Éducation sentimentale*', *Romanic Review*, 50 (1959), 35–40
HIDDLESTON, J. A., *Baudelaire and 'Le Spleen de Paris'* (Oxford: Clarendon Press, 1987)
HITCHCOCK, HENRY-RUSSELL, *Architecture: Nineteenth and Twentieth Centuries*, (New Haven, CT: Yale University Press, 1987)
HOUSSAYE, ARSÈNE, *Poésies complètes* (Paris: Charpentier, 1850)
JACKSON, JOHN E., *La Mort Baudelaire: essai sur 'Les Fleurs du mal'* (Neuchâtel: La Baconnière, 1982)

―― 'Vers un nouveau berceau? Le rêve de palingénésie chez Baudelaire', in *L'Année Baudelaire 2: figures de la mort, figures de l'éternité*, ed. by John E. Jackson and Claude Pichois (Paris: Klincksieck, 1996), pp. 45–61

JACQUIER, JOSÉPHINE ALIDA, 'From Paris to Rome: Virgil's Andromache Between Politics and Poetics in Charles Baudelaire's "Le Cygne"', in *Augustan Poetry and the Roman Republic*, ed. by Joseph Farrell and Damien P. Nelis (Oxford: Oxford University Press, 2013), pp. 161–79

JOHNSON, BARBARA, 'Apostrophe, Animation, and Abortion', *Diacritics*, 16.1 (1986), 28–47

JULLIEN, DOMINIQUE, 'Entre psychiatrie et philosophie : la folie dans *Adieu* de Balzac', *Littérature*, 162 (2011), 24–35

KAMM, LEWIS, 'People and Things in Zola's *Rougon-Macquart*: Reification Re-humanized', *Philological Quarterly*, 53.1 (1974), 100–09

KAPLAN, EDWARD K., 'Baudelaire's Portrait of the Poet as Widow: Three "Poëmes en prose" and "Le Cygne"', *Symposium*, 34.3 (1980), 233–48

KELLY, DOROTHY, 'Balzac, Gender and Sexuality: *La Cousine Bette*', in *The Cambridge Companion to Balzac*, ed. by Owen Heathcote and Andrew Watts (Cambridge: Cambridge University Press, 2017), pp. 111–26

―― 'Gender, Metaphor, and Machine: *La Bête humaine*', *French Literature Series*, 16 (1989), 110–22

―― 'The Living Death of the Past: Body Parts, Money, and the Fetish in *La Peau de chagrin*', *Lingua Romana*, 8.1 (Fall 2009), no pagination

―― 'The Marriage of Don Juan: Balzac and the Inheritance of Culture', *Dix-Neuf*, 11.1 (2008), 49–58

―― 'Toxic *Doxa* in Baudelaire: "À celle qui est trop gaie" and "Une charogne"', *Symposium*, 66.4 (2012), 194–205

KNIGHT, DIANA, 'Celibacy on Display in Two Texts by Balzac: *Le Cabinet Des Antiques* and the Preface to *Pierrette*', *Dix-Neuf*, 2.1 (2004), 1–15

KOPP, ROBERT, 'Le "Balzac" de Walter Benjamin', *L'Année Balzacienne*, 7 (1986), 339–48

KROEN, SHERYL, *Politics and Theater: The Crisis of Legitimacy in Restoration France, 1815–1830* (Berkeley: University of California Press, 2000)

LABARTHE, PATRICK, *Baudelaire et la tradition de l'allégorie*, Histoire des idées et critique littéraire, 380 (Genève: Droz, 1999)

―― 'La Douleur du cygne', in *Baudelaire: une alchimie de la douleur: études sur 'Les Fleurs du mal'*, ed. by Patrick Labarthe (Saint-Pierre-du-Mont: Eurédit, 2003), pp. 143–61

LAFORGUE, PIERRE, 'Écrire le fantasme, ou masculin et féminin dans "Une martyre"', in *Baudelaire, une alchimie de la douleur: études sur 'Les Fleurs du mal'*, ed. by Patrick Labarthe (Saint-Pierre-du-Mont: Eurédit, 2003), pp. 163–74

―― '"Falsi Simoentis ad undam" — autour de l'épigraphe du "Cygne": Baudelaire, Virgile, Racine et Hugo', *NCFS*, 24.1–2 (Fall-Winter 1995–96), 97–110

LAMARTINE, ALPHONSE DE, *Œuvres d'Alphonse de Lamartine*, 2 vols (Paris: Jules Boquet, 1826)

LEAKEY, F. W., *Baudelaire, Collected Essays, 1953–1988*, ed. by Eva Jacobs, Cambridge Studies in French (Cambridge: Cambridge University Press, 1990)

―― *Baudelaire: 'Les Fleurs du Mal'* (Cambridge: Cambridge University Press, 1992)

―― 'The Originality of Baudelaire's "Le Cygne": Genesis as Structure and Theme', in *Order and Adventure in Post-romantic French Poetry: Essays Presented to C. A. Hackett*, ed. by Ernest M. Beaumont (New York: Barnes & Noble, 1973), pp. 38–55

LEE, SCOTT, 'Le Réalisme au risque de Balzac: témoignage et récit dans *Adieu*', *Études Françaises*, 37.2 (2001), 181–202

LIONNET, FRANÇOISE, 'Reframing Baudelaire: Literary History, Biography, Postcolonial Theory, and Vernacular Languages', *Diacritics*, 28.3 (1998), 63–85

LLOYD, ROSEMARY, *Baudelaire's World* (Ithaca, NY: Cornell University Press, 2002)

LOK, MATTHIJS M., '"Un oubli total du passé"? The Political and Social Construction of Silence in Restoration Europe (1813–1830)', *History and Memory*, 26.2 (Fall-Winter 2014), 40–75

LOYER, FRANÇOIS, *Paris Nineteenth Century: Architecture and Urbanism*, trans. by Charles Lynn Clark (New York: Abbeville Press, 1988)

MANNONI, OCTAVE, *Clefs pour l'imaginaire, ou l'autre scène* (Paris: Seuil, 1969)

MARDER, ELISSA, *Dead Time: Temporal Disorders in the Wake of Modernity (Baudelaire and Flaubert)* (Stanford, CA: Stanford University Press, 2001)

MARINI, MARCELLE, 'Chabert mort ou vif', *Littérature*, 13.1 (1974), 92–112

MARION, FULGENCE, *L'Optique* (Paris: Hachette, 1867)

MARTINE, JEAN-LUC, '*Adieu*! de Balzac, un texte qui soigne ou un texte qui tue?', *Études Épistémè*, 13 (2008), 121–41

MATHIEU, JEAN-CLAUDE, '"Une charogne"', in *Les Fleurs du Mal: actes du colloque de la Sorbonne, des 10 et 11 janvier, 2003*, ed. by André Guyaux and Bertrand Marchal (Paris: Sorbonne, 2003), 161–80

MCGRATH, CAITLIN, '"Crippled by Sight": Detail in *Au Bonheur des Dames*', *Modernism / Modernity*, 21.3 (2014), 641–64

MELTZER, FRANÇOISE, *Seeing Double: Baudelaire's Modernity* (Chicago: University of Chicago Press, 2011)

MÉNARD, SOPHIE, *Émile Zola et les aveux du corps: les savoirs du roman naturaliste* (Paris: Classiques Garnier, 2014)

——'Les Fantômes nuptiaux chez Zola', *Romantisme*, 149.3 (2010), 97–110

MILLER, D. A., 'Balzac's Illusions Lost and Found', *Yale French Studies*, 67 (1984), 164–81

MILLER, MICHAEL B., *The Bon Marché: Bourgeois Culture and the Department Store, 1869–1920* (Princeton, NJ: Princeton University Press, 1981)

MITTERAND, HENRI, 'The Genesis of Novelistic Space: Zola's *La Bête humaine*', in *Naturalism in the European Novel: New Critical Perspectives*, ed. by Brian Nelson (New York & Oxford: Berg, 1992), pp. 666–79

——'Une archéologie mentale: le roman experimental et *La Fortune des Rougon*', in *Le Discours du roman* (Paris: PuF, 1980), pp. 164–85

——'Zola devant la Commune', *Les Lettres françaises*, 732 (3 July 1958), 5–6

MIZOUNI, SOPHIA, 'Nineteenth-century Paris, Capital of Illusion' (unpublished doctoral thesis, Boston University, 2016)

MULVEY, LAURA, *Fetishism and Curiosity* (Bloomington: Indiana University; London: British Film Institute, 1996)

NELSON, BRIAN, 'Zola and the Counter Revolution: *Au Bonheur des Dames*', *Australian Journal of French Studies*, 30.2 (1993), 233–40

NELSON, LOWRY, 'Baudelaire and Virgil: A Reading of "Le Cygne"', *Comparative Literature*, 13.4 (1961), 332–45

NERVAL, GÉRARD DE, *Petits châteaux de bohême: prose et poésie* (Paris: E. Didier, 1853)

NESCI, CATHERINE, 'De l'histoire-panorama à l'histoire-mémoire: Balzac et la "fantasmagorie" du passé', in *Balzac dans l'histoire*, ed. by Nicole Mozet and Paule Petitier (Paris: SEDES, 2001), pp. 55–67

NEWMARK, KEVIN, 'Off the Charts: Walter Benjamin's Depiction of Baudelaire', in *Baudelaire and the Poetics of Modernity*, ed. by Patricia Ward and James Patty (Nashville, TN: Vanderbilt University Press, 2001), pp. 72–84

——'Who Needs Poetry? Baudelaire, Benjamin, and the Modernity of "Le Cygne"', *Comparative Literature*, 63.3 (2011), 269–90

NOIRAY, JACQUES, 'La Symbolique de l'espace dans *La Curée*', *L'Information Littéraire*, 39.1 (1987), 16–20

―― 'Une "mise en abyme" de *La Curée*: les amours du beau Narcisse et de la nymphe Echo', *Littératures*, 16.1 (1987), 69–77

NORA, PIERRE, ed., *Les Lieux de mémoire: La République, La Nation, Les France 1* (Paris: Gallimard, 2004)

―― *Realms of Memory*, trans. by Lawrence D. Kritzman (New York: Columbia University Press, 1998)

OEHLER, DOLF, 'Baudelaire's Politics', in *The Cambridge Companion to Baudelaire*, ed. by Rosemary Lloyd (Cambridge: Cambridge University Press, 2006), pp. 14–30

―― 'L'Explosion baudelairienne', *Europe: Revue Littéraire Mensuelle*, 70 (August-September 1992), 62–68

―― *Le Spleen contre l'oubli, juin 1848: Baudelaire, Flaubert, Heine, Herzen* (Paris: Payot, 1996)

OLMSTED, WILLIAM, 'Immortal Rot: A Reading of "Une charogne"', in *Understanding 'Les Fleurs du mal': Critical Readings*, ed. by William J. Thompson (Nashville, TN: Vanderbilt University Press, 1997), pp. 60–71

PAGANO, TULLIO, 'Allegorizing *La Curée*', *Excavatio*, 6–7 (January 1995), 166–76

PARASCHAS, SOTIRIOS, '*Illusions perdues*: Writers, Artists and the Reflexive Novel', *The Cambridge Companion to Balzac*, ed. by Owen Heathcote and Andrew Watts (Cambridge: Cambridge University Press, 2017), pp. 97–110

PARSONS, DEBORAH L., *Streetwalking the Metropolis: Women, the City, and Modernity* (Oxford & New York: Oxford University Press, 2000)

PAUW, CLARA, '(Un) Dressing Renée: Clothing and Identity in Zola's Novel *La Curée*' (unpublished doctoral thesis, Emory University, 2011)

PETERSON, SAMANTHA, 'Experimenting on Difference: Women, Violence, and Narrative in Zola's Naturalism' (unpublished doctoral thesis, Boston University, 2015)

PETREY, SANDY, 'Balzac's Empire: History, Insanity, and the Realist Text', in *Historical Criticism and the Challenge of Theory*, ed. by Janet Levarie Smarr (Urbana: University of Illinois Press, 1993), pp. 25–41

―― 'The Reality of Representation: Between Marx and Balzac', *Critical Inquiry*, 14.3 (1988), 448–68

―― 'Stylistics and Society in *La Curée*', *MLN*, 89.4 (1974), 626–40

PILBEAM, PAMELA, *The French Revolution of 1830* (New York: St Martin's Press, 1991)

PIREDDU, NICOLETTA, 'Between *fantasque* and *fantasmagorique*: A Fantastic Reading of Balzac's *La Peau de chagrin*', *Paroles Gelées: UCLA French Studies*, 9 (January 1991), 33–47

POT, OLIVIER, '"Une charogne" de Baudelaire: autopsies d'une rencontre', in *Mémoire et oubli dans le lyrisme européen*, ed. by Dagmar Wieser, Patrick Labarthe, and Jean-Paul Avice (Paris: Champion, 2008), pp. 113–48

POULET, GEORGES, *Qui était Baudelaire?* (Geneva: Skira, 1969)

PRENDERGAST, CHRISTOPHER, 'Melodrama and Totality in *Splendeurs et misères des courtisanes*', *Novel*, 6.2 (1973), 152–62

―― *The Order of Mimesis: Balzac, Stendhal, Nerval, Flaubert*, Cambridge Studies in French (Cambridge & New York: Cambridge University Press, 1986)

QUARANTINI, FRANCA ZANELLI, '"Andromaque" au Carrousel: une lecture de "Le Cygne"', *Revue italienne d'études françaises*, 2 (2012), 1–12

RAMAZANI, VAHEED, 'Gender, War, and the Department Store: Zola's *Au Bonheur des Dames*', *SubStance*, 36.2 (2007), 126–46

RICATTE, ROBERT, 'Espace et temps dans *La Fortune des Rougon*', in *Les Critiques de notre temps et Zola*, ed. by Colette Becker (Paris: Garnier, 1972), pp. 135–40

RINCÉ, DOMINIQUE, 'Vers, vermines, vermisseaux et autres bestioles contaminantes dans l'œuvre poétique de Charles Baudelaire', *Nottingham French Studies*, 58.2 (2019), 146–55

ROBB, GRAHAM, *Baudelaire, lecteur de Balzac* (Paris: Corti, 1988)

ROLLS, ALISTAIR, *Paris and the Fetish* (Amsterdam: Rodopi, 2014)
ROULIN, JEAN-MARIE, and COLETTE WINDISH, 'The Return of the Undead: The Body Politic in *Le Colonel Chabert*', *South Central Review*, 29.3 (2012), 20–35
RYKNER, ARNAUD, 'Les Fulgurances du corps muet: Zola, les tableaux vivants et la pantomime', *Studies in French Literature: Naturalisme et excès visuels: pantomime, parodie, image, fête. Mélanges en l'honneur de David Baguley*, ed. by Catherine Dousteyssier-Khoze and Edward Welch (Newcastle upon Tyne: Cambridge Scholars Publishing, 2009), pp. 17–35
—— 'The Power of Tableaux Vivants in Zola: The Underside of the Image', *Image & Narrative*, 12.3 (2011), 98–112
SALISBURY, LAURA, 'Michel Serres: Science, Fiction, and the Shape of Relation', *Science Fiction Studies*, 33.1 (March 2006), 30–52
SALOTTO, ELEANOR, *Gothic Returns in Collins, Dickens, Zola, and Hitchcock* (New York: Palgrave Macmillan, 2006)
SAMUELS, MAURICE, 'Metaphors of Modernity: Prostitutes, Bankers, and Other Jews in Balzac's *Splendeurs et misères des courtisanes*' *Romanic Review*, 97.2 (2006), 169–84
—— 'Realizing the Past: History and Spectacle in Balzac's *Adieu*', *Representations*, 79.1 (2002), 82–99
—— *The Spectacular Past: Popular History and the Novel in Nineteenth-century France* (Ithaca, NY: Cornell University Press, 2004)
SANYAL, DEBARATI, *The Violence of Modernity: Baudelaire, Irony, and the Politics of Form* (Baltimore, MD: Johns Hopkins University Press, 2006)
SARTRE, JEAN-PAUL, *Baudelaire* (Paris: Gallimard, 1947)
SCHEHR, LAWRENCE R., 'Fool's Gold: The Beginning of Balzac's *Illusions perdues*', *Symposium*, 36.2 (1982), 149–65
SCHOR, NAOMI, 'Devant le château: femmes, marchandises et modernité dans *Au Bonheur des Dames*', in *Mimesis et Semiosis: littérature et représentation*, ed. by Philippe Hamon and Jean-Pierre Leduc-Adine (Paris: Nathan, 1992), pp. 179–86
—— 'Mythe des origines, origine des mythes: *La Fortune des Rougon*', *Les Cahiers Naturalistes*, 52 (1978), 124–34
—— *Zola's Crowds* (Baltimore, MD: Johns Hopkins University Press, 1978)
—— 'Zola: From Window to Window', *Yale French Studies*, 42 (1969), 38–51
SCHWARTZ, VANESSA R., 'The Morgue and the Musée Grévin: Understanding the Public Taste for Reality in Fin-de-Siècle Paris', in *Spectacles of Realism: Gender, Body, Genre*, ed. by Margaret Cohen and Christopher Prendergast (Minneapolis: University of Minnesota Press, 1995), pp. 268–93
SERRES, MICHEL, *Feux et signaux de brume: Zola* (Paris: Grasset, 1975)
SHUH, RACHEL, 'Madness and Military History in Balzac's *Adieu*', *French Forum*, 26.1 (Winter 2001), 39–51
SMITH, MICHAEL STEPHEN, *The Emergence of Modern Business Enterprise in France, 1800–1930* (Cambridge, MA: Harvard University Press, 2006)
SMITH, RIGGS ALDEN, *The Primacy of Vision in Virgil's Aeneid*, (Austin: University of Texas Press, 2005)
SPRENGER, SCOTT, 'Quand "je" est un autre pays: archéologie, folie et espace identitaire dans *Adieu* de Balzac', in *Balzac voyageur: parcours, déplacement, mutations*, ed. by Nicole Mozet and Paule Petitier (Tours: Université François Rabelais, 2004), pp. 151–71
STAMELMAN, RICHARD, 'The Shroud of Allegory: Death, Mourning and Melancholy in Baudelaire's Work', *Texas Studies in Literature and Language*, 25.3 (Fall 1983), 390–409
STAROBINSKI, JEAN, *La Mélancolie au miroir: trois lectures de Baudelaire* (Paris: Julliard, 1989)
STRAUSS, JONATHAN, *Human Remains: Medicine, Death, and Desire in Nineteenth-century Paris* (New York: Fordham University Press, 2012)

SZAKÁCS, LÁSZLÓ, 'Les Vivants et les morts dans *La Fortune des Rougon*', *Acta Litteraria Scientarium Hungaricae*, 32.1–2 (1990), 91–95

TERDIMAN, RICHARD, *Present Past: Modernity and the Memory Crisis* (Ithaca, NY: Cornell University Press, 1993)

—— 'Structures of Initiation: On Semiotic Education and Its Contradictions in Balzac', *Yale French Studies*, 63 (1982), 198–226

THOMPSON, HANNAH, *Naturalism Redressed: Identity and Clothing in the Novels of Émile Zola* (Oxford: Legenda, 2004)

—— '"Une perversion du désir, une névrose nouvelle": Female Sexuality in Zola's *Au Bonheur Des Dames*', *Romance Studies*, 16.2 (Autumn 1998), 81–92

THOMPSON, WILLIAM J., 'Order and Chaos in "À une passante"', in *Understanding 'Les Fleurs du Mal': Critical Readings* ed. by William J. Thompson (Nashville, TN: Vanderbilt University Press, 1997), pp. 145–59

TILBY, MICHAEL, 'Poetry, Image, and Post-Napoleonic Politics: Baudelaire's "Le Squelette laboureur"', *Studi Francesi*, 56.3 (September-December 2012), 422–36

TWOREK, AGNIESZKA, 'Death Masks in *Thérèse Raquin*', *Excavatio*, 23.1–2 (2008), 195–202

VACHON, STÉPHANE, 'Le Désir de l'homme est le désir de l'autre: *Adieu* d'Honoré de Balzac', in *Balzac, pater familias: études réunies par Claudie Bernard et Franc Schuerewegen* (Amsterdam: Rodopi, 2001), pp. 85–94

VERNON, JOHN, *Money and Fiction: Literary Realism in the Nineteenth and Early Twentieth Centuries* (Ithaca, NY: Cornell University Press, 1984)

VINKEN, B., 'Forget Vergil? The Truth of Modernity', *Literary Imagination*, 8.3 (2006), 417–36

—— 'Mourning Woman: Andromache', *Pequod: A Journal of Contemporary Literature and Literary Criticism*, 35 (1993), 47–65

—— 'Temples of Delight', in *Spectacles of Realism: Gender, Body, Genre*, ed. by Margaret Cohen and Christopher Prendergast (Minneapolis: University of Minnesota Press, 1995), pp. 247–67

WALKER, PHILIP D., 'Life Continuing and Recommencing', in *'Germinal' and Zola's Philosophical and Religious Thought*, Purdue University Monographs in Romance Languages, 14 (Amsterdam & Philadelphia: John Benjamins, 1984)

WALLS, ALISON, 'Symbolism and Commodified Identity in Rachilde and Zola's Department Store Novels', *New Zealand Journal of French Studies*, 28.2 (November 2007), 36–48

WATTS, ANDREW, 'Les Spectres muets: l'adaptation de Balzac dans *Narayana* et *The Conquering Power*', *L'Année Balzacienne*, 13.1 (2012), 213–29

WEBER, JEAN-PAUL, *Genèse de l'œuvre poétique* (Paris: Gallimard, 1960)

WEBER, SAMUEL, *Unwrapping Balzac: A Reading of 'La Peau de chagrin'* (Toronto & Buffalo: University of Toronto Press, 1979)

WHITE, NICHOLAS, 'Family Histories and Family Plots', in *The Cambridge Companion to Zola*, ed. by Brian Nelson (Cambridge: Cambridge University Press, 2007), pp. 19–38

WIESER, DAGMAR, 'Témoignage de Baudelaire: du fétichisme dans "Une martyre"', *Versants*, 25 (1994), 97–115

WILLIAMS, ROSALIND H., *Dream Worlds: Mass Consumption in Late Nineteenth-century France* (Berkeley: University of California Press, 1982)

WILSON, STEVEN, 'Nana, Prostitution and the Textual Foundations of Zola's *Au Bonheur des Dames*', *NCFS*, 41.1–2 (2012), 91–104

WING, NATHANIEL, 'On Reading Baudelaire's Allegories', in *Pre-text, Text, Context: Essays on Nineteenth-century French Literature*, ed. by Robert L. Mitchell (Columbus: Ohio State University Press, 1980), pp. 135–44

WITT, CATHERINE, 'Passages Through Baudelaire: From Poetry to Thought and Back', in *Thinking Poetry*, ed. by Joseph Acquisto (New York: Palgrave Macmillan, 2013), pp. 25–42

WRIGHT, BARBARA, 'Baudelaire's Poetic Journey in *Les Fleurs du mal*', in *The Cambridge Companion to Baudelaire*, ed. by Rosemary Lloyd (Cambridge: Cambridge University Press, 2006), pp. 31–50
YEE, JENNIFER, 'Mementoes and the Memory of the Reader in *L'Éducation Sentimentale*', *Dix-Neuf*, 14.1 (2010), 1–12
ZIELONKA, ANTHONY, 'Renée et le problème du mal', in *La Curée de Zola ou 'la vie à outrance': actes du colloque du 10 janvier 1987*, ed. by David Baguley (Paris: SEDES, 1987), pp. 161–70
ZIMMERMANN, ÉLÉNORE M., 'Notes sur la forêt du "Cygne"', *Bulletin Baudelairien*, 26.2 (1991), 51–56
ZOLA, ÉMILE, *The Kill*, trans. by Arthur Goldhammer (New York: Modern Library, 2005)
—— *The Ladies' Paradise*, trans. and intro. by Brian Nelson (Oxford: Oxford University Press, 2012)
—— *The Ladies' Paradise*, intro. by Kristin Ross (Berkeley: University of California Press, 1992)
—— *Le Naturalisme au théâtre: les théories et les exemples* (Paris: Charpentier, 1895)
—— *Les Rougon-Macquart*, ed. by Henri Mitterand, 5 vols, Bibliothèque de la Pléiade (Paris: Gallimard, 1960–67)
—— *Thérèse Raquin* (Paris: Librairie Générale Française, 1997)

INDEX

Agamben, Giorgio 8, 147–48, 150, 154 n. 11
Ahearn, Edward 79
allegory 1, 7, 12, 21, 22, 31, 32, 33, 39, 41, 47 n. 57,
    52, 56, 58, 74, 75, 76, 82–84, 86 n. 21, 87 n. 33,
    91 n. 91 & 93, 94 n. 131 & 133 & 136, 103, 114,
    116, 117, 126, 130, 149, 153
androgyny 62, 65–67, 87 n. 43 & 44, 152
Andromache 6, 52, 73–79, 84, 89 n. 79 & 81, 89 n. 84,
    90 n. 90, 92 n. 99 & 100 & 103 & 108, 93 n. 109
    & 111 & 113, 147, 150, 151, 154 n. 11
Angoulême 28–30, 39, 152
animal 11, 23–24, 41, 44 n. 12, 58–60, 75, 76, 79,
    90 n. 86, 127, 137 n. 27, 148, 149, 150, 153
apostrophe 65, 78, 80, 82, 93 n. 112, 94 n. 129
Arcades 111, 112–14, 122
Armstrong, Marie-Sophie 136 n. 11
artifice 5, 7, 13, 15, 18, 22, 32–33, 35, 46 n. 30, 63,
    64, 67, 73, 74, 87 n. 38, 116, 118, 120–21, 122,
    123, 126, 128, 132, 134, 140 n. 60, 142 n. 84,
    143 n. 90, 145 n. 117, 151–52
    and clothing 17–19, 26, 33, 35, 44, 117, 122, 126,
        142 n. 84
    of human identity 5, 18–19, 122, 126, 128,
        142 n. 84, 146 n. 129
    mixed with natural 5, 32–33, 64, 67, 116, 126
    as simulacrum 11, 13, 46 n. 30, 74, 78
    as surface 26, 30, 31, 33, 35, 46 n. 30, 50 n. 85,
        63, 68, 87 n. 38, 122, 125, 132, 140 n. 63,
        142 n. 84

Babuts, Nicolae, 89 n. 81, 92 n. 99
Balzac, Honoré 1–2, 4, 5, 6–7, 9–51, 52, 66, 77,
    89 n. 82, 90 n. 85, 90 n. 90, 94 n. 128, 95, 104,
    108, 115, 118, 130, 132, 135 n. 5, 147, 149, 151, 152
    fiction:
        Adieu 6, 7, 9–14, 15, 18, 19, 28, 42, 44 n. 3 & 6
            & 7 & 8 & 9 & 10 & 12, 45 n. 13 & 15 &
            17 & 18 & 19 & 20 & 24, 46 n. 30, 108, 115,
            147, 148, 151–52
        Le Colonel Chabert 5, 7, 9, 15–19, 28, 32, 34, 35,
            41, 43, 44 n. 3, 15 n. 23 & 26, 46 n. 29 &
            30 & 34 & 36 & 38, 50 n. 96, 131, 147, 148,
            149, 152
        La Cousine Bette 90 n. 85 & 90
        'L'élixir de longue vie' 135 n. 5
        La Fille aux yeux d'or 66

Illusions perdues 19, 27–34, 37, 49 n. 74 & 77 &
    78 & 82, p. 50 n. 88 & 96, 144 n. 106, 147,
    149, 152, 153
La Peau de chagrin 4, 7, 19–27, 28, 30, 94 n. 128,
    132, 147, 148–49, 153
Le Père Goriot 15, 35, 130
Splendeurs et misères des courtisanes 5, 19, 27, 34–44,
    49 n. 78, 50 n. 86 & 88 & 91 & 93, 147,
    149–50, 151, 152, 153
other works:
    'Physiologie de la Toilette' 17
bare life 8, 147–51
Baudelaire, Charles 1, 2, 4, 5, 6, 7, 8, 19, 21, 49 n. 83,
    52–94, 98, 99, 108, 111, 125, 136 n. 11, 146 n. 11,
    147, 150, 151, 152, 153, 153 n. 2, 154 n. 11
poems:
    'L'Aube spirituelle' 87 n. 34
    'Au lecteur' 57, 86 n. 22
    'À une passante' 7, 21, 71–73, 88 n. 69 & 70,
        89 n. 72 & 73 & 74 & 75, 146 n. 125, 147
    'Les Aveugles' 88 n. 53
    'Le Beau Navire' 88 n. 66
    'Les Bijoux' 66–68, 72, 87 n. 36
    'Brumes et pluies', 85 n. 17
    'Une charogne' 7, 56, 57–62, 63, 65, 75, 86 n. 25
        & 27 & 30, 89 n. 79
    'La Chevelure' 76, 85 n. 7
    'Le Cygne' 4, 7, 72, 73–79, 80, 83, 99, 147, 150,
        151, 153
    'Danse macabre' 5, 63, 65
    'Un fantôme' 54, 62, 87 n. 34
    'Femmes damnées : Delphine et Hippolyte',
        87 n. 34
    'Le Flacon' 7, 52–57, 60, 61, 62–63, 64, 65, 70, 75,
        83, 87 n. 35, 89 n. 79, 152
    'Je n'ai pas oublié' 92 n. 103
    'Le Léthé' 62, 67
    'Une martyre' 7, 63–70, 72, 87 n. 38 & 40 & 45,
        88 n. 46 & 56, 150, 152
    'Le Masque' 63
    'Les Métamorphoses du vampire' 63
    'Les Petites Vieilles' 79, 87 n. 34, 89 n. 81
    'Les Phares' 84 n. 2, 86 n. 32
    'Que diras tu ce soir, pauvre âme solitaire,
        87 n. 34
    'La Rançon' 81

'Remords posthume' 85 n. 6
'Le Rêve d'un curieux' 93 n. 124
'Les Sept Vieillards' 79, 89 n. 81, 90 n. 90, 93 n. 124
'Spleen, "J'ai plus de souvenirs"' 85 n. 17
'Spleen, "Je suis comme le roi"' 85 n. 17
'Le Squelette laboureur' 4, 7, 80–81, 85 n. 17, 94 n. 124, 152, 153
'La Vie antérieure' 84
'Un Voyage à Cythère' 87 n. 34
prose poem:
  'Les Veuves' 75, 147, 150
other works:
  Fusées 94 n. 130
  Les Paradis artificiels 74, 82
  Le Peintre de la vie moderne 7, 49 n. 83, 61, 69, 83
  Théophile Gautier (I) 94 n. 130
Becker, Colette 98, 126, 141 n. 71, 145 n. 117
Beizer, Janet 10, 44 n. 9, 45 n. 18, 145 n. 115
Bell, David F. 47 n. 47, 110, 139 n. 43
Bell, Dorian 137 n. 23
Bell, Michael Mayerfeld 138 n. 33
Benhaim, André 140 n. 62
Benjamin, Walter 2–4, 21, 23–24, 47 n. 50, 49 n. 68, 52, 57, 68–70, 71, 72, 77, 80, 82, 83, 84, 91 n. 91, 93 n. 124, 94 n. 131, 112–14, 122, 123, 125, 139 n. 53, 143 n. 91, 147, 154 n. 11
Bersani, Leo 67, 87 n. 44
Berthier, Philippe 49 n. 78, 140 n. 63, 142 n. 86
Blanqui, Louis Auguste 3
Blood, Susan 82, 89 n. 75
bones 16, 59, 99–100, 104, 130, 131, 152, 153
Borie, Jean 136 n. 15, 141 n. 73, 144 n. 101
Bourdieu, Pierre 6, 105, 122
Bowlby, Rachel 22, 129, 133, 144 n. 104 & 111 & 112, 145 n. 122, 146 n. 127
Bray, Patrick 47 n. 46, 89 n. 84
Brombert, Victor 92 n. 101, 93 n. 119
Broom, Peter 54, 84 n. 5, 85 n. 20
Buck-Morss, Susan 142 n. 82, 143 n. 91
burial 15, 16–17, 25, 27, 35, 37, 38, 41, 46 n. 34, 50 n. 90, 68, 90 n. 90, 98, 99, 103, 107, 111, 112, 115, 136, 136 n. 11, 139, 142 n. 77
Burton, Richard D.E. 55, 78, 85 n. 9 & 11, & 18, 87 n. 36 & 37 & 44, 89 n. 81 & 84, 90 n. 86 & 88, 92 n. 103 & 107 & 108

cadavers:
  as commodity 114
  living 11, 15, 23, 27, 56, 57, 68, 80–81, 82, 86 n. 21, 87 n. 41, 98, 107, 111, 112, 139 n. 47
Caruth, Cathy 17
Castle, Terry 66
Chambers, Ross 61, 71, 75, 82, 84, 85 n. 16, 87 n. 33, 88 n. 70, 89 n. 72 & 84, 91 n. 91 & 92 & 96 & 97, 93 n. 122

change 1–2
  in Balzac 9, 14, 15–16, 28–29, 31, 35–44, 46 n. 41, 49 n. 85, 50 n. 89 & 91
  in Baudelaire 57, 63, 76, 83
  in Zola 104–05, 116–17, 119, 134, 140 n. 62, 144 n. 105, 148, 149–50, 154 n. 11
Charles, David 103, 136 n. 12, 137 n. 21
Chateaubriand, François René 140 n. 62
chronotope 108–09, 138 n. 34
clothing:
  in Balzac 4, 5, 17–18, 20, 25–26, 30, 31, 32, 33, 34–35, 38, 46 n. 32 & 37, 49 n. 84
  in Baudelaire 63, 65, 69, 72, 82, 87 n. 38
  in Zola 97, 113, 117–18, 122–25, 132–33, 134, 141 n. 66 & 67 & 68, 142 n. 84, 143 n. 89, 146 n. 129
  see also artifice
coffins 54–57, 64, 70, 97
Cohen, Margaret 8, 24, 69, 113
Cohen-Vrignaud 20
Cohn, Robert Greer 85 n. 12
commerce 1, 28, 32, 42, 110, 113–14, 128–30, 133, 135, 138 n. 40, 145 n. 120, 153
commodities 4–5, 22–26, 31–32, 33, 43, 47 n. 51 & 54, 68–71, 77–78, 88 n. 56, 92 n. 103, 95, 113–14, 118, 125, 133, 139 n. 53, 146 n. 127, 153
commodity fetishism 21, 26, 47 n. 49, 67–69, 71, 78, 84, 87 n. 38
  human-like objects 4, 5, 25, 30, 48 n. 65 & 67, 69–70, 108, 109, 138 n. 35, 139 n. 55, 146 n. 127, 152
  human objects 7, 20, 25, 48 n. 65, & 67, 50 n. 87, 67–70, 77, 88 n. 56, 92 n. 100, 104, 109, 112, 113–14, 122–27, 128, 133, 135, 138 n. 40, 139 n. 55, 141 n. 72, 151, 152, 153
  selling humans 4, 21, 23, 25, 27–28, 30–31, 32, 33–35, 40, 43, 50 n. 86, 69–70, 77, 104, 109–10, 113–14, 118, 123, 139 n. 55, 149, 152, 153
  see also prostitution, reification
Compagnon, Antoine 88 n. 69
consumerism 7, 8, 25, 97, 128, 131, 134, 144 n. 111, 149, 153
consuming as burning 97
consuming as eating 60, 98
containment, containers 34, 54, 56–57, 65, 67, 70, 73, 81, 84, 89 n. 79
Counter, Andrew 137 n. 27
Cuvier, Georges 23

decomposition 23, 56–57, 58, 59, 61, 75, 85 n. 15, 86 n. 27 & 29 & 30, 96, 127, 144 n. 114,
degeneration 129
Delavigne, Casimir 95
Deleuze, Gilles 137 n. 26 & 27
Delvau, Alfred 90 n. 86
De Man, Paul 83–84

Derrida, Jacques 98
Dezalay, Auguste 135 n. 6, 141 n. 71
disillusionment 30, 33, 49 n. 74
dispossession 116–18, 135, 141 n. 70, 149
dream 5, 22–28, 29–30, 32, 33, 41, 42–43, 49 n. 76, 65, 70, 85 n. 15, 86 n. 29, 90 n. 90, 111, 121–22, 132, 142 n. 82, 145 n. 117 & 119
Duval, Jeanne 62, 79

Faudemay, Alain 84 n. 5, 85 n. 13
féerie 29, 48 n. 67, 123, 125–26, 132, 142 n. 87, 143 n. 92, 145 n. 117
Ferguson, Priscilla Parkhurst 140 n. 64, 142 n. 82
fetish 4, 21, 26, 47 n. 49, 62, 63, 67–72, 78, 84, 87 n. 38, 89 n. 74, 92 n. 106, 113, 132–33, 139 n. 53, 145 n. 120
  woman and the 26, 63, 67–72, 132–33, 145 n. 120
Finch-Race, Daniel A. 89 n. 81
Fischer, Caroline 86 n. 21
Fisher, Dominique 66, 87 n. 44
Flaubert, Gustave:
  L'Éducation sentimentale, 141 n. 69
  Madame Bovary, 117
fossils 23, 41
Foucault, Michel 39, 148, 150
Freud, Sigmund 10, 67–68, 87 n. 38, 88 n. 52 & 54, 97, 133
Fuss, Diana 66

Gaillard, Françoise 47 n. 49, 105, 137 n. 26
Gasarian, Gérard 86 n. 29, 87 n. 41, 89 n. 77, 91 n. 91, 93 n. 109 & 111
Gascar, Pierre 9, 44 n. 3, 45 n. 26
Gautier, Théophile 90 n. 87, 94 n. 130
ghostliness 1, 3–4, 5, 152
  in Balzac 9–10, 13–14, 23–26, 28, 31, 33, 43–44, 44 n. 5, 48 n. 62 & 67, 90 n. 90
  in Baudelaire 1, 6, 49 n. 83, 53–55, 56, 57, 60–62, 65–71, 74, 75, 77–79, 83, 84, 84 n. 2, 85 n. 10, 86 n. 32, 86 n. 29, 87 n. 33 & 34, 89 n. 73 & 81, 90 n. 90, 93 n. 111 & 119
  and the commodity 4, 24, 26, 33, 69–71, 78, 113–14, 125, 132–33
  and lesbianism 66–67, 88 n. 46
  of the past 1, 3–4, 5, 9–10, 13–14, 43, 65, 74, 77, 83–84, 131
  in Zola 1, 102, 107, 112–14, 119, 121, 125, 127, 129, 131, 132, 133, 136 n. 19, 137 n. 23 & 24, 138 n. 30, 138 n. 33, 139 n. 43 & 44 & 45, 145 n. 115, 146 n. 128
Godfrey, Sima 87 n. 43, 91 n. 95
Goldhammer, Arthur 144 n. 102
graves 15, 16, 45 n. 17, 53–54, 55, 68, 78, 80, 81, 92 n. 107, 99, 104, 111, 130
Griffiths, Kate 136 n. 19, 137 n. 24, 138 n. 30, 140 n. 61
Grimm, Richard E. 92 n. 108

Guys, Constantin 61, 83

habitus 6, 45 n. 23, 105
Hallucination 42–43, 99, 111, 121, 139 n. 46, 151, 149, 151
Harrow, Susan 139 n. 46, 141 n. 72, 142 n. 75 & 78 & 84, 144 n. 98, 146 n. 127
Harvey, David 1–2, 3
Haunting 1–2, 9, 14, 36, 37, 43, 53, 61, 65, 67, 69–70, 74, 83, 92 n. 99, 97, 106, 107, 108, 111, 113, 120, 127, 131, 133, 136 n. 19, 138 n. 29, 150
Haussmann 1–3, 20, 73, 116, 140 n. 64
heredity 6, 7, 95–97, 100–03, 105–07, 115, 122, 127, 129, 135, 136 n. 14, 137 n. 20 & 26, 139 n. 59, 152
Hiddleston, J. A. 84 n. 5
Homosexuality 66, 87 n. 45
Honour 9, 18–19, 40, 42–43
Houssaye, Arsène 90 n. 90
humanity 3–5
  loss or death of 5, 8, 10–11, 31, 35, 46 n. 30, 95, 105, 112–14, 122–23, 125, 127–28, 131–35, 146 n. 127, 148, 152, 53

identity 5, 6, 7, 9, 10, 11, 15–19, 20, 25, 29, 31, 34–41, 45 n. 21 & 23, 46 n. 38, 50 n. 86, 53, 66, 69, 83, 92 n. 99, 117, 122–23, 127, 138 n. 30, 147, 148, 150, 153
illusion 4, 5, 13, 22, 24, 26–35, 42, 49 n. 74, 50 n. 98, 70, 90 n. 90, 121–22, 126–27, 132
intoxication 26, 29, 56, 61, 82, 119–20, 132, 141 n. 72

Jackson, John E. 57, 85 n. 6, 86 n. 28
Jacquier, Joséphine Alida 92 n. 105
Johnson, Barbara 65, 78, 94 n. 129

Kamm, Lewis 138 n. 35, 145 n. 124
Kaplan, Edward 93 n. 118, 147, 153 n. 3
Knight, Diana 50 n. 87
Kroen, Sheryl 16

Labarthe, Patrick 80, 85 n. 14, 89 n. 81, 92 n. 98
Laforgue, Pierre 88 n. 46, 93 n. 115
Lamartine, Alphonse de 56
Lazarus 1, 52, 53, 55, 56, 61, 70, 82, 83
Leakey, F. W. 87 n. 45, 91 n. 95 & 97, 93 n. 111
lesbian 66–67, 88 n. 46 & 50, 145 n. 120
Lévi-Strauss, Claude 127
lieux de mémoire 9, 73, 151
limbic state 12, 34, 55, 56, 60, 63, 64, 65–68, 72–73, 75, 85 n. 18, 151, 152
liminality 5, 11–12, 29, 32, 39, 47 n. 47, 53, 115, 129
Lionnet, Françoise 93 n. 112 & 115 & 117
living death 1–6, 147–49
  in Balzac 1, 2, 4, 5, 6, 7–8, 9–44, 44 n. 6, 47 n. 47 & 51, 50 n. 87 & 97, 90 n. 90, 95, 110, 115, 135 n. 5, 147, 148–50, 149, 151, 152

in Baudelaire 52–84, 84 n. 3, 85 n. 13 & 18 & 20, 86 n. 30, 87 n. 37 & 41, 88 n. 53, 90 n. 90, 92 n. 98 & 99 & 108, 93 n. 124, 111, 136 n. 11, 147, 150, 151, 152, 153
in Zola 1, 2, 4–5, 7–8, 36, 47 n. 51, 95–135, 135 n. 7 & 8, 139, nn. 47 & 48 & 59, 142 n. 78, 147, 152, 153
Lloyd, Rosemary 153 n. 2
Lok, Matthijs M. 17

machines:
human-like 110
human machines 5, 104–05, 110, 112, 113, 125, 129, 135
living death, and 139 n. 48
madness 119–20, 150
Mannoni, Octave 92 n. 106
Marder, Elissa 88 n. 69, 89 n. 71
marketing 29, 47 n. 54, 129, 134
Marx, Karl 2, 4, 8 n. 7, 69, 113, 139 n. 53
Mathier, Jean-Claude 86 n. 25
McGrath, Caitlin 142 n. 75
Meltzer, Françoise 89 n. 73
memory 1, 6
in Balzac 10, 11, 13–14, 15, 16, 45 n. 26
in Baudelaire 53–56, 57, 59, 60–62, 65, 67, 72–76, 77, 83, 85 n. 7 & 9, 86 n. 22 & 29 & 32, 91 n. 92 & 96 & 97, 92 n. 105, 93 n. 109
mémoire involontaire 76
in Zola 98, 107, 111, 148, 151, 153
Ménard, Sophie 137 n. 23, 139 n. 44
Michelangelo 84 n. 2
milieu, formation by the 7, 15, 35, 36, 39, 43, 96, 100, 103, 105–06, 110–11, 112, 114–16, 121–23, 126, 128–29, 132, 137 n. 26, 144 n. 105, 153
Miller, D.A. 28, 30, 39, 49 n. 74, 50 n. 94
Miller, Michael B. 47 n. 53
Mitterand, Henri 135 n. 4, 136 n. 12 & 15, 138 n. 34 & 38
Mizouni, Sophia 143 n. 88
modernization 1, 7, 20, 28, 52, 104–05, 110, 114
money 4–8, 9, 14, 18–19, 20–22, 25, 32, 34, 35, 39–41, 46 n. 37, 47 n. 48, 48 n. 67, 95, 104, 107, 118–19, 120, 134, 138 n. 29 & 40, 145 n. 117, 148, 149, 153
Mulvey, Laura 87 n. 38
mummies 23, 34, 43, 48 n. 60, 80–81, 153

nakedness 67, 114, 117–18, 122, 123, 125, 127
Nelson, Brian 144 n. 111, 146 n. 125
Nelson, Lowry 73, 78, 91 n. 96
Nerval, Gérard de 90 n. 90
Newmark, Kevin 86 n. 32, 94 n. 133
newness 1–8, 147, 149–52, 154 n. 11
in Balzac 14, 17, 18–19, 20, 23, 27–30, 35, 36, 37, 39–44, 45 n. 24 & 26, 48 n. 58, 50 n. 96
in Baudelaire 56, 57, 58–60, 73–74, 77–78, 79, 86 n. 28, 89 n. 77 & 81 & 84, 91 n. 95, 92 n. 105

in Zola 95, 99, 101, 102, 103, 104, 113, 116, 117, 127, 128–29, 130, 131, 132, 135, 140 n. 62 & 64, 143 n. 88, 144 n. 102 & 106 & 112 & 113, 145 n. 119, 147, 149– 152, 154 n. 11
Noiray, Jacques 140 n. 63, 144 n. 96 & 99
Nora, Pierre, 151

objects, *see* commodities
Oehler, Dolf 57, 74, 79, 85 n. 20
Olmstead, William 86 n. 30
orphans 8, 79, 97, 128, 136 n. 18, 147, 150, 151

Pagano, Tullio 142 n. 80
Paris 1, 3, 5, 7–8
in Balzac 16, 19, 20, 28, 29, 30–39, 40, 41, 43, 46 n. 41, 48 n. 67, 49 n. 78
in Baudelaire 52–53, 68, 69, 71, 72, 73–74, 76, 77, 79, 80, 83, 89 n. 8, 90 n. 90, 91 n. 91, 92 n. 103, 93 n. 112
Bois de Boulogne 115–16, 50 n. 89, 140 n. 62
Conciergerie/Palais de Justice 34, 41–43, 108, 149, 151
Doyenné 73–75, 77, 79, 90 n. 90, 152
Galeries de Bois 31–33, 43, 49 n. 82, 89 n. 82, 153
Halles 2
Louvre 74–75, 76, 77, 87 n. 43, 90 n. 87 & 90, 151–52
Morgue 114, 138 n. 42, 139 n. 56
Palais Royale 19, 20, 30, 34
Passage du Pont Neuf 111
place du Carrousel 73–74, 77, 84, 89 n. 77 & 84, 90 n. 86, 91 n. 92 & 95, 92 n. 105, 99, 108
rue de Langlade 30, 34, 152
Seine 21, 74
Tuileries 21
woman and the street 71–73, 87 n. 33, 88 n. 69 & 70, 113, 120, 123–26, 141 n. 73
in Zola 109, 110, 112, 114–15, 116–17, 118, 119–20, 122, 123, 125, 128, 129, 130, 140 n. 60 & 61 & 63, 141 n. 66 & 70 & 73, 142 n. 74, 143 n. 88 & 90 & 94, 144 n. 106, 149, 151, 152, 153
Parsons, Deborah 145 n. 120 & 122
past:
dead past 1, 3, 4, 5–6, 10, 11, 13, 22, 36, 52, 73–74, 76, 77, 89 n. 79, 91 n. 92, 95, 98, 102, 108, 111, 128, 131, 140 n. 62
forgetting of 16–17, 45 n. 26, 46 n. 29, 62–63
living-dead past 5, 75, 95
in objects and spaces 84, 53–54, 107–09
present past 2, 13–14, 43, 52, 53, 54, 73, 75–77, 89 n. 81
Pauw, Clara 141 n. 67
penetration:
by the milieu 116, 121, 140 n. 60
by poetry 53, 57
of scents 53–54, 56–57

Peterson, Samantha 138 n. 31
Petrey, Sandy 16, 17, 46 n. 30 & 38, 140 n. 62
phantasmagoria 2–4, 7, 19, 21, 23–28, 30, 31, 49 n. 70, 68–70, 113, 114, 119, 120–22, 125, 131–32, 134, 139 n. 53, 142 n. 76, 143 n. 93 & 94, 145 n. 119, 153
Pichois, Claude 58, 66, 88 n. 50
poison 38, 50 n. 93, 56–58, 62, 96, 113, 115, 118, 141 n. 73
Pot, Olivier 86 n. 27
Poulet, Georges 84 n. 3, 85 n. 15, 87 n. 37, 92 n. 102, 92 n. 102
power 6, 15, 19, 21, 25, 26, 33, 37, 39–40, 43, 50 n. 92 & 94 & 96, 53, 96, 103–04, 107, 110, 117, 130, 144 n. 105, 148–49, 150
Prendergast, Christopher 18, 33, 46 n. 32, 49 n. 80, 50 n. 91 & 93
prostitution 4, 8 n. 8, 17, 19, 28, 29, 30–34, 35, 36–37, 39, 42, 49 n. 85, 50 n. 93, 51 n. 99, 69, 113–14, 118, 123–26, 133, 139 n. 55, 141 n. 72, 143 n. 89 & 90 & 93, 145 n. 120 & 122, 149, 150 152, 153
  of author 4, 32, 33, 153
Proust, Marcel 76, 108

Quarantini, Franca Zanelli 89 n. 84
Quinlan, Karen 147, 148

Ramazani, Vaheed 144 n. 113, 145 n. 115
reification 5, 7, 25, 30–31, 69, 88 n. 56, 92 n. 100 & 103, 104–05, 109, 113–14, 122, 125–26, 128, 131, 133–34, 144 n. 98 & 101, 145 n. 123 & 124
return:
  cycles 103, 136 n. 14 & 15
  of the dead 1–4, 6, 24, 42–43, 53–55, 56, 57, 70, 83–84, 101, 102, 103, 106, 107, 111–12, 131, 135, 136 n. 17 & 18, 137 n. 20, 139 n. 59
  eternal return 101, 103, 106, 112, 136 n. 12 & 15
  of the past 1, 2, 3, 11, 13, 36, 37, 46 n. 30, 54, 83, 91 n. 91, 98, 101, 102, 107, 112, 131, 151
  of political regimes 2, 14, 16, 103
  repetition 3, 6, 10, 11, 12, 21, 45 n. 15, 55, 56, 68, 76, 77, 78, 89 n. 81, 91 n. 91, 95, 102, 109, 116, 126, 137 n. 21
  of the repressed 67, 97–98
Ricatte, Robert 136 n. 10
Robb Graham 90 n. 90
Rolls, Alistair 89 n. 74
Ross, Kristin 131, 144 n. 104, 145 n. 123
Rousseau, Jean-Jacques 3, 20
Rühle, Otto 4
ruins 5, 12, 16, 22, 28, 43, 45 n. 15, 73, 74, 83, 90 n. 90, 94 n. 131, 103, 130, 147, 149, 151, 152
Rykner, Arnaud 142 n. 87

Salisbury, Laura 110
Salotto, Eleanor 146 n. 128

Samuels, Maurice 12–13, 46 n. 30, 50 n. 86
Sanyal, Debarati 8 n. 9, 64, 69–70, 88 n. 55 & 56
Sardou, Victorien 77
Sartre, Jean Paul 85 n. 18
Schor, Naomi 100, 101, 102, 104, 136 n. 14 & 19, 144 n. 114, 145 n. 115
Schwartz, Vanessa R. 139 n. 56
seduction 7, 29–30, 131–33
Sergent, Élise (la reine Pomaré), 88 n. 50
Serres, Michel 110
shopping 4, 7, 19, 21–25, 28, 31, 32–33, 34, 47 n. 51 & 53, 110, 116, 119, 128, 131–33, 135, 145 n. 122, 149
  sexuality and shopping 132–33
  shop lifting 132
  shoppers 133, 145 n. 117 & 122
Shuh, Rachael 12, 45 n. 19
skeleton 1, 3, 4, 5, 23, 52, 57, 63, 65, 80–81, 96
  in Baudelaire 4, 63, 65, 80
sleep 13, 23, 24, 30, 55, 62, 65, 68, 80–81, 99, 100, 106, 111, 120, 121, 140 n. 61
Smith, Riggs Alden 74
spaces 1–2, 5–6, 7–8, 147, 148, 149, 151–53
  in Balzac 9, 11, 15, 16, 19, 21, 22, 23, 31, 32, 33, 39, 43, 44 n. 6, 47 n. 46
  in Baudelaire 52, 53, 72, 73, 77, 79, 84, 87 n. 38, 91 n. 92 & 97, 92 n. 105, 94
  Beresina 10–14, 151, 44 n. 10, 46 n. 30
  buildings 5, 7–8, 9, 12, 16, 20, 22, 30, 32, 33, 41, 48 n. 59, 52, 74–75, 76, 77, 79, 83, 84, 90 n. 90, 108, 117, 120, 130, 131, 142 n. 77, 151, 152
  cemetery 7, 57, 107, 111, 136 n. 11, 136 n. 12
    Saint-Mittre cemetery 96, 99–101, 103–05, 107, 115, 131, 140 n. 61, 152
  of living death 5, 7, 9, 11, 15–16, 21, 22, 43, 52, 53, 84, 105, 108, 111, 116, 122, 129, 147–49, 151–53
  and memory 91 n. 97
  and trauma 5–7
  in Zola 100, 101, 104–05, 108, 109, 111, 116, 122, 128–29, 130, 134, 138 n. 33 & 34, 141 n. 73, 143 n. 93
  see also Paris, tomb
spectacle 3, 5, 24, 25, 28, 29, 30, 31, 48 n. 67, 114, 123, 125–26, 129, 132, 134, 139 n. 56, 143 n. 90 & 93, 144 n. 95, 145 n. 117
Stamelman, Richard 86 n. 21, 91 n. 95, 94 n. 136
Starobinski, Jean 93 n. 112 & 113 & 115
Stoltz, Rosine 88 n. 50
stores 4, 7–8, 47 n. 53, 48 n. 59, 138 n. 40, 143 n. 93, 149, 153
  in Balzac 16, 19, 21–25, 26, 27, 31–32, 34, 43, 46 n. 40, 47 n. 55, 48 n. 58 & 65, 50 n. 97
  in Baudelaire 75, 77, 86, 94 n. 128
  in Zola 123, 125, 128
    Au Bonheur des Dames 113, 128–35, 144 n. 112, 145 n. 117, 153
    living death, and 4, 7–8

Raquin shop 110–11, 112–13, 114, 116, 128–30, 131, 138 n. 42
   Au Vieil Elbeuf 129, 153
Strauss, Jonathan 139 n. 48
surface, *see* artifice
Szakács, László 135 n. 8

tableaux vivants 121, 123, 125, 126, 139 n. 58, 142 n. 87, 144 n. 95 & 99
Taine, Hippolyte 113
Terdiman, Richard 6, 50 n. 92, 74, 76, 91 n. 93
Thompson, Hannah 141 n. 68, 142 n. 84, 145 n. 120 & 121, 146 n. 129
Thompson, William J. 88 n. 69
threshold 5, 9–12, 15, 19, 21, 22–23, 25, 43, 46 n. 40, 48 n. 64, 52, 99, 101
Tiedemann, Rolf 139 n. 53
Tilby, Michael 93 n. 124
tomb 3, 6, 15, 33, 45 n. 17, 55, 56, 57, 68, 70, 73, 74, 76–77, 78, 84, 85 n. 20, 90 n. 90, 99, 100, 101, 105, 111, 136 n. 12, 140 n. 62, 141 n. 67, 145 n. 115, 147, 150, 151, 152
   see also spaces
trauma 5–6, 7, 8 n. 9–10, 14, 43, 150
trees 11, 12, 93 n. 111, 95–96, 99, 100, 103, 115, 135 n. 2 & 4, 140 n. 60
Tworek, Agnieszka 138 n. 42, 139, nn. 47 & 55

veils 19, 26–28, 46 n. 39, 69,
Vinken, Barbara 92 n. 98 & 103, 144 n. 110
Virgil 78, 92 n. 98, 93 n. 112

waking 5, 12, 15, 23, 26, 27, 56, 83, 88 n. 53, 99, 106, 112, 114, 121, 127, 132, 140 n. 61,
Walker, Philip D. 136 n. 15
Walls, Alison 146 n. 127

White, Nicholas 135 n. 2
widows 8, 73, 75, 77, 78, 92 n. 99 & 103, 111, 147, 150, 151, 153 n. 2 & 3
Wieser, Dagmar 87 n. 38
Williams, Rosalind 144 n. 104 & 107, 145 n. 118 & 119
Wilson, Stephen 144 n. 105, 145 n. 114
Wing, Nathanial 91 n. 93
Witt, Catherine 89 n. 71
Wright, Barbara 86 n. 22

Yee, Jennifer 141 n. 69
Yost, Matthew 138 n. 32

Zielonka, Anthony 139 n. 59
Zimmerman, Élénore M. 90 n. 90
zoetrope 143 n. 93
Zola, Émile 1, 150
   novels:
      La Bête humaine 7, 36, 100, 105–10, 112, 119, 121, 132, 135, 138 n. 28, 138 n. 29, 138 n. 31 & 32, 147, 151
      Au Bonheur des Dames 4, 5, 7, 113, 116, 119, 128–35, 145 n. 117, 147, 151
      La Curée 5, 7, 114–28, 135, 140 n. 61 & 64, 147, 151, 152
      Le Docteur Pascal 127, 137 n. 20
      La Faute de l'abbé Mouret 142 n. 79
      La Fortune des Rougon 1, 7, 95–105, 115, 128, 130, 135, 137 n. 21, 138 n. 40, 139 n. 47, 147, 150, 152
      Germinal 100
      La Mort d'Olivier Bécaille 139 n. 47
      Thérèse Raquin 7, 107, 110–14, 116, 121, 128, 132, 133, 135, 139 n. 49, 147, 151
   other work:
      Le Naturalisme au théâtre 143 n. 92

www.ingramcontent.com/pod-product-compliance
Lightning Source LLC
LaVergne TN
LVHW061252060426
835507LV00017B/2030